RETHINKING THE WELFARE RIGHTS MOVEMENT

Lasting from the early 1960s to the mid 1970s, the welfare rights movement crossed political boundaries, fighting simultaneously for women's rights, economic justice, and black women's empowerment through welfare assistance. The welfare rights movement was an interracial protest movement of poor women receiving Aid to Families with Dependent Children who demanded reform of welfare policy, greater respect and dignity, and financial support to properly raise and care for their children. In short, they pushed for a right to welfare. Its members challenged stereotypes, engaged in Congressional debates, and developed a sophisticated political analysis that combined race, class, gender, and culture, crafting a distinctive, feminist, anti-racist politics rooted in their experiences as poor women of color.

Rethinking the Welfare Rights Movement provides a short, accessible overview of this important social and political movement, highlighting key events and figures, the movement's strengths and weaknesses, and how it intersected with other social and political movements of the time, as well as its lasting effect on the country. It is perfect for anyone wanting to obtain an introduction to the welfare rights movement of the twentieth century.

Premilla Nadasen is Associate Professor of African American History at Queens College, City University of New York.

American Social and Political Movements of the Twentieth Century

Series Editor: Heather Ann Thompson

RETHINKING THE WELFARE RIGHTS MOVEMENT

Premilla Nadasen

Routledge
Taylor & Francis Group

NEW YORK AND LONDON

First published 2012
by Routledge
711 Third Avenue, New York, NY 10017

Simultaneously published in the UK
by Routledge
2 Park Square, Milton Park, Abingdon, Oxon OX14 4RN

Routledge is an imprint of the Taylor & Francis Group, an informa business

Library of Congress Cataloging in Publication Data

Nadasen, Premilla.
  Rethinking the welfare rights movement / by Premilla Nadasen.
    p. cm. – (American social and political movements of the
    twentieth century)
  Includes bibliographical references and index.
    1. National Welfare Rights Organization (U.S.) 2. Welfare
rights movement–United States–History–20th century. 3. Public
welfare–United States–History–20th century. 4. Welfare
recipients–Political activity–United States–History–20th century.
5. Poor–Political activity–United States–History–20th century.
6. United States–Social policy. I. Title.
HV91.N123 2011

362.5´56140973–dc23

ISBN: 978-0-415-80085-3 (hbk)
ISBN: 978-0-415-80086-0 (pbk)
ISBN: 978-0-203-13804-5 (ebk)

Typeset in Bembo
by Cenveo Publisher Services

Printed and bound in the United States of America on acid-free paper by
Walsworth Publishing Company, Marceline, MO.

CONTENTS

EDITOR'S SERIES INTRODUCTION

Welcome to the *American Social and Political Movements of the Twentieth Century* series at Routledge. This collection of works by top historians from around the nation and world introduces students to the myriad movements that came together in the United States during the twentieth century to expand democracy, to reshape the political economy, and to increase social justice.

Each book in this series explores a particular movement's origins, its central goals, its leading as well as grassroots figures, its actions as well as ideas, and its most important accomplishments as well as serious missteps.

With this series of concise yet synthetic overviews and reassessments, students not only will gain a richer understanding of the many human rights and civil liberties that they take for granted today, but they will also newly appreciate how recent, how deeply contested, and thus how inherently fragile, are these same elements of American citizenship.

Heather Ann Thompson
Temple University

ABBREVIATIONS

ACLU	American Civil Liberties Union
ADC	Aid to Dependent Children
AFDC	Aid to Families with Dependent Children
ANC	Aid to Needy Children
BWR	Baltimore Welfare Rights Organization
CAP	Community Action Program
CARASA	Committee for Abortion Rights and Against Sterilization Abuse
CORE	Congress of Racial Equality
CUFAW	Citizens United for Adequate Welfare
FAP	Family Assistance Plan
ICPP	Inner City Protestant Parish
IFCO	Interreligious Foundation for Community Organizations
JOIN	Jobs or Income Now
MAW	Mothers for Adequate Welfare
OSCAW	Ohio Steering Committee for Adequate Welfare
NAACP	National Association for the Advancement of Colored People
P/RAC	Poverty/Rights Action Center
NCC	National Coordinating Committee
NCSC	National Council of Senior Citizens
SCLC	Southern Christian Leadership Organization
SDS	Students for a Democratic Society
TANF	Temporary Assistance to Needy Families
WSO	West Side Organization
WIN	Work Incentive Programme
WRDA	Welfare Recipients Demand Action

INTRODUCTION

On June 30, 1966, thirty-five people, mostly women and children, arrived in Columbus, Ohio, weary but jubilant, after a ten-day walk from Cleveland. Their 150-mile "Walk for Decent Welfare" drew attention to the inadequacy of welfare benefits in Ohio. When the marchers left Cleveland they were 100 strong and several hundred supporters joined them as they passed through towns and cities along their journey. Indicative of the era's anti-welfare hostility, bystanders heckled and harassed the marchers, calling them "bums" and chanting "work, work, work!" One night a cross was burned nearby as they slept.[1] Upon their arrival in Columbus a crowd of 2,000 met them at East High School, where they gathered before the last leg of their march to the steps of the state capitol. The Ohio Rally for Decent Welfare sought to ensure that recipients received 100 percent of the amount of money the state welfare department decided was necessary for a minimum standard of living.[2] At the time, the state paid only 70 percent of the amount. The Ohio Steering Committee for Adequate Welfare (OSCAW), which planned the demonstration, demanded that the governor call a special session of the state legislature to raise welfare grants to the full standard of need.[3]

Protesters in Ohio were not alone in their efforts to reform the welfare system. On the same day that the Ohio marchers arrived in Columbus, recipients and their supporters around the country gathered at their state capitols, in public squares, and at local welfare departments to stage the first nationwide demonstration of recipients of Aid to Families with Dependent Children (AFDC). AFDC was a cash assistance program for poor single mothers and their children that was funded jointly by the state and federal governments, but administered by the state.[4] In Chicago 200 poor people marched to the city's downtown welfare office. In Newark, seventy-five welfare recipients went to the state capitol to demand higher welfare benefits.[5] In New York City, 2,000 mostly black women and children demanded an end to the "indignities" of the welfare system.[6] Other protests occurred in Los Angeles, Baltimore, Trenton, Louisville, Boston, Washington, and San Francisco. An estimated 6,000 people demonstrated in twenty-five cities across the country.

Although the 1966 welfare protests didn't garner the same publicity as the civil rights marches led by Martin Luther King, Jr., they nevertheless managed to grace the front pages of many national newspapers. The welfare rights protests signaled a new phase in the struggle for black equality—one addressing more directly the problem of economic deprivation. By the mid-1960s, the civil rights movement had desegregated most public facilities in the South, delivered the ballot to millions of previously disenfranchised African Americans, and set an important national precedent for equal access to public education. Engulfed in convulsive internal debates about what future struggles were necessary to fully ensure the freedom of millions of impoverished black Americans, many African American political leaders, including Martin Luther King, concluded that economic justice was vital for social equality. Although unemployment was at one of its lowest points in the postwar period, millions of Americans lived in dilapidated housing and were malnourished and inadequately clothed. Michael Harrington, author of an influential book on poverty, *The Other America*, estimated in 1962 that 40 to 50 million Americans were poor.[7] The problem crossed racial and ethnic boundaries, but the African American community bore the brunt of it. In 1962, for example, 15 percent of white families, but 40 percent of black families, earned less than the poverty line of $3,000.[8] Social movement activists contemplated how to alleviate or, better yet, eradicate poverty. The welfare rights movement offered one solution: provide sufficient public assistance.[9] The emergence of the welfare rights movement reflected the increasing attention to economic justice among civil rights and student activists, social scientists, policymakers, and government officials in the mid-1960s. Many Americans had come to believe that some level of economic security or opportunity was essential for domestic tranquility and prosperity. Antipoverty proposals ranged from job creation to direct cash assistance to expanded educational opportunity. Many of these programs targeted unemployed men or turned to jobs and education as the best remedy for poverty. The welfare rights movement, on the other hand, sought to improve the lot of single mothers on public assistance. It challenged much of the conventional wisdom about fighting poverty: that single parenthood was a bad thing; that "welfare dependency" fostered negative behavior; that welfare recipients should be shamed rather than embraced.

The welfare rights movement also fits into a much longer trajectory of poor people's activism. Throughout the twentieth century poor people fought for governmental assistance, claimed rights, and mobilized to protect their interests. In the 1930s, the Communist Party formed unemployed councils to demand jobs, seek better relief from government officials, and to halt evictions of the unemployed. These grassroots councils of unemployed workers planned mass demonstrations, hunger marches, and nationwide political protests. In the 1920s and 1930s, a tenant movement organized militant rent strikes. There is also a long history of consumer boycotts, perhaps most notably those launched by house-wives throughout the twentieth century to oppose rising food prices. Part of what sets the welfare rights movement apart, however, was its constituency of poor black women on welfare and they way in which they advocated on their own behalf.

June 30, 1966, a date commemorated annually for many years by welfare activists around the country, marked the official start of the welfare rights movement in the United States. Welfare rights activists and supporters had met a few months earlier at a conference in Chicago and designated June 30 a national day of action around welfare, in solidarity with the already planned Ohio Walk for Adequate Welfare. Conference attendees asked George Wiley, head of the Poverty/Rights Action Center (P/RAC), a Washington D.C.-based nonprofit group committed to assisting organizing efforts by the poor, to coordinate and promote the event. Wiley and his staff at P/RAC accepted the task and traveled around the country informing recipients of the upcoming march and providing technical support to local groups. These early contacts resulted in the founding in 1967 of the National Welfare Rights Organization (NWRO), which comprised most local welfare rights groups, and would lead the struggle for welfare rights over the next decade. Many of the recipients from local organizations participating in the first national demonstration would come to play prominent roles in the national movement.

Comprising an alliance of grassroots groups, this movement gave political voice to one of the most disenfranchised sectors of US society.[10] Women on AFDC encountered a welfare system that left them unsure day-to-day whether they could pay rent or feed and clothe their children; that showed them little respect; by stigmatizing them as lazy, licentious, and unfit mothers. Transforming both the administration and the public perception of AFDC was a central goal of the welfare rights movement. It sought to organize AFDC recipients to reform the program and make it more humane. Welfare rights protesters rallied and marched, picketed and protested to pressure public officials to address the inadequacies in the welfare system. They held sit-ins, wrote letters, blockaded buildings, testified before Congress, and organized rent strikes. They demanded that welfare officials guarantee them a basic standard of living and eliminate regulations that violated their civil rights. They believed that welfare should be distributed in a nondis-criminatory and dignified manner to everyone who needed it.

Through their organizing, women in the welfare rights movement formulated a distinctive radical black feminism that saw gender as linked to and shaped by class, race, culture, and sexuality. This radical black feminism spoke to their needs as poor women. It called for racial justice, economic empowerment, reproductive rights, and autonomy for women on welfare. They demanded a right to welfare and a decent standard of living based on the work they performed as mothers, regardless of behavior or personal morality. They insisted on participation in the making of welfare policy and wanted a role in shaping those rules and regulations that affected them. By defending their status as single mothers, they modeled an alternative to the traditional two-parent family. They challenged the discourse of welfare that labeled black women lazy and unfit and in the process hoped to recast popular perceptions of black womanhood. Theirs was a multiracial movement that highlighted the problems of racism and sexism in the disbursement of welfare. They built a broadly based, if somewhat tenuous, alliance among diverse constituencies of women. These women did not understand their situation only as welfare recipients or poor people. Instead, they had complex multiple identities that integrated their experiences with racism in the welfare system, their work as mothers, as well as their involvement in myriad community issues. The welfare rights movement is important because it provides a new perspective on the struggle for rights in the postwar period. The movement's demands for rights were tied to both civil rights and economic rights. Through their intersectional analysis, they began to chart an independent political course that would eventually redefine the meaning of black freedom and women's liberation in the 1960s.

This book offers a brief overview of the welfare rights movement and some of its key campaigns. Chapter 1 provides an introduction to the welfare system and chronicles some of the earliest welfare rights activity, explaining how poor women came together to address the many inadequacies of the welfare system prior to the 1966 march. Chapter 2 explores the larger political climate of the 1960s—both the civil rights movement and the antipoverty discourse—that helped lay the foundation for the emergence of the National Welfare Rights Organization. Chapter 3 discusses NWRO's first effort to influence federal welfare legislation and how women on welfare crafted a politics of motherhood to justify welfare assistance. Chapter 4 examines the movement's grassroots campaigns for a right to welfare. Chapter 5 traces NWRO's struggle for a national guaranteed annual income. Chapter 6 looks at some of the emerging tensions around race, class, gender, and political control that plagued the movement. Chapter 7 chronicles the external backlash and rising hostility the movement encountered and the ensuing differences between the middle-class male staff and the poor women of color about the direction of the movement. Chapter 8 explains the emerging radical black feminist politics of women in the welfare rights movement and the subsequent decline of the movement. The Conclusion assesses some of the important legacies of the welfare rights movement.

1

THE ORIGINS OF THE WELFARE RIGHTS MOVEMENT

The 1966 Ohio March was a milestone for the welfare rights movement. Grassroots activists from around the country participated in this historic protest and established networks of solidarity that would sustain the movement over the next nine years. But rather than a starting point, the march was more accurately a turning point. Prior to the march women welfare rights activists had formed neighborhood associations or local support groups to challenge the unfair practices and policies of the welfare system—in some cases a decade before the Ohio March. Their political initiatives reflected the multiple identities and the issues with which recipients were engaged on the ground and were rooted in the women's day-to-day experiences with welfare.

"Welfare" can refer to any range of government assistance programs, including social security for the elderly or student aid programs or even farm subsidies. But, in most cases, when people talk about welfare they are referring to cash assistance to the poor. Over time "welfare" has become synonymous with AFDC or what is today Temporary Assistance to Needy Families (TANF), a specific program for poor single mothers. During the postwar period as more African American women joined the welfare rolls, AFDC became more punitive and officials instituted tougher regulations and eligibility criteria. In many ways, welfare became a program that disciplined poor women rather than supported them. In addition, AFDC achieved unparalleled importance in American political discourse. It was a touchstone for debates about government bureaucracy, single motherhood, and inner-city decline. These issues informed both the unfolding reform efforts in the 1960s and 1970s, as well as the political evolution of the welfare rights movement.

Welfare rights activists organized first and foremost against the dehumanizing and surveillance-based components of welfare. The welfare program aimed to regulate the lives of poor women, deciding how they should raise their children, whom they could see, how to spend their money, and when they should enter the labor market. Although initiated to aid poor mothers, in the post-war period race came to dominate the politics of AFDC, as welfare became more punitive and exerted greater control over recipients' lives. The welfare rights movement emerged in part because of this dramatic transformation in AFDC.

History of AFDC and Support for Single Mothers

When initially established in 1935, AFDC was known as Aid to Dependent Children (ADC) and was part of the Social Security Act, a package of legislation passed in the midst of the Great Depression that sought to create an economic safety net for most Americans. The Social Security Act had two primary components: social insurance and public assistance. Social insurance programs, such as social security and unemployment compensation, were federally run, depended upon payroll contributions from workers, who were more likely to be male and white. Public assistance included ADC, Old Age Assistance for the elderly poor, and Aid to the Disabled. Public assistance was less generous and more restrictive than social insurance and served a greater proportion of women and people of color.[1] Unlike social insurance, which did not have income requirements— so everyone regardless of need could receive benefits if they paid into the program—public assistance was means-tested: recipients had to be poor in order to qualify. The federal government provided oversight and matching funds for public assistance, but states controlled eligibility criteria, determined budgets, and essentially ran the program. Consequently, ADC payments varied widely from state to state, and local politics, to a large degree, shaped the program.[2]

Through ADC, states granted monthly stipends to poor single mothers. ADC reinforced traditional gender roles of the male breadwinner and female caretaker because it offered assistance to mothers who did not have a husband to support them.[3] The rationale was that if the husband or father could not financially support the family, the state should step into that role, so mothers could care for their children. And, although the idea that single mothers should be encouraged in their work as mothers prevailed in the political discourse, in practice, most ADC recipients worked or supplemented their monthly allowance, which was simply too little to support their children. Local welfare departments often expected recipients to work even though they saw them primarily as mothers.[4] To deflect potential criticism, caseworkers made assistance available only to recipients they believed were blameless for their current situation, morally pure, and properly disciplining and caring for their children. Beginning in the 1940s and continuing into the 1950s local officials passed regulations to limit eligibility.[5] These included: "suitable home" laws denying aid to mothers who bore children out of wedlock or engaged in other behavior that caseworkers considered immoral or inappropriate; "substitute father" or "man-in-the-house" rules denying aid to women if there was any evidence of a male present in her home; employable mother laws refusing assistance to women physically able to work; and residence laws denying assistance to migrants from outside the state.[6] Despite the limited benefits and strict eligibility criteria, ADC did provide an allowance to help some mothers raise their children.[7]

Patterns of discrimination in the program were widespread. Racial, cultural, and class biases shaped social workers' views of who was a worthy and unworthy recipient. White women, most of whom were widows or deserted by their husbands, overwhelmingly populated the welfare rolls in the late 1930s.[8] Caseworkers expected poor single mothers receiving assistance to conform to white middle-class notions of proper motherhood and used noncompliance as grounds to deny assistance. Countless needy African American women never received aid, especially in the South and other areas where large numbers of African Americans lived. Although laws restricting eligibility were not race-specific, they were applied disproportionately to African American women. In 1943 the state of Louisiana refused assistance to women during cotton-picking season. Georgia passed an employable mother rule in 1952. Michigan and Florida passed suitable home laws in 1953 and 1959, respectively.[9]

Employable mother laws, in particular, were often designed to ensure an adequate supply of laborers to the workforce. They were directed primarily at African American women, who had a long history of employment outside the household. A field supervisor in a southern state explicitly made this connection:

> The number of Negro [welfare] cases is few due to the unanimous feeling on the part of the staff and board that there are more work opportunities for Negro women and to their intense desire not to interfere with local labor conditions. The attitude that "they have always gotten along," and that "all they'll do is have more children" is definite … [They see no] reason why the employable Negro mother should not continue her usually sketchy seasonal labor or indefinite domestic service rather than receive a public assistance grant.[10]

Consequently, southern officials routinely tightened eligibility and forced recipients into the labor market during periods of labor shortage.[11] Thus, black women's status as welfare recipients was bound up with their relationship to the labor market. Black women, more often seen as laborers than as mothers, were considered less deserving of public assistance than other women.[12]

Black Women's Entry onto the Welfare Rolls

Between 1950 and 1960 there were increasing attacks on and criticism of AFDC. Some of this had to do with the expansion of the rolls. The number of families on welfare grew from 652,000 in 1950 to 806,000 in 1960.[13] While a substantial increase, this alone does not explain the outcry. Public concern about welfare centered more on the particular welfare recipients joining the welfare rolls. By 1960, women of color, divorced and never-married women were a larger portion of those receiving welfare. The 1939 Amendments to the Social Security Act encouraged this trend by extending social security insurance coverage to widows and their children. The Amendments moved "deserving" women and children, whose husbands and fathers had died, from the ADC rolls into the more respectable social security program, leaving ADC with a larger percentage of divorced and unmarried mothers. In 1961, widows made up only 7.7 percent of the ADC caseload, down from 43 percent in 1937.[14]

The percentage of African Americans on ADC rose from 31 percent in 1950 to 48 percent in 1961.[15] This can be attributed in part to growing migration to the North. African Americans fled both Jim Crow racism and declining job opportunities in the South. Mechanization and other changes in agricultural production in the postwar South left many African Americans without work. Between 1940 and 1960, more than three million African Americans made their way from the South to northern cities in search of employment. Although many found work, deindustrialization in conjunction with widespread race and gender employment discrimination led to a disproportionately large number of unemployed or underemployed African Americans. In 1960, the official unemployment rate was 4.9 percent for whites and 10.2 percent for nonwhites.[16] Those arriving in the North may have turned to welfare departments for economic support as a last resort.

In addition, nonwhite and African American women were disproportionately single mothers. In 1960 the official non-marital birth rate for whites was 23 out of 1,000 births. For nonwhites it was 216.[17] Although single motherhood increased for all racial groups after World War II, white women becoming pregnant were well hidden from the public eye. They were sent off to birthing homes and their babies quietly put up for adoption. Black women had fewer institutional resources available. The lack of avenues for adoption, in addition to community values discouraging mothers from giving up their children, meant that unmarried black women kept their children and raised them at a far higher rate than unmarried white women.[18] This higher rate of black single motherhood coupled with higher poverty rates translated into a higher ADC rate for African American women. Taking into account their poverty and non-marital birth rates, black women were actually underrepresented on ADC.

Nevertheless, the increase in the number of black single mothers on welfare caused public alarm.[19] Using hyperbole and inflammatory rhetoric, politicians and the press hammered away at the apparent overrepresentation of black women on ADC. Increasingly, the politics of welfare converged on the stereotypical image of a black unmarried welfare mother who was lazy and dishonest. This image, more than any other, fed the fires of the welfare controversy.

In the late 1950s and early 1960s a welfare backlash by local politicians, the conservative press, and many ordinary white Americans exposed purported welfare fraud. Special investigative committees documented and ferreted out recipients allegedly unworthy of support. They charged that women recipients had several children outside of marriage, fathers took no responsibility for raising their children, and parents simply did not want to work. In most cases, the stereotypical welfare recipient was an African American woman. Further investigations into these claims, however, rarely revealed widespread fraud and found little abuse in the system. In Detroit, for example, a 1948 study revealed only two cases of fraud and in neither case was the recipient convicted of criminal wrongdoing.[20] Nevertheless, the investigations aroused public passion about welfare and planted in the minds of many Americans inextricable associations between receipt of ADC, race, immorality, and disdain for employment.

The press also highlighted the problems of cultural pathologies and sexual immorality. One investigator reported that 93 percent of ADC recipients in Washington, D.C. in 1962 were African American and that "Women with several illegitimate children, by several different fathers, were often found living with men who were bringing home regular paychecks."[21] Unlike when ADC was first established and financial assistance was deemed necessary for single mothers to raise healthy and well-adjusted children, by the early 1960s welfare for single mothers was considered detrimental. In 1963, an author for the *Saturday Evening Post* commented: "Today's welfare child, raised in hopelessness and dependency, becomes tomorrow's welfare adult, pauperized and helpless."[22] *US News and World Report* reported in 1965 that the rise in welfare rolls was due to the "mass migrations of unskilled Negroes from the South" and their "high rate of illegitimacy." The increasing number of "welfare babies" would "breed more criminals, more mental defectives, more unemployables of almost every type." The paper profiled the typical ADC recipient in Chicago: "A poor Negro girl: … She is insecure, uneducated, unsophisticated, frightened."[23] One official referred to children on welfare as the "children of illegitimate parents."[24] Clearly the target in the welfare debate had become African American men and women who were characterized as not wanting to work, unable to properly raise their children, and perpetuators of social and cultural pathologies.

"Illegitimacy," in particular, had become the catchword for evidence of the "degeneracy" of the black population and was justification for denying welfare to African American women. Popular and social welfare journals gave undue attention to the rise in non-marital births among women on AFDC and attributed this to male unemployment and female promiscuity.[25] In 1965, *US News and World Report* explained that as a result of migration, black men, unable to get jobs, abandoned their families: "Deserted wives, sometimes turning to any man who comes along, add to the high rate of illegitimacy in the self-perpetuating breeding grounds of city slums."[26] Thus, the concern about ADC was shaped and sold to the public in large part by racial ideology. Promiscuity and laziness became synonymous with black women on welfare. "Illegitimacy" became a code word for black single mothers on ADC and came to signify bankrupt moral values and community disintegration. White racism, gender norms, and assumptions about the moral dangers of "dependency" converged on ADC.[27]

By the late 1950s the discourse about welfare, particularly among politicians and some sectors of the public, interwove race, sex, class, and morality. Local welfare officials and legislators responded by attempting to uncover alleged welfare fraud and corruption, limiting eligibility, reducing welfare payments, and putting welfare recipients to work.[28] A number of cities, counties, and states, including Washington, D.C., Milwaukee, WI, Los Angeles, CA, Cuyahoga County, OH, Wayne County, MI, and the states of Illinois, Louisiana, and Pennsylvania formed special units within the welfare department to investigate whether a substitute parent, or potential breadwinner, resided in the house.[29] Caseworkers routinely checked up on recipients, sometimes conducting "midnight raids" to ensure that a recipient was not involved in a relationship with a man. These unannounced searches of recipients' homes violated their privacy and stripped them of their dignity. Caseworkers applied stringent and humiliating eligibility criteria to prevent women with alternate sources of support from receiving assistance. Under constant scrutiny, recipients had to prove the soundness of their character, their destitution, and, increasingly, their willingness but inability to work. Intake workers produced piles of application documents and asked probing questions about the candidate's personal and sexual history. Even when recipients qualified for assistance, their income was not always secure. Caseworkers frequently cut them off assistance without notice or explanation or reduced their grants arbitrarily. Those getting their monthly check found the amount hardly enough to provide the basic necessities for their children.[30]

The charges of fraud and attacks on the morality of welfare recipients were paralleled by cuts in monthly budgets. In Cleveland, Ohio, for example, the point of departure for the Ohio Walk for Adequate Welfare, officials instituted a number of punitive measures in response to an increase in black migration. Cuyahoga County, Ohio cut welfare checks in June 1959 by 10 percent and denied assistance to all able-bodied single men. In Cleveland, the City Council cut welfare, it stated, because of the rising number of relief cases due to "recent migrants" and increasing costs of welfare. Indeed, the proportion of Cleveland's nonwhite population had nearly doubled between 1950 and 1960, from 16 percent to 29 percent.[31] Eighty-seven percent of the AFDC caseload in the city in 1966 was African American.[32] In May 1960, it denied assistance to all employable single women and childless couples.[33] Although welfare cuts were explained in terms of rising costs, in 1962, AFDC payments were well below other public assistance levels in Ohio. Families on AFDC received $31 per person per month. Recipients of Old Age Assistance, Aid to the Blind, Aid to the Disabled, and General Assistance received between $75 and $80 per person.[34] Clearly, when budgets tightened officials turned to AFDC rather than other programs because welfare recipients were an easy target. These increasingly restrictive ADC policies made it harder for all women, but particularly black women, to receive assistance.[35] While southern states had always implemented racially punitive welfare policies and had consistently pushed black women into the labor force when necessary, black migration to the North and the changing composition of the welfare rolls fostered similar reforms in the northern and western states and on a national level in the 1960s. These trends illustrate changes in local policy as well as the national shift in the discourse about welfare and government responsibility over the course of the postwar period.

The Earliest Welfare Rights Groups

In the context of a harsher AFDC program, welfare recipients in cities, towns, and rural communities across the country began to discuss, and in some cases demonstrate about, their day-to-day experiences with poverty, racism, and the many abuses they endured from the welfare system. Well before the Ohio march and the formation of NWRO, welfare recipients had formed local welfare rights groups in response to their difficulties with ADC, which was renamed Aid to Families with Dependent Children (AFDC) in 1962. They met in the cramped kitchens or sparse living rooms of poor single mothers. They initiated neighborhood groups, often informally, to share stones about life on welfare. These women—some with a history of organizing—reached out to other women in their housing projects, their churches, and their neighborhoods. The first welfare rights organizers spearheaded collective efforts that questioned unfair welfare policies and practices. Ruth Pressley, for example, founded Welfare Recipients in Action in central Harlem in 1964, hoping to create an "organized, determined, and united group to fight the power structure."[36]

In the late 1950s and early 1960s recipients in California, Ohio, New York, Mississippi, Nevada, Michigan, and New Jersey were mobilizing.[37] Dorothy Moore headed a welfare rights group in Los Angeles. The Welfare Action and Community Organization started in 1958 in South Central and East Los Angeles. Moore formed a welfare recipients' union after the department mistakenly gave her a weekly check for only $1.50 and she had nowhere to turn for help.[38] She described the overwhelming power of caseworkers:

> The worst thing is the way [caseworkers] use fear. People depend on their checks so much that they're afraid to speak up for their rights … they are afraid to assert themselves and ask for what's theirs because if they do the worker may threaten to cut them off entirely.[39]

In 1961, Moore, along with other local leaders, established the Los Angeles County Welfare Rights Organization.[40] Shortly after that recipients in northern and southern California formed a statewide welfare rights organization.

Sometimes the bureaucratic red tape of the welfare department triggered organizing among recipients. In Chicago, for example, "Stringent and inflexible rules of the system, interpreted and applied by punitive caseworkers, created great frustration among the women recipients."[41] In 1965 the staff of the West Side Organization (WSO), a Chicago antipoverty group, helped the women form a union, which provided mutual assistance and enabled them to "take collective action in their own interests."[42] By the summer of 1966, the WSO Welfare Union had attracted over 1,500 welfare recipients.[43]

In other cases, the discretionary power of caseworkers prompted recipient organizing. An early welfare activist, who became prominent in Mothers for Adequate Welfare (MAW) in Boston, had several run-ins with the welfare department in the 1950s. Two caseworkers, she explained, "had very peculiar ways of dealing with public assistance families ... They visited late at night ... If ... you were going to have a male visitor, you knew that you were subject to visits during any time of the 24 hour period." If the caseworkers suspected something, the client stopped getting a check.[44] The MAW member explained that prior to the formation of a welfare rights group, recipients in Boston challenged this kind of treatment:

> Occasionally, [women] who may live in the same building or in the same block in the street would go together directly to the local field office and quarrel with the welfare office supervisor or they would move from the supervisor and go straight to the central office and try to get an appointment with the Director...This was in the early fifties through to about 1957 or '58.[45]

MAW was formed when several Boston welfare mothers, whose children were in the same after-school program, attended the 1963 March on Washington and learned from other participants about the surplus food program.[46] When they returned home, this group of friends reconvened to discuss how to start a surplus food program. In 1965, with the help of student organizers, they formed MAW.[47] The recipient who organized the first meeting reported that "she had become very scared of what she had started, and had been filled with misgivings and worry that her children might in some way be hurt by the publicity."[48] Despite the early hesitation, the group flourished. Three years later the organization had six branches in the Boston area with a membership of between fifty and sixty.

As is clear from the case of MAW, the civil rights movement was also a motivating factor in welfare rights organizing and served as an important model of social change. It fueled concerns about justice and equality, inspired people to question daily indignities, and provided countless examples of grassroots organizing to transform discriminatory institutions. Thousands of residents of Montgomery, Alabama boycotted the city busses for over a year because of segregation and mistreatment. Student protestors sat in and endured verbal and physical assaults to integrate lunch counters. And throughout the South, many African Americans found the courage to register to vote despite the many obstacles and almost certain retaliatory violence. Empowering individuals as agents of social change, the movement gave a voice to the disenfranchised and articulated a moral code of human rights, racial equality, and social justice. Women in the welfare rights movement drew on the example, language, and tactics of the civil rights movement to develop a collective identity and form a social movement. The civil rights movement spoke to the women's concerns about racism and inequality and provided a framework for understanding their oppression. For some welfare recipients the connection was more direct because the civil rights movement proved to be a training ground for their later welfare rights activism.

Many welfare recipients and organizers who first became involved in the civil rights movement later joined the struggle for welfare rights. In Boston, prior to initiating welfare rights organizing the leaders of MAW worked on a number of civil rights campaigns, including a Congress of Racial Equality (CORE) rent strike in 1962 and a battle led by the National Association for the Advancement of Colored People (NAACP) to end de facto school segregation in 1963 and 1964.[49] In another case, Mrs. Mildred Calvert, chairman of the Northside Welfare Rights Organization in Milwaukee, rooted her welfare rights activity in the civil rights movement. She explained that although "I was afraid of those kind of things ... when the kids decided that they were going [on the march] ... I had to go with them." The newspapers reported that the marchers "were doing all the bad things ... [but] we were the ones being fired upon with rocks and bricks and sticks." She read the black newspapers and started "seeing things in a different light."[50] This was when she joined the welfare rights movement. Whether or not they participated in the civil rights movement, the larger context and political climate of the postwar period gave welfare recipients both the optimism and opportunity to effect change. Inspired by the numerous instances of ordinary people refusing to submit to unjust, or racist policies, they began to agitate for themselves.

Although the civil rights movement provided inspiration, the indignities of the welfare system brought these women together and served as the glue for their social movement. Recipients became involved because of their difficulties with poverty, trying to survive on a meager monthly check, the embedded racism within the welfare system, as well as the reality of their lives as mothers. They encountered high food prices, exorbitant rent, and dehumanizing treatment by social service caseworkers. The meager monthly allowance and stigma associated with welfare deterred many poor mothers from applying for assistance. Those receiving aid were subjected to a bureaucratic maze of rules and regulations, leaving them powerless and at the mercy of caseworkers, who, at some moments, required them to discuss deeply personal matters and, at other times, expected them to be voiceless, passive subjects. By coming together and organizing, these women challenged some core features built into the public assistance program for poor mothers.

The Challenges of Welfare Organizing

For most people on AFDC, welfare was part of a web of social problems, which included inadequate housing, segregated schools, unsafe playgrounds for children, police harassment, and high food prices. The multiple issues in which they engaged meant that recipients in the welfare rights movement had complex identities. They were not only "poor people" or "welfare recipients," but also black, brown, or white mothers, tenants, consumers, and community members. Welfare rights activists were involved in grassroots organizing, before or simultaneously with welfare rights, that addressed an array of issues such as civil rights, housing, and labor organizing. Many confronted the specific problem of welfare through multi-issue neighborhood and community associations.

The multiple identities of welfare recipients were exemplified by the way in which welfare rights organizing in the early 1960s was often an extension of other kinds of community activism. Housing was deeply intertwined with welfare. The economic security that welfare rights activists sought depended to a large degree on the availability of adequate shelter. Their poverty limited their housing options. So, many opposed evictions and gentrification and advocated affordable housing. In Mount Vernon, NY in 1966 the Committee of Welfare Families had been

> protesting for several weeks against slum housing conditions that welfare recipients are forced to endure. Their action has included a sit-in at City Hall demanding temporary shelter and prompt relocation within Mt. Vernon for those evicted; an end to evictions for filing slum housing complaints. They plan to erect a tent in the center of the city for people already evicted who have no place to live.[51]

A welfare rights group in Waltham, Massachusetts declared in 1968, "Housing is a main complaint of most of the mothers, since many of them pay more than half their incomes for housing."[52]

Beulah Sanders, chair of the Citywide Coordinating Committee in New York from 1966 until 1971 and a national leader of the welfare rights movement, first engaged in the fight for housing rights for the poor. Born and raised in Durham, North Carolina, Sanders moved to New York City in 1957 in search of work. In 1966, unable to find work, she lived on the Upper West Side of Manhattan on a small welfare check in a neighborhood designated for urban renewal. The urban renewal program, known among some black activists as "Negro removal," sought to eradicate "slum" housing by moving poor people out to make way for better housing and wealthier families. Sanders joined the effort to reform urban renewal policies and end the demolition of homes of the poor. She defended the rights of neighborhood families, many of whom were welfare recipients, to remain in their homes. In the midst of this work she helped organize a citywide welfare movement in New York.[53]

One of Sanders' friends and another New York City welfare activist, Jennette Washington, moved from Florida to Manhattan in 1945 at the age of ten to live with her mother who had set out in search of work. She went to school until 10th grade and eventually found a job in a factory, but was laid off during a recession. She turned to welfare to help provide for her three children. Washington was always rebellious, someone who questioned authority and stood up for her beliefs. As a youngster this landed her in trouble with her mother, school authorities, and a judge who sent her to a juvenile home for a period of time. As an adult, her indomitable personality was well suited for the political organizing that marked the 1950s and 1960s. Washington organized for many years in urban renewal, housing rights, parent–teacher associations, and a community group called the Stryckers Bay Neighborhood Council, before getting involved in welfare rights activity. Well before the formation of NWRO she and Beulah Sanders started the West Side Welfare Recipients League. Washington was at the founding NWRO convention and served on the executive board of the Citywide Coordinating Committee in New York from 1968 until 1971.[54] Washington, Sanders, and other members of the Welfare Recipients' League attended the 1966 Chicago meeting where the Ohio march was initially discussed.

Both Sanders and Washington were part of a larger network of a New York-based welfare coalition known as the Welfare Recipients League. The League grew out of a grassroots storefront office, the East New York Action Center, started in 1964 by Puerto Rican activist Frank Espada.[55] The handful of people working in the East New York storefront in this predominantly black and Puerto Rican neighborhood organized rent strikes and protested inadequate garbage pickup. They soon identified welfare as a critical community problem and formed the Welfare Recipients' League. The League grew quickly, and soon incorporated twenty-four chapters in Brooklyn, with some meetings drawing hundreds of people. Throughout Brooklyn a number of other storefront action centers served as a meeting ground for welfare recipients. In another initiative in Brooklyn three nuns and two priests from local parishes assisted in establishing several storefront action centers in 1966. These neighborhood groups formed the base for the Brooklyn Welfare Action Center. By 1968, the Brooklyn Welfare Action Center had 8,000 members.[56]

Many welfare rights groups in the early sixties grew out of community organizations. In Chicago the Kenwood-Oakland Community Organization (KOCO) had on its agenda, among other issues, education, housing, and urban renewal. In one campaign, for example, it opposed the Board of Education's decision to relocate residents to build a new school. After welfare surfaced as a central problem, KOCO started a welfare union, with recipients who were designated "union stewards" acting as counselors and advocates to other recipients.[57] In early 1966, KOCO Welfare Commission, as the union was known, published a welfare rights pamphlet and planned sit-ins and pickets to pressure the welfare department.[58] The pattern was repeated in Louisville, Kentucky. The West End Community Council initially addressed problems of housing, education, tenants organizing, and recreational activities. Welfare, however, quickly became the main focus. Members planned "a series of workshops to inform local recipients of their rights; a membership drive; and a presentation of recipients' demands to welfare officials in Louisville and Frankford in conjunction with nation-wide welfare demonstrations on June 30."[59] These examples demonstrate that for most AFDC recipients, welfare was not an isolated issue, but part of a broader set of concerns.

Forming a Multiracial Movement

One of the biggest challenges welfare rights activists encountered was to build an interracial movement that identified the universal problems faced by poor women while recognizing the centrality of race. The welfare rolls in the mid-1960s were 48 percent African American. The welfare rights movement, however, was overwhelmingly African American, perhaps 85 percent.[60] Women in the welfare rights movement believed that racism was the scaffolding for the welfare system, which did not regard all poor people or welfare recipients as equal. Black women welfare rights activists articulated their political engagement in part because of the racism they experienced as AFDC recipients. MAW in Boston explained the different treatment of black and white recipients:

> White recipients will almost automatically be granted special allowances at some offices, while black recipients in similar circumstances will be met with delaying tactics plus a full quota of red tape, and then will probably be turned down. Likewise, case-workers are accused of using their power to disapprove moving allowances for the purpose of keeping white recipients out of disreputable neighborhoods while black recipients are kept in.[61]

For most welfare rights activists, their race or nationality was inseparable from their day-to-day experiences as welfare recipients. Mrs. Clementina Castro, Vice Chairman of the Union Benefica Hispana WRO and Sergeant-at-Arms of the Milwaukee County WRO, explained:

> When I first came on welfare, they didn't have any Spanish-speaking caseworkers at all…I was so shy because I had never talked to white people, because I had been working in the fields…Some whites can speak it, but they just know the language, they don't know the problems. Latins can

understand better because they know, they have already passed through the same problems. They know our culture.[62]

Welfare recipients such as Mrs. Castro saw race and culture mediating their inter-actions with caseworkers and their relationship with the welfare department. These welfare recipients articulated their problem with the welfare system as one of racial discrimination as well as poverty. The discretionary acts of racism by caseworkers and the systematic mistreatment of black and Latino recipients fostered among welfare rights activists a consciousness rooted as much in their experiences as black, brown, and white people as their status as poor. As racial identity became a salient and more frequent part of political discussion in the 1960s, welfare rights activists used a language of racial consciousness and voiced their struggle as partly for racial liberation. They developed an analysis linking their race to their experiences as poor women on welfare.

For welfare activists, however, a racial consciousness did not preclude the pos-sibility of working in an interracial setting; and organizing in a multiracial setting did not mean a movement devoid of an analysis of race. Although they situated racism as integral to the disbursement of welfare they remained committed to interracial activism and invited people of any color to join them. Beverly Edmon, the founder of the Welfare Recipients Union in Los Angeles said: "There's as many white people, probably a lot more, who have the very same kind of prob-lems we get here from welfare. Poor people have the same problems, black or white. What we have to offer is good for anybody who comes in."[63] Welfare lead-ers formulated a welfare rights agenda that attempted to toe a line, on the one hand, of addressing the racism of the welfare system and wanting to empower black women and, on the other hand, recognizing the class-based nature of their oppression. Despite the way in which racism divided women and operated to stigmatize AFDC recipients, it seems that momentarily and for a small group of women, the welfare rights movement was able to bridge the racial divide. The movement fostered an interracial organizing model that brought together women of different racial backgrounds around their common concerns of poverty, welfare, and motherhood. By welcoming all women on welfare, welfare rights activists suggested that racist attitudes, while pervasive, were not inherent.

Perhaps the life of Johnnie Tillmon best encapsulates the movement's early organizing efforts and its complex relationship to race. Tillmon, an African American woman, was the first chairwoman and later executive director of NWRO, and was one of the most important ideological influences within the welfare rights movement. Born in 1926 in Scott, Arkansas, Johnnie Lee Percy was a sharecropper's daughter, whose itinerant farming family was forever in search of a better economic situation. Although poor, she had fond childhood memories of her family's self-sufficiency since they made or grew nearly every-thing they needed—clothing, soap, lard, fruit, and vegetables. When she was five years old, her mother died while giving birth. Her father and stepmother raised her and her two younger brothers. Tillmon's father instilled in her a strong sense of racial pride and taught her about her forebears' migration from Africa and their history of enslavement. In Arkansas, Jim Crow segregation mandated separate public facilities for blacks and whites, especially in urban areas. But Tillmon learned to live with these publicly drawn racial boundaries. Moreover, formal segregation might not have been as profound in shaping her world view as the economic forces that impoverished families like hers. She observed white poverty first hand, and recognized similarities between her own situation and that of poor white people: "Some of the white people in Little Rock were just as poor as I was … where I lived there was always white people who worked on the farms. They weren't treated any better … than I was."[64]

As Tillmon tells it, far from being "shiftless and lazy,"—as welfare recipients were often described in the 1960s—she began her working career in the cotton fields at the age of seven. She attended one- or two-room schoolhouses in rural Arkansas, until she moved in with her aunt in Little Rock to attend high school. Although a good student, she took a job and never graduated. For a short time she did domestic work. But when the family asked her to eat lunch with the dog, she made a pledge to never again work in anybody's house. During World War II she was employed in a war plant, then got a job in a laundry where she remained until she left Little Rock. At the laundry, an integrated workplace, Tillmon noticed little racial animosity: "For those of us who worked there, it wasn't about white and black. It was about green. Were you going to get paid at 12:00 on Saturday?"[65] In 1946, she married James Tillmon and had two children, but she and her husband separated after two years. She subsequently had four more children. Tillmon worked during and after her marriage ended and also supported her father who lived with her. After her father died in 1960, she headed to California to join her two brothers.

While pregnant with her sixth child, Tillmon moved in with her brother in Los Angeles. To support herself and her five children, she worked as a shirt line operator in a laundry—a job her sister-in-law helped her land—where she ironed 120 shirts an hour. She eventually moved into a place of her own, but found it impossible to care for an infant and five other children while working full time. She sent her six-month-old baby girl to live with her youngest brother in Richmond, California. At the laundry facility, where African Americans, Mexican Americans, and poor whites worked side-by-side, Tillmon advocated for better working conditions and wages. She quickly rose to a position as union shop steward, undoubtedly learning organizing skills that she would later use in the struggle for welfare rights. She also helped register voters and joined a community association, the Nickerson Gardens Planning Organization, which planted flowers, arranged after-school activities for children, and improved living conditions in her housing project.

In 1963, Tillmon contracted a severe case of tonsillitis and was hospitalized. The president of the neighborhood association, Mr. Garringer, suggested that

Tillmon apply for welfare so she could devote more time to raising her children. Her teenage daughter—who had been skipping school—needed her attention. In addition, welfare assistance would enable her to be reunited with her two-year-old baby who was still living in northern California with her brother. Imbued with negative ideas about welfare, she hesitated, but eventually agreed because of concern for her children.

Tillmon was struck by the differences between her life as a recipient and as a working woman. Caseworkers inventoried Tillmon's refrigerator, questioned such decisions as purchasing a television, and provided her with a welfare budget that outlined how she should spend her money. She contrasted this unrelenting supervision to her relative independence as a worker: "[W]hen I left my job in the evening. I was through until the next morning. And on the weekend I didn't have no one peeping and peering, telling me what to do or what I couldn't do."[66] The policing of her intimate life angered Tillmon. She later recounted: "When I was working every day, if I wanted to have male company, then I had male company. But when you're on welfare, you can't have too much male company."[67]

Just eight months after getting on welfare, Tillmon began to organize her fellow recipients. She and five of her friends surreptitiously obtained a list of all Aid to Dependent Children (ADC) recipients in the housing project where they lived. They sent out letters asking the women to come to a meeting to discuss their lease and grant. Three hundred people showed up to the first meeting.[68] In August 1963, the Los Angeles-based Aid to Needy Children (ANC) Mothers Anonymous opened an office staffed by welfare recipients to help people who had been cut off from assistance or had other welfare problems. As Tillmon explained, her goal was "to be independent and if you weren't independent, to be treated with dignity."[69]

Tillmon's life, in many ways, reflects many of the important themes in early welfare rights organizing. She had a long history of employment and only went on welfare when it seemed impossible to combine work and mothering. Although she engaged in activism previously, the humiliation she experienced as a welfare recipient prompted her to begin organizing a local welfare rights group. And despite her strong racial identity, economic hardship enabled her to recognize how poverty crossed racial lines.

Conclusion

Although these women came from different backgrounds, lived in different regions of the country, and had different social networks, they all had one thing in common: they were recipients of AFDC. Whatever particular problems recipients encountered with welfare, uniting to address them was tremendously empowering. Collectively, welfare recipients could more effectively navigate the welfare bureaucracy, challenge caseworkers, share information, or simply support one another. Welfare rights activity empowered recipients, most of whom had silently suffered the humiliation of being on welfare. Sharing experiences taught them that their problems were not exceptional; but that abuse and arbitrary treatment were a systematic part of AFDC, designed to discourage them from being on welfare or to prevent them from knowing and asserting their rights. The very act of coming together challenged the stigma long associated with AFDC and embodied the idea that welfare was not charity, but a right. Many women on AFDC, for the first time, publicly identified and spoke about their experiences as welfare recipients.

AFDC recipients often coalesced as a result of friendships or connections to a neighborhood association. These kitchen-table discussions enabled recipients to share experiences about the indignities of the welfare system, the first step in the formation of local welfare rights organizations. Through these discussions people came to believe that they should not have to be demeaned in order to receive a welfare check, that the grant should be enough for them to live decently, and that they had rights that ought to be protected. By meeting to talk about their problems as welfare recipients and turning social networks into political ones, these women embarked on a process that ultimately led them to challenge the rules and regulations governing their lives.

Local organizing was not widespread before the emergence of a national movement in 1966. But this early agitation and welfare recipients' initiative is an important part of the story of how the welfare rights movement emerged. Its existence demonstrates that the impetus for the movement lay not with civil rights activists and middle-class organizers but with the daily experiences of welfare recipients and their belief that they could make gains—a belief no doubt influenced by the liberal political climate and the example of other social movements. The heart of the movement comprised largely poor, uneducated, single black mothers who were, as former sharecropper and civil rights leader Fannie Lou Hamer said, "sick and tired of being sick and tired."

If it were not for the prior organizing by welfare rights activists, the June 1966 nationwide march could not have been pulled off. Local communities would not have been prepared to participate. But the success of the 1966 march also illuminated the benefits of local groups cooperating and connecting with one another. And that watershed moment set them on a course of establishing the National Welfare Rights Organization. NWRO brought together local grassroots activists and middle-class allies to transform fledgling neighborhood welfare rights groups into a national political movement.

2

FORMING A NATIONAL ORGANIZATION

The 1966 March for Adequate Welfare was the first coordinated national demonstration of welfare recipients. Thousands of local activists protested throughout the country, bringing a previously unknown visibility to the welfare rights movement. Grassroots organizers who participated in the 1966 march came together a few months later to form the National Welfare Rights Organization. The formation of NWRO was a defining moment in the history of the welfare rights movement. As the first national organization of welfare recipients, it gave a collective voice to women on public assistance—enabling them to participate more effectively in policy debates. It emboldened community activists by offering resources and a network to which they could turn for help. And it provided a much-needed intervention by the poor in the political discourse.

Middle-class allies and supporters were essential to the formation of NWRO. Many of these middle-class allies were veteran activists who had numerous contacts, an arsenal of organizing skills, and extensive experience navigating the political bureaucracy. They raised money, coordinated meetings, distributed literature, and provided staff. The national structure, which grew out of these efforts, was responsible for much of the movement's national influence. But in some ways, NWRO's structure, which included both middle-class staff and grassroots welfare recipient activists, proved in the long run to be constricting for welfare recipients who dissented from some of the strategies and tactics the organization pursued. Differences of class, race, gender, and political philosophy, especially between staff and recipients, bubbled just below the surface. Nevertheless, during the early years the organization forged a coherent political agenda for welfare rights and created an opening for recipients to participate in national legislative debates about AFDC. The larger political climate and the emerging concern about poverty were decisive as welfare recipients and their supporters established a national political movement.

Antipoverty Policy

The question of poverty was central to national political discourse as the decade of the 1960s opened. Academics and policymakers discussed, documented, and analyzed poverty and its social consequences. These academic and political debates fostered a climate that was conducive for the expansion of a movement for welfare rights.

One reason for the concern about poverty was its intellectual "discovery" in the midst of an era of dramatic economic growth and prosperity. In the 1960s, the US experienced one of the longest uninterrupted economic expansions in the country's history. For most of the decade, unemployment was very low, hovering around 5 percent, but even falling below that. Economic growth and worker productivity increased. By 1960 the income of the average worker was 35 percent higher than in 1945. Working-class Americans could afford to purchases suburban homes, automobiles, televisions, and numerous other appliances to fill their countertops and cabinets. Much of the economic expansion was made possible with massive federal expenditures on health care, education, highway construction, and defense, which created well-paying jobs in both the public and the private sectors. But there was another side to the story. Although the poverty rate declined substantially in the postwar period, in the late 1950s 20 percent of Americans still lived below the poverty line. So, while many Americans benefitted from economic expansion, a swathe of the American public remained untouched.

In 1958 renowned Harvard economist John Kenneth Galbraith assessed this period of economic growth in his best-selling book *The Affluent Society*. [1] Galbraith did not present an uncritical view of American prosperity. While recounting the material benefits of consumerism for many Americans, Galbraith also called for an enlargement of the public sector and greater government investment in education, health care, public parks, housing, and sanitation, to remedy what he called a "social imbalance." Michael Harrington published in 1962 a much more probing critique of economic growth.[2] In *The Other America,* Harrington documented the existence of poverty amidst the wealth of the nation. He asserted that the tentacles of economic prosperity had not reached every nook and cranny of the nation; that some people had been left behind through no fault of their own. Perhaps most importantly, he argued that the persistence of poverty belied the assumption that a rising tide lifts all boats. Clearly, economic growth and impressive GDP numbers in and of themselves were not enough. Harrington and other scholars of poverty proposed government intervention through job training and educational programs—strategies that would prepare the poor to take advantage of expanding opportunities.

The emerging concern about poverty was perhaps best reflected in the federal government's "War on Poverty," officially launched in 1964. The origins of the War on Poverty lay with President John F. Kennedy, who, after touring parts of Appalachia in 1961, hoped that a concerted government effort might aid impoverished rural residents, many of whom were white. After Kennedy's assassination, President Lyndon Johnson ushered through Congress in 1964 the Economic Opportunity Act, the most important piece of legislation to come out of the War on Poverty. Johnson, who in part hoped to pacify flaring anger about persistent racial discrimination and ongoing racial violence, promised "equality as a fact."[3] The Economic Opportunity Act initiated a whole range of programs and waged a multi-pronged attack on poverty. These included job training, work experience programs for disadvantaged youth, early childhood education to prepare poor children for elementary school, local health centers, work-study programs, free legal services for the poor, and, perhaps most controversially, a community action program, which facilitated poor people's organizing.

The War on Poverty was the boldest government effort to ameliorate poverty since Franklin Roosevelt's New Deal. But unlike the New Deal which grew from the depths of economic desperation of the Great Depression, the War on Poverty was the fruit of economic growth and abundance. As Lyndon Johnson said in his speech announcing the program in January 1964, "This administration today, here and now, declares unconditional war on poverty in America. I urge this Congress and all Americans to join with me in that effort. It will not be a short or easy struggle, no single weapon or strategy will suffice, but we shall not rest until that war is won. The richest Nation on earth can afford to win it." Indeed, for many people the riches of the nation held out the promise of eradicating poverty once and for all.

The War on Poverty's main strategy provided opportunity for the poor, rather than income support. The slogan for the Office of Economic Opportunity, the Washington office that coordinated the government's antipoverty efforts, was "a hand up, not a hand out." This encapsulated the OEO's goal of helping people to help themselves through job training, education, and social services. The social service and job training model was in part premised on the belief that there was nothing fundamentally wrong with the economic system, but that poor people needed to be prepared, trained, and taught how to take advantage of the opportunity the economy provided. So, the War on Poverty offered them tools to compete in the labor market. This approach differed from that of the welfare rights movement, which demanded higher monthly benefits—income support—so poor mothers could adequately raise their children.

The other thread of concern about poverty in the 1960s came out of the civil rights movement, which had drawn the nation's attention to the visible and sometimes brutal realities of racial segregation and violence. But many civil rights activists had never confined their attention only to dismantling southern-based Jim Crow laws and had argued that economic progress was essential for mitigating racial inequality. The large number of impoverished African Americans in both the rural South and the urban North was stark evidence of the debilitating effects of racism. The 1963 March on Washington, for example, was billed as a march for jobs and freedom. Civil rights leaders also observed that despite the removal of formal barriers of equality with the passage of the Civil Rights Act of 1964, many African Americans were still mired in poverty. The Southern Christian Leadership Organization (SCLC), founded by Martin Luther King, Jr., began Operation Breadbasket in Chicago in 1965 to improve housing and job opportunities for African Americans in this northern city. As if to drive home the point about the needs of the economically marginalized, in the mid-1960s several inner-city neighborhoods—Harlem and Watts among them—violently exploded into what some called "uprisings" directed at an unjust racial and economic system.

The antipoverty rhetoric of the early 1960s had a two-fold impact on the welfare rights movement. First, it opened up a dialogue about poverty by suggesting that no American should be deprived of basic necessities in the midst of economic abundance. All of these theorists and activists identified poverty as a social problem that had to be rectified. Although the reports, studies, and government programs of the early 1960s did not speak to the specific needs of women on welfare or single parents, the antipoverty rhetoric probably heightened recipients' expectations for raising their own standard of living and gave them hope that a struggle for reform might yield results. Middle-class proclamations about alleviating poverty increased the likelihood of recruiting allies and securing funding for a movement for welfare rights.

Second, most theorists framed the discussion of poverty within the circumscribed boundaries of male unemployment. Scholars such as Harrington, policymakers, foundation heads, and even civil rights activists, grappled with how to prepare unemployed men for available jobs, redevelop de-industrialized areas, and increase the minimum wage. The main concern of poverty researchers was not single motherhood or even racial discrimination. Instead, they studied the impact of broad structural changes, especially deindustrialization, on able-bodied but unemployed men. Countless reports echoed the concern with male unemployment and its attendant social problems. Lost in the discussion were the inability of single mothers to support themselves, the lack of available day care, and paltry AFDC payments. The optimistic public dialogue about the affluence of the nation and the possibility of eradicating poverty stood in stark contrast to the concerted efforts to cut AFDC budgets, restrict the number of people on the rolls, and attack the moral character of recipients. Many believed that black women on AFDC were unworthy of support and ended up on welfare because of debauchery and personal failings. On the other hand, they cast unemployed and poor working men as victims of impersonal structural forces. The emphasis on male unemployment rather than female independence foreshadowed a fierce debate within the welfare rights movement and in other policy circles about single motherhood, gender, and poverty. These parallel trends of AFDC cuts and antipoverty rhetoric produced a formula that encouraged women on welfare and their allies to begin to fight back.

Middle-Class Support for Welfare Rights

The increasing attention to poverty among social movement activists, politicians, policymakers, and ordinary Americans in the mid-1960s led to an outpouring of resources devoted to eradicating poverty. Some of this facilitated welfare rights organizing. Local welfare rights groups acquired support in their political work from student activists, churches, legal aid societies, civil rights groups, and the federal government. Middle-class allies provided meeting space for recipients, gave legal advice, funded local welfare rights groups, and hired staff to work with welfare rights leaders. Some supporters offered basic necessities like the use of a telephone while others helped initiate and maintain welfare rights groups. Whatever the level of support, middle-class organizations and individuals proved indispensable in the creation of a national welfare rights movement.

The War on Poverty's Community Action Program (CAP) directly aided welfare rights organizing. It provided federal money to encourage the participation of poor people in neighborhood and community associations that advocated for their interests. It called explicitly for "maximum feasible participation" of the poor with the rationale that poor people needed to be engaged politically in order for reform to be most effective. In some ways the welfare rights organizations were tailor-made for the CAP program: here were poor people interested in participating in community-based groups to reform the welfare system. Welfare rights organizers and leaders applied for federal CAP grants to hire organizers, print leaflets, and operate storefront offices. As Johnnie Tillmon explained, "Community action programs and agencies began to form and we began to participate. I'm sure whoever wrote those words 'maximum feasible participation of the poor,' wished they had not done that!"[4] Another War on Poverty program, VISTA, a domestic version of the Peace Corps, enabled dozens of young people to serve as organizers for welfare rights organizations.[5]

Student activists were another important source of support. Perhaps the most influential student group was the largely northern, predominantly white Students for a Democratic Society (SDS). SDS was formed in 1963 after several white college students traveled South to participate in the civil rights movement and show solidarity and support for the black-led grassroots campaigns. But SDS soon developed its own agenda, which included opposition to the Vietnam War and also a critique of hierarchy and authoritarianism on college campuses. In addition, SDS launched a community organizing project. Intense discussions within SDS led many to conclude that students could organize inner-city communities and construct a model of participatory democracy. From 1963 to 1965 students in SDS took up full-time residence in several cities across the country to build "an interracial movement of the poor." Intending to organize unemployed men, students were forced to consider the specific problems of welfare recipients by poor women who responded to their calls for community participation.[6]

Cleveland was one of SDS's antipoverty sites. Cleveland had a long history of welfare rights protest, even before student activists arrived. In 1954, several ministers founded the Inner City Protestant Parish (ICPP), a cooperative interdenominational and interracial church network to assist the poor. ICPP provided religious leadership for the welfare rights movement in Cleveland. Rev. Paul Younger, minister at Fidelity Baptist Church, part of the ICPP, worked with the civil rights movement in Cleveland in the early 1960s and helped form Citizens United for Adequate Welfare (CUFAW). Younger worked tirelessly to mobilize welfare recipients to demand their rights through CUFAW, which drew its membership from two Cleveland churches that served different racial communities, but came together around welfare rights. Co-chaired by Erla Jones and Mabel Swanson, the group educated the public about inadequate welfare grants, fair hearings, and the free school lunch program. With the support of churches and other community groups, they organized letter-writing campaigns and public forums and picketed at the State House.[7]

When SDS organizer Sharon Jeffrey moved into Cleveland's Near West Side to work with CUFAW, the organization was somewhat dormant. The presence of SDS and its infusion of resources and energy revived CUFAW, and it quickly became a functioning organization. Throughout Ohio, recipients, with the help of supporters, organized regional committees for adequate welfare. In the spring of 1966 the local and regional groups in Ohio came together to form the Ohio Steering Committee for Adequate Welfare, which launched the Ohio Walk for Adequate Welfare.[8]

Lillian Craig's story provides a good example of how middle-class support in Cleveland facilitated organizing among women on welfare. Lillian, a white woman recipient, was born in 1937 in Cleveland, Ohio. Her mother died of asthma and pneumonia when Lillian was twelve. Lillian spent much of the rest of her childhood in foster homes and a girls' reform school. She worked after high school, married, had three children, divorced, and went on welfare. She learned of welfare rights through St. Paul's Community Church, a member of Cleveland's ICPP and came in contact with Paul Younger.

Craig became part of a close-knit group of women, mostly welfare recipients, who provided mutual support to one another. In 1964, when SDS established the Cleveland Community Project in the Near West Side, Lillian became involved. SDS worked in both the predominantly black east side and the largely white west side, and brought these groups together. As poor white women and poor women of color began to work together, they remarked how eye-opening the experience of cross-race organizing was for them. Speaking of her first encounter with the organization, Lillian explained in her memoir: "It was scary. I had never been around groups of black people. I didn't even know how to express my fear of blacks. But I began to get to know them through Paul [Younger] and because he was just plain folks, we soon discovered that we all were just plain folks."[9] The campaign in Cleveland typifies how church, student, and civil rights contexts in Ohio shaped activism.

On a national level, churches provided most of the financial support for NWRO. Protestant denominations, including the United Church of Christ, Methodists, Presbyterians, and Episcopalians, funded nearly half of NWRO's budget in 1968. Other support came from Catholic and Jewish groups. The largest single funding source for NWRO was the Interreligious Foundation for Community Organizations (IFCO), an arm of the National Council of Churches. Between 1967 and 1971, IFCO gave $500,000 to NWRO.[10] Formed in early 1967 by the United Presbyterian Church, the United Church of Christ, and the Episcopal Church, IFCO supported community organizing in poor neighborhoods. The formation of IFCO and Protestant and Catholic support for community organizing was part of a religious inclination in the 1960s and 1970s, called liberation theology, emphasizing social action over service and advocating liberation and empowerment of the poor and oppressed. In concrete terms, this meant a huge network of financial and political support for the welfare rights movement.

In some cases sympathetic caseworkers encouraged recipient activism. Caseworkers were often a target of recipient discontent, but in the 1960s, many social workers were sensitive to clients' predicaments. Social-work students radicalized on college campuses rejected the traditional casework approach to social welfare as well as the overriding concern for professionalism of many social workers in the early postwar period.[11] This led to, according to Richard Cloward, "an important activist segment that was very supportive" of welfare rights.[12] A significant minority of social workers supported a more generous and liberal welfare system and worked with WROs, becoming themselves advocates for welfare rights. According to one study that surveyed members of the National Association of Social Workers, 45 percent of respondents in 1968 believed that poor people must organize to demand better treatment.[13] These social workers assisted welfare recipients in articulating and pushing for their rights. Betty Niedzwiecki, chairman of a WRO in Milwaukee County, illustrates this point:

> When I went on welfare, they stuck me in an experimental zone. The case-workers in there were working for the people as much as they possibly could. They even belonged to Milwaukee's Friends of Welfare Rights. They told me about Welfare Rights in the first place. They informed me of a lot of things that go on.[14]

These are some of the most important examples of middle-class support, but they are not the only ones. Foundations and nonprofit organizations offered their support as well. The Highlander Folk School in Tennessee, for example, hosted workshops on community organizing for a welfare rights organization in Boone County, West Virginia.[15] Mobilization for Youth in New York City, funded by the Ford Foundation, helped start a number of welfare rights organizations.[16] Legal aid societies and the Columbia University School of Social Work also played critical roles in defending the rights of welfare recipients and offering legal advice and representation. In the mid- and late-1960s the antipoverty fervor and commitment to social activism touched many Americans. Some may have devoted their lives to helping the needy; others simply donated money or applauded the many efforts under way. Whatever their chosen level of support, this collective effort aided the welfare rights movement in tangible and long-lasting ways.

Leadership

Perhaps the individual most instrumental in establishing a national welfare rights movement was George A. Wiley, a black chemistry professor at Syracuse University who served as NWRO's executive director for most of its history. Born in 1931 in New Jersey and raised in Warwick, Rhode Island, a semi-rural, nearly all white middle-class town near Providence, Wiley attended the University of Rhode Island and earned his Ph.D. in Chemistry at Cornell. While a professor at Syracuse University in the early 1960s, Wiley chaired the local Congress of Racial Equality (CORE) chapter, which fought for integrated public schools and equal employment and housing opportunity.

In 1964 Wiley left his teaching post at Syracuse to work full-time for CORE as associate national director, second in command under James Farmer. When Farmer announced his resignation in late 1965, Floyd McKissick, chairman of CORE's policymaking body the National Action Council, and Wiley both vied for Farmer's position. Wiley was at a disadvantage, however, partly because of the rising tide of nationalism within CORE. By 1966, many CORE members questioned the strategy of nonviolence and the benefits of interracial organizing. Wiley's sophisticated and cultured background did little to ingratiate him with the young militants. In addition, in his ambitious pursuit for power within the organization, Wiley had curried disfavor with Farmer, who in the end supported McKissick.[17] After the unsuccessful attempt to win Farmer's position, Wiley resigned from CORE and turned his attention to antipoverty activism.

In April 1966, using money raised from friends and $3,000 of his own savings, Wiley started the Poverty/Rights Action Center (P/RAC) in Washington, D.C. Edwin Day, a graduate student in public affairs at Syracuse who had worked with Wiley in CORE and left the organization with him, helped start P/RAC.[18] Wiley and Day envisioned P/RAC as a communications clearinghouse for poor people's organizations around the country, linking efforts already under way. The increased welfare rights activity around the country and the persistent urging of two academics, Frances Fox Piven and Richard Cloward, convinced Wiley to focus on welfare.

Wiley stood out from other civil rights leaders because of his commitment to welfare rights. Some civil rights leaders opposed organizing African Americans to claim welfare benefits because they believed welfare fostered dependency, encouraged the break-up of black families, and stigmatized the African

American community. When Richard Cloward and Francis Fox Piven sought to convince civil rights leaders to encourage African American women to join the welfare rolls as a strategy to federalize AFDC, they approached Whitney Young of the National Urban League. Revealing his own class biases, Young responded to the two social scientists by saying: "I would rather get one black woman a job as an airline stewardess than I would to get fifty black mothers on welfare."[19] Wiley, on the other hand, was deeply committed to those "fifty black mothers" and soon began an independent organizing effort.

Wiley met Cloward and Piven at the "Poor People's War Council on Poverty" in Syracuse in January 1966. That year, the two scholars wrote an article in *The Nation* magazine arguing that the current welfare system should be replaced with a guaranteed annual income, a basic federally guaranteed minimum income for all poor families. After extensive research, they discovered that nearly half the people qualifying for AFDC did not receive it and proposed that organizers recruit these people onto the welfare rolls. This, they predicted, would "precipitate a profound financial and political crisis" in the welfare system. City governments, unable to handle the large influx of new recipients, would pressure the national government to implement a guaranteed annual income.[20] George Wiley, on the other hand, was more interested in building an organization of poor people. He wanted "to unite public assistance recipients around the country into an organized bloc that can push for better welfare legislation and demand with some authority that abuses in the system be corrected."[21] He believed that marches, sit-ins, and threats of disruption would reap electoral and economic power for the poor if they were organized. To this end, Wiley hoped to create a mass-based national organization.[22] Although Piven's and Cloward's strategy was not adopted—NWRO chose to recruit current recipients rather than mobilize potential recipients—the two academics, nevertheless, were important in the intellectual development of the movement. Piven and Cloward met periodically with Wiley to discuss the direction of the movement, attended conferences and meetings, and raised money. They differed with Wiley and other organizers about NWRO's strategy, but Cloward's and Piven's idea for a guaranteed annual income would ultimately become a central goal of NWRO.[23]

Wiley recruited Tim Sampson, who eventually managed NWRO's headquarters as associate director for three years, to work with him and Day at P/RAC.[24] Sampson, a white organizer and social worker, helped start the Alameda County Welfare Rights Organization in California. The first P/RAC staff members set up shop in an old pink row house in Northwest Washington, D.C. and during the first few months traveled around the country speaking to welfare rights leaders. Day contacted Johnnie Tillmon in Los Angeles. When Tillmon got word that an organizer from Washington was looking for her, she called a friend and asked him to "check out" this guy. When her friend confirmed that Day was "okay," Tillmon met and spoke to him about her work with Aid to Needy Children. Within a year, twenty people worked in the P/RAC office in Washington.[25]

Formation of a National Welfare Rights Group

While setting up P/RAC, Wiley attended a Guaranteed Income Conference at the University of Chicago in the spring of 1966, at which grassroots welfare rights leaders were also present.[26] After the conference recipient and non-recipient welfare activists from around the country met up, including Johnnie Tillmon, Beulah Sanders, and a group from Ohio that was planning a Walk for Decent Welfare. They came from Chicago, Ann Arbor, Newark, Syracuse, New York City, Detroit, and Cleveland.[27] This was, in fact, the first time welfare rights leaders from around the country got together.

This meeting laid the basis for a nationally coordinated campaign. The Ohio group had planned their protest for June 30, and asked other activists from around the country to join them. Since it was impractical for welfare recipients who had little money to travel to Ohio, they decided that groups would hold their own demonstrations to coincide with the Ohio Walk. June 30 would be a national day of action for welfare rights.[28] They also decided to form a national coordinating committee which would meet again in Chicago in August to discuss plans for a national welfare rights organization.[29] Two days after the Chicago conference Wiley returned to Washington for the official opening of P/RAC. He then turned his energies to making June 30 a success. A shrewd fundraiser, he got a $5,000 loan from Irving Fain, an industrialist in Providence, RI.[30] He also sought financial assistance from people such as Katherine Graham, publisher of the *Washington Post*, Harold Taylor, former president of Sarah Lawrence College, and Maurice Tempelsman, diamond owner in South Africa.[31] He traveled around the country meeting with welfare rights leaders and recruiting help from community and religious leaders and social service workers. He mailed out literature, contacted the press, and helped form local and regional welfare rights committees to coordinate activity.[32]

Although a citywide welfare rights group already existed in New York, Wiley worked with several welfare recipients active there, including Beulah Sanders and Jennette Washington, and spoke to them about coordinating the demonstration. The group decided to hold the June 30 protest at City Hall in Manhattan. By August 1966, New York's Citywide Coordinating Committee included forty-five affiliated groups and claimed to represent 5,000 clients. Wiley asked Hulbert James to serve as executive director of Citywide. Born in the Virgin Islands and raised in Harlem, James was active in the student movement and the NAACP while in college. During the mid-1960s he was working on welfare issues for a Louisville anti-poverty agency. James accepted Wiley's offer, and by August 1967, was working full time with the Citywide Coordinating Committee of Welfare Rights Groups.[33]

In addition to working with specific local chapters, Wiley also coordinated welfare rights activity nationally. A savvy political organizer adept at dealing with journalists, politicians, and welfare officials of all colors and stripes, Wiley managed at once to bring both much needed publicity and funds to the efforts of local welfare rights groups. More importantly, he created a space and an opportunity for welfare recipients from around the country to come together around national campaigns and to lend support to local groups. He helped transform the incipient struggle against welfare into a coherent national political movement. An important function of NWRO was, according to Wiley, the

> encouragement that the local group gets from knowing that it is part of a movement greater than its own local situation. The national visibility we have given to the welfare problem by linking together what would otherwise appear to be disparate activity pulls together matters of really great importance.[34]

Welfare recipients concurred. Beulah Sanders believed that if the "system were to be effectively changed, a strong, cohesive organization would have to be formed to link together the activities and purposes of the many neighborhood welfare rights groups that existed."[35] This networking and organizing for the June 30 demonstration that grew out of the Chicago meeting signaled the emergence of a national welfare rights movement.

Wiley and his allies were important in the development of a national welfare rights movement. They did not, however, start the movement. Welfare recipients around the country were already fighting for their rights on a local level around issues of welfare, housing, education, and community services. In fact, Catherine Jermany, a participant in the Los Angeles County WRO explained, "We were not particularly interested in a national organization and being a part of it because we had our own thing going in California."[36] Frances Fox Piven reflected on this period of organizing:

> There's a sort of arrogance in the...way George and all of the organizers really believed that they were moving people...That organizers got people to come to a meeting, or a march, or to get arrested or to scream or erupt... Organizers played a role. But people were ready to move. People were ready to join [an] organization.[37]

So, Wiley and other middle-class supporters expanded and strengthened organizing already under way on the local level and created a national forum to discuss the goals of a movement.

In August 1966, one hundred representatives from seventy-five welfare rights organizations around the country came to the first NWRO meeting in Chicago to set up a national coordinating committee and to formulate goals and strategies for a nationwide movement. The following spring, 375 people attended a meeting in Washington and laid plans for a formal organization. Because of concerns about domination by middle-class people, NWRO limited membership and voting privileges to the poor.[38] Wealthier supporters were invited to join a Friends of Welfare Rights group, which would provide financial and moral support for the movement. Local welfare rights organizations could affiliate with NWRO when they recruited twenty-five members and sent the national office $1 dues per member per year. This earned them the right to send a delegate to the annual national convention. Most local groups required members to pay yearly dues of $1 to the local welfare organization and another $1 for national membership. In this way, NWRO was more of a federation of local groups than a direct member-ship organization. The national office encouraged, but did not require, local groups to adopt "WRO" as part of their name to display affiliation with the national association.

The yearly convention of representatives from welfare rights organizations around the country set the general program and goals of NWRO. The National Coordinating Committee (NCC), made up of elected delegates from each state with affiliated welfare rights organizations, was the policymaking body between national conventions and met four times a year. In addition, an executive commit-tee, composed of nine welfare recipients elected at the national convention, car-ried out policy decisions made by the NCC or the membership at the convention. The executive committee met eight times a year and decided policy between conventions and NCC meetings.[39] George Wiley, the executive director of the national office in Washington, hired a staff to help him fundraise, distribute information to welfare rights organizations around the country, and coordinate campaigns. The staff included people who worked in the national office, as well as organizers who were placed in different locations around the country. In the first few years, paid staff positions went primarily to middle-class, mostly white, supporters of the movement. The official role of the staff was to implement the decisions of the national convention, the NCC, and the executive committee.

At the first convention in August 1967, welfare recipients from around the country elected officers. Johnnie Tillmon, head of ANC Mothers in Los Angeles, was chosen chairman of the new organization.[40] Tillmon would prove to be a powerhouse, a savvy organizer with an astute sense of politics who left an indeli-ble mark on the welfare rights movement. The group also outlined four major goals of their organization: adequate income, dignity, justice, and democracy. These four themes embodied the multiple strategies of the welfare rights move-ment, which included not just higher benefits, but respect, equality, and political participation. The themes would emerge and re-emerge in the various campaigns the movement waged.

Conclusion

The formation of NWRO was a critical turning point in the history of the wel-fare rights movement. NWRO provided invaluable material and moral support for women welfare rights activists. Staff members wrote grants and raised money.

They established a communications network with other political organizations that could provide assistance to local welfare rights struggles. NWRO sought national venues where recipients could be represented. It transformed disparate local groups into a national political force and served as a microphone for the collective voice of women on welfare. One of the first opportunities to engage national welfare policy occurred just one year after NWRO's founding—in Washington D.C. as Congressional representatives debated new welfare legislation that significantly shifted the goal of welfare assistance.

3

MOTHERHOOD AND THE MAKING OF WELFARE POLICY

NWRO held its first national convention in August 1967 in Washington D.C. It did so deliberately. Washington, of course, was the home of P/RAC, where Wiley and his staff were based. But, more importantly, that summer Congressional representatives were in the throes of discussing and debating new welfare regulations and NWRO intended to weigh in. NWRO used its first national convention as an opportunity to express its opposition to the proposed amendments to AFDC. Welfare recipients were most disturbed by the mandatory work requirements that Congress was considering. Proponents of the work requirements believed that black women were lazy and promiscuous and needed to be disciplined.[1] Women in the welfare rights movement framed their opposition to the work requirements by making a moral claim for assistance as mothers. They fought for their right to stay home and care for their children, enter or reject intimate relationships, and to legitimate their status as single mothers. Their position was very much at odds with the larger discourse of welfare reform and with many of their middle-class allies within the welfare rights movement, who opposed the work requirements for different reasons. Nevertheless, welfare rights activists' intervention in the debate about welfare and articulation of their needs is an important indication of the contestation of welfare policy.

The welfare rights movement's participation in the 1967 welfare debates is one example of how the movement sought to engage, reshape, and redefine the meaning of welfare. Recipients did this through grassroots campaigns for higher monthly benefits and protection of their civil rights and also through demands for participation and representation—suggesting that welfare policy cannot and should not be crafted without input from those people most directly affected. The campaign around the welfare amendments illustrated both the strengths and weaknesses of NWRO speaking "for" welfare recipients. The weaknesses became most obvious when staff members, shortly after the passage of the bill, signed a government contract to help implement the new work requirements. NWRO's lobbying effort revealed differences and divisions within the organization—not about whether recipients should have a voice—but whose voice would represent them and what that voice would say.

The Poor and Policymaking

In the 1960s, recipients engaged in a number of campaigns to transform the meaning of welfare on their own terms. The welfare system did not function only in the interests of the powerful to control and regulate the less powerful. Nor did the poor have complete freedom to shape it. The welfare rights movement's campaigns demonstrate that the meaning of welfare was contested terrain. Public assistance to the poor had always been a site of struggle.[2] This occurred in the day-to-day battles between caseworker and client. Clients may have reshuffled their budget categories to reflect their needs in a way that caseworkers were unaware and may not have approved of. Occasionally, they might have earned unreported income, or accepted money from family members or ex-husbands. Or they could have turned down job opportunities as a way to spend more time with their children. Welfare recipients employed these strategies to resist constricting rules and regulations and to make the welfare program work in their interests.

With the emergence of the welfare rights movement, the day-to-day battles continued, but opposition to the dehumanizing regulatory aspects of welfare was also more overt. Sometimes, as with demands for special minimum-standards grants from caseworkers, which recipients were legally entitled to, activists organized on terms set by welfare departments. In other ways, such as when they insisted on the right to be involved in intimate relationships, women on welfare defined their needs and the nature of their claims. They also demanded a role in the formulation of welfare policy. Welfare policy was an evolving process. As welfare activists organized and found strength in numbers, they questioned decisions by caseworkers about their monthly budget and standard of living. They rejected anything tainted of charity, made claims as mothers, and sought to make their own and their children's lives more comfortable. By speaking up and speaking out, welfare recipients transformed a political discourse that silenced and marginalized poor black women on welfare.[3]

Members of the welfare rights movement demanded participation of the poor and welfare recipients in both welfare policy and electoral politics. In the 1960s, democratic participation was a broader concept than simply voting, placing a representative on a board, or submitting a proposal for reform. Many grassroots groups organized to participate in political institutions, community boards, and policymaking bodies. Welfare rights activists hoped to be included in the policymaking process as a group with special concerns; to be recognized as a community with a collective voice and shared interests. Johnnie Tillmon echoed the need to acknowledge the existence of the poor:

> A major problem we had to face was to get recognition. That was a hard thing to do. The fact is that we do have recognition now—whether it is on the subversive lists or whatever. We are still recognized. Maybe people aren't saying the kind of things that we want them to say about us, but the point is that they at least recognize that we are here.[4]

Leaders of the welfare rights movement demanded representation on policy-making bodies at the local and national levels. When Beulah Sanders spoke before the President's Income Maintenance Commission, a government-appointed committee that was considering a federal subsidy for all poor people, she reiterated the importance of recipient participation. "We have our own ideas on what kind of system we should have. It seems to us as organized welfare recipients … that the recipients of the program should have the largest say as to what goes into it."[5] Similarly, a welfare rights activist from Beaufort County, SC testifying before Congress about the food-stamp program argued:

> We came to participate in the formulation of plans that would get at the needs of hunger and malnutrition in Beaufort County. For too long, people have been making decisions about what will affect other people's lives. The people that these programs will affect directly have nothing at all to say about them. We want to participate in some of those decisions about how the new program can best meet the needs of the poor people.[6]

For welfare rights activists, the goal of participation was twofold. They wanted to transform the welfare system and to empower welfare recipients through the process of participation.[7] Jon Van Til, a sociologist and participant-observer of three welfare rights organizations in Delaware County, Pennsylvania explained:

> [Welfare recipients] participated intelligently. They participated in a civil fashion. And they participated in a productive fashion. It's a real testimony to the ability of individual citizens who are [recipients]…These folks know the system. They know how it works. And actively having them participate in shaping it, and critiquing it, and tweaking it, and fine tuning it, and improving it…makes for better policy.[8]

Recipients expecting to transform the system through democratic participation paralleled the idea of some union organizers that if workers helped run the factories, the factories might look quite different. But, in addition, for welfare rights activists, democratic participation was part of the process of individual transformation.[9] By demanding representation and insisting that their voices were heard, welfare recipients challenged their social/political/economic marginalization. As black feminist scholar bell hooks suggests, the very act of speaking out begins a process of political empowerment.[10] From this perspective, participation was an act of political resistance that enabled welfare recipients to alter a political landscape that silenced and rendered them powerless.[11]

Including the poor in policymaking was not always successful and, even when it was, the question loomed of exactly how much power and influence a few welfare recipients had. Welfare administrators sometimes placated protesters by giving them nominal positions without real power or influence. Or, they encouraged recipient participation as a way to defuse political mobilization. An aide to the governor of Massachusetts suggested that the state recognized Mothers for Adequate Welfare (MAW), a welfare rights group, and its members, who "have been brought into the system via the appointment of [a welfare recipient] to the State Advisory Board" and no longer have a power base.[12] In this case, the real authority to make decisions lay with the welfare department and not the clients.

Nevertheless, including the poor in decision making was a watershed development in the history of social welfare. Prior to the 1960s there had been no precedent to seek recipient participation. Caseworkers and administrators rarely recognized recipients as active agents. The 1962 Amendments to the Social Security Act, however, included a provision for local welfare centers to create advisory committees to improve communication between welfare centers and clients. In most cases, administrators only formed advisory committees after clients began to organize as a way to either preempt or undermine their political organizing. In New York City, for example, advisory committees were set up after recipients formed a citywide WRO.[13] So, the impetus for recipient participation in policymaking came from the welfare rights movement. As scholar Neil Gilbert summed up:

> Over the past fifteen years a significant increase in client–group–member participation on governing boards of public and private nonprofit social welfare agencies has reinforced the mission and capacity of these bodies to represent the varied interests of the community. This marked change in board composition was perhaps the most important legacy of the citizen participation movements of the 1960s. One might almost say that those movements fashioned a new norm which mandates client-group representation on social welfare agency boards.[14]

An OEO official similarly pointed out how participation of the poor transformed welfare policy:

> The concept of participation in program operation and decision making by the resident of the target areas, thought to be completely unworkable,

has become an accomplished fact...Prior to this development, social welfare could be adequately characterized as a noblesse oblige responsibility of one group for the less fortunate.[15]

Thus, the demands for participation altered recipients' relationship to the welfare department and its governing structures. Previously marginalized and silenced in decision–making, recipients began to have a voice in the welfare system. Both local welfare rights organizations as well as NWRO facilitated and created avenues for welfare recipients to participate in the making of welfare policy. Scholar Nancy Fraser has argued that the state assumes the authority to define welfare recipients' needs. She suggests that even though state processes operate in such a way as to make the interpretation of people's needs a foregone conclusion, how we define needs is very much a site of contestation. The welfare rights movement did indeed challenge state authority and prevailing interpretations. Recipients' articulation of their needs and the means of distributing welfare became a part of the dialogue and discussion about what the welfare system ought to look like. The discourse about needs is important, according to Fraser, because it "functions as a medium for the making and contesting of political claims."[16] The welfare rights movement's participation in this discourse made it difficult to implement welfare policy without, at least in a token way, consulting poor people. Although both middle-class NWRO organizers and grassroots welfare activists agreed on the importance of welfare recipient participation in welfare reform, they differed somewhat on the nature of the reform. Middle–class allies pushed for more money, a dignified program, and restoration of the two–parent family. Welfare rights activists saw dignity and economic security as inextricably tied to motherhood and women's independence.

Welfare and Motherhood

Perhaps the welfare rights movement's most important contribution to the debate about welfare was highlighting their roles as mothers.[17] Since the movement's inception, motherhood was a central theme for activists. Many women in the welfare rights movement identified as mothers and were motivated in large part to provide adequately for their children. They wanted the state to support and recognize their work as mothers. Local welfare rights organizations often had the word "mother" in their name. In northern Colorado a group calling itself the AFDC Mothers Club organized to protect their rights.[18] In Minnesota, recipients established AFDC Mothers Leagues beginning in 1964.[19] Welfare rights activists also framed their campaigns as benefitting their children. In Pennsylvania in mid-June 1966, 700 mothers on welfare planned a "crusade for children" asking for an immediate increase in the basic AFDC grant.[20] The Citywide Coordinating Committee of Welfare Rights Groups in New York wanted to ensure that "our children ... have the same advantages, the same education, the same hospital services, the same opportunities as other children."[21] The needs of children were a primary issue for many women joining the welfare rights movement.

Lois Walker, a member of the Rockbridge County WRO in Virginia, understood her welfare rights activity in terms of quality of care for her children. Several of her children had health problems including a son with eczema who needed oil baths twice a day, a nearly blind daughter who needed close supervision, and an epileptic son who required medication daily. She explained:

> I was working at the time I became a member because the Welfare Department had really forced me to leave my five children with just any unreliable babysitter...I was told if I didn't work my children would be taken away from me. So by being in the group I learned my rights by being an ADC mother, and I am constantly fighting for the beneficial changes that would improve the living conditions for both me and my children.[22]

Ethel Dotson, participant in the Richmond, California WRO and a Northern California representative to the NCC, explained her situation. Working until she became pregnant with her first child, she initially drew unemployment and then in 1965 started receiving welfare. She recounted:

> I had seen a lot of kids where the parents worked and they had babysitters and the kids would end up calling the babysitter 'momma.' And calling mother something else. And I stayed at home and made sure I did not work for at least two years, so that my son, you know, we had our time together with me raising him. So, he was calling me 'momma' and not the babysitter momma.[23]

The welfare rights movement's claims to motherhood was a critical intervention in the political debate about welfare at a time when welfare mothers, and black welfare mothers in particular, were under attack. It attempted to redirect the conversation away from lazy and irresponsible AFDC recipients; away from the question of employment of welfare recipients; and away from the so-called "crisis of the black family" that had come to dominate social science research.

The Black Family and Welfare

In the 1960s, the black family became a subject of scholarly interest and national concern. A plethora of articles, studies, and conferences examined the rising number of single parents, relations between black men and women, and cultural traits of African Americans. This focus on the black family, which eventually came to be defined as a "crisis," forged two major concerns on the domestic agenda—racism and poverty. The concentration of poor black people in urban areas, the increasing number of black women on welfare, as well as protests and demonstrations by civil rights activists and welfare recipients highlighted the problem of black poverty. Academics explained the prevalence of poverty among African Americans by looking at patterns of racism and how this shaped characteristics of the black family.[24] Abram Kardiner and Lionel Ovesey, for example, in *The Mark of Oppression* outlined the psychological and cultural damage caused by racial discrimination. Other scholars, such as Kenneth Clark in *Dark Ghetto* and Lee Rainwater in *Behind Ghetto Walls,* examined structural barriers to economic success for urban African Americans and the resulting "pathological" behavior. Pathology, in most cases, was defined by male unemployment and female-headed families. So, even if the point of departure was structural economic forces, many of these theorists concluded that the black family was damaged. Like the antipoverty researchers, they resolved to find work for men and reestablish the two-parent household.

Some analysts pointed to the rising number of black welfare recipients as one of the most reliable indicators of the widespread problem of poverty and racism. The best-known study to connect welfare, poverty, and race was *The Negro Family: A Case for National Action* by Daniel Patrick Moynihan, Assistant Secretary of Labor under President Johnson. Published in 1965, the *Moynihan Report*, as it is more popularly known, argued that "At the heart of the deterioration of the fabric of Negro society is the deterioration of the Negro family. It is the fundamental source of the weakness of the Negro community." Moynihan attributed the disproportionate number of black single parent families, which he called a "tangle of pathology" to the "matriarchal" black family structure. A long history of slavery, exploitation, racism, and unemployment led to a high divorce rate, male desertion, a large number of "illegitimate" children, and a rapid growth in AFDC families. The solution, Moynihan claimed, was to establish a stable black family structure.[25]

The Moynihan Report reflected a "culture of poverty" thesis that gained currency in the 1960s. The culture of poverty argument attributed the persistence of poverty to familial and cultural traits within particular communities. Anthropologist Oscar Lewis first popularized the term in the early 1960s in his writings about impoverished communities in Mexico and Puerto Rico. Lewis argued that among his subjects, poverty had become a way of life, passed from generation to generation through the cultural transmission of a series of traits: the lack of a work ethic, resignation, dependence, lack of impulse control, and the inability to delay gratification, among others.[26] In some distant past, such traits developed in response to prolonged economic deprivation, but Lewis argued that these traits now prevented individuals in these communities from escaping poverty. In other words, culture perpetuated—even caused—poverty. Of course, culture of poverty arguments failed to take into account the complex reasons for the persistence of poverty, including residential segregation, racially discriminatory hiring policies, and inadequate schools. By narrowly focusing on one issue—personal behavior—culture of poverty theorists missed the larger picture of why poverty exists and, moreover, assumed that culture is an attribute "passed on" generationally rather than something created and crafted in a particular historical moment.

The *Moynihan Report* and its culture of poverty argument had a profound impact on welfare policy. It ultimately reinforced welfare's racial stigma and proved to be invaluable to critics and reformers of welfare policy. His analysis that the "deteriorating" black family, i.e. single motherhood, was the source of many problems in the black community fueled criticism of AFDC, enabling conservative and liberal politicians and policymakers to demand a retrenchment in the welfare state. They argued that assistance from the government discourages two-parent families, promotes out-of-wedlock births, gives fathers little incentive to pay child support, and, according to Moynihan's logic, leads to myriad other social and economic problems. These critics concluded that poor women should not have access to a source of income independent of men. Strengthening age-old beliefs about why poor single mothers should not get government assistance, the *Moynihan Report* also cemented the issue of race to welfare and single-parent families in a way that made it difficult to talk about one without the others.[27] Moynihan's report shifted the debate about urban poverty from structure and economics to culture and values. Although Moynihan suggested expanding employment opportunities for black men, his emphasis on black family cultural practices overshadowed his other points. The ensuing debate centered on changing the "domineering" position of black women, bringing black men back into the household, and ending the "cycle of poverty."

Reclaiming Black Families

George Wiley, like most black leaders of the time, was outraged by the *Moynihan Report*. He questioned whether the patterns of family breakdown that Moynihan identified pertained only to the black family. He argued that if statistics of single parenthood were broken down by race and income, the same trends could be applied to white families as well.[28] He suggested that poverty, not black culture, explained high rates of single parenthood. Like countless others, Wiley challenged Moynihan's focus on race rather than income to explain the deterioration of two-parent families. He objected to Moynihan's characterization of the black family as "matriarchal" but did not dispute the dubious link between matriarchy and social pathology.

Like Wiley and Moynihan, most people in the NWRO national office assumed that single motherhood was a social problem and, like many other black and white activists in the 1960s, ascribed to traditional notions of proper family forms. Richard Cloward, one of the most ardent defenders of the rights of welfare recipients, wrote in 1965:

> Men for whom there are no jobs will nevertheless mate like other men, but they are not so likely to marry. Our society has preferred to deal with the

resulting female-headed families not by putting the men to work but by placing the unwed mothers and dependent children on public welfare-substituting check-writing machines for male wage earners. By this means we have robbed men of manhood, women of husbands, and children of fathers. To create a stable monogamous family, we need to provide men (especially Negro men) with the opportunity to be men, and that involves enabling them to perform occupationally.[29]

White and black organizers within NWRO supported strategies that reinforced the traditional family. White male staff members at the national office wrote in the platform for the Poor People's Campaign in 1968 that "there is a desperate need for jobs in the ghettoes for men to permit them to assume normal roles as breadwinners and heads of families."[30] Dovetailing with mainstream policy analysts, many male leaders of NWRO agreed that single motherhood was a social pathology, every family needed a male breadwinner, and male employment was a long-term solution to poverty.[31] The debate around the *Moynihan Report* demonstrated the widespread consensus among people on both the left and the right of the "problem" of single motherhood in the black community.[32]

Women in the welfare rights movement, on the other hand, attempted to debunk the notion that single motherhood signaled culture deficiency and challenged the assumption that poor single mothers needed a male breadwinner.[33] Reclaiming their own definition of functional families, they argued that there was nothing inherently wrong with women raising children alone. Welfare rights activists in West Virginia counseled recipients to get a "paupers' divorce" if the welfare department won't pay for a divorce, suggesting that women separate from their husbands and plead ignorance about their whereabouts.[34] When women did marry someone who was not the father of their children, they wanted to continue to receive welfare and maintain their economic independence. Westside ADC Mothers of Detroit sought to overturn a policy making the new husband financially liable for the children of the recipient.[35]

Welfare rights activists criticized intimate relationships that oppressed women. According to reporter Gordon Brumm, Mothers for Adequate Welfare (MAW) believed that marriage with its "fixed rules and obligations" was a "means for domination more than a means for expressing love."[36] Although they valued motherhood, they did not promote marriage or encourage women to accept a subordinate status as mother and homemaker. They believed women should have autonomy in choosing their partners and suggested alternative family and relationship models—where women had control of their personal lives and could strive for fulfilling relationships. MAW explained, "Instead [of institutional marriage], they favor love, ... responsibility toward other persons, and freedom to whatever extent that responsibility allows."[37] Welfare rights activists asserted their right to date without negative repercussions from the welfare department. In Morgantown, West Virginia activists wrote in a handbook that "an AFDC mother can have male visitors as often as she wants and go out on dates if she leaves her children in the care of a responsible person."[38]

Women in the welfare rights movement tackled head-on criticisms that welfare recipients' "dependency" distinguished them from other women. There were many women and mothers, they suggested, who were dependent. Women in MAW argued that women on AFDC "supported out of public funds" were not much different from wives dependent on wages paid to men and also supported by public funds in the form of taxes or higher prices. The family-wage system assumed that men had families to sustain and justified paying them higher wages. Yet the same consideration was not given to women supporting their families. Working mothers "need nearly the same income as a family man, yet they are expected to take jobs ordinarily occupied by young unmarried women."[39] Welfare rights activists explored how the disparate realities of men and women caring for families were socially constructed. The critical factor determining their entitlements was not their familial responsibility, but their gender, race, and class status.

Women in the welfare rights movement attempted to legitimate their status as single parents and assert their right to marry or date on their own terms free of social stigma or repercussions from the welfare department. At a time when welfare recipients—black recipients in particular—were increasingly attacked as immoral and licentious women not worthy of receiving public assistance, these welfare recipients stood up to declare their right to be single mothers.[40] Welfare rights activists supported poor women's right to public assistance whether or not they conformed to the dominant norm of a heterosexual, patriarchal family model. Their ultimate goal was not restoration of the two-parent family, but autonomy and economic support for poor women. They defended their status as single mothers and disputed arguments vilifying them. For these welfare activists, autonomy meant preserving their right to be women and mothers independent of men.

Women, Welfare, and Work

The debates about single motherhood, rising welfare rolls, inadequate budgets, and the black family were reflected in welfare reform policies of the 1960s, which for the first time sought to require women on welfare to work. When AFDC was established in 1935, it was rooted in the male breadwinner model of the family. Poor women without a breadwinner, the architects reasoned, should be supported in their work as mothers so they could carry out their domestic responsibilities. Although AFDC benefits were too low for mothers to avoid all paid employment, the program lauded women's mothering role. This began to change, however, when more black women joined the rolls. In the early 1960s, national welfare policy shifted to encourage women on welfare to enter the labor force rather than to support them in their work as mothers. Work incentives were first passed as part of the 1962 Social Security Amendments, which permitted states to require adult recipients to work in exchange for benefits and allowed them to deduct work-related expenses when computing welfare benefits.[41]

The shift in the goals of AFDC was embodied most clearly in the 1967 Amendments to the Social Security Act. The Amendments had several components. It included a provision requiring states to establish a minimum level of "health and decency" for welfare recipients. The provision, which sought to improve the living standards of welfare recipients, was later used as a basis for legal struggles by the welfare rights movement to increase monthly stipends. The proposed Social Security Amendments also made employment of welfare recipients a mandatory and permanent feature of federal welfare policy. The Work Incentive Program (WIN) required states to refer a portion of their AFDC population with school-age children to accept either job training or employment, provided funding for day care, and allowed recipients to keep the first $30 of their monthly income and one-third of anything beyond that. Recipients refusing to participate in work or training lost their benefits. By mandating work, the 1967 Amendments reversed a basic premise of the original welfare program: to support single mothers. WIN undermined the idea that welfare was an entitlement for poor single parents and their children and more firmly tied benefits to the behavior of recipients.

In addition to the new work program, the bill also capped increases in AFDC because of parental absence from the home due to desertion or a child born outside of marriage. Repealed before it ever took effect, the inclusion of this clause was nonetheless important. The House Ways and Means Committee, for example, reported that it was "very concerned about the continued growth" of the ADC rolls due to "family breakup and illegitimacy."[42] The 1967 Social Security Amendments, then, aimed to resolve the problems that many people believed plagued AFDC—rising caseloads, inadequate budgets, out-of-marriage births, and black women's tenuous work ethic. For women in the welfare rights movement, the work requirement was the most appalling aspect of the proposed Amendments.

The new welfare proposals represented a widespread consensus in the 1960s that women on welfare should work. Liberals, conservatives, and many radicals, concurred that employment would solve the immediate problem of rising welfare rolls and the long-term problem of poverty.[43] Democrats and Republicans did not agree completely on all aspects of the WIN proposals. President Johnson offered amendments for child care and a work incentive allowing recipients to keep a portion of their earnings and suggested making mandatory the AFDC–Unemployed Parent program, which started in 1961 and extended benefits to two-parent families. But even these revisions reinforced the dominant view about the need to bolster the two-parent family and require recipients to work.

NWRO lobbied against the proposed work requirements. In August 1967, it held a public hearing and members spoke to a roaring crowd of several hundred, in the presence of what one reporter called an "unusual force" of police officers.[44]

The delegates then adjourned to the Mall in downtown Washington for a "Mothers' March" which drew 1000 people and later a picket at the Department of Health, Education and Welfare. At the rally, Margaret McCarty, welfare rights leader in Baltimore, invoked the historical oppression of African Americans as well as the racial pride of period, when she said "lousy, dirty, conniving brutes" devised the bill to "take us back to slavery…I'm black and I'm beautiful and they ain't going to take me back."[45] NWRO aimed to ameliorate the problem of poverty through an adequate income, not employment and argued that "having a job is no guarantee against poverty." In a pamphlet called the "Six Myths about Welfare" written a few years after passage of the bill, NWRO wrote that under WIN, the welfare department would force a mother "to take any job, even if it's not covered by minimum wage laws. In the South, especially, where cheap 'domestics' are in greatest demand, the WIN program can be tantamount to involuntary servitude."[46] They called the bill "a betrayal of the poor, a declaration of war upon our families, and a fraud on the future of our nation."[47]

The next month, NWRO testified before the Senate Finance Committee about the impending legislation. Fifty women attended, many with their children in tow. Welfare recipients with prepared testimony denounced the regulations as "disgraceful." Beulah Sanders explained the potential impact of the work requirements on their children: "When our children are picked up by the police, they'll ask them where their parents are. And we'll have to tell the police that we've been forced to let them roam the streets because the Government says we have to go to work."[48] Only two of the seventeen Senators were present to hear their testimony, however. In protest, the women staged a three-hour sit-in until all seventeen members of the Senate Finance Committee appeared. Committee Chairman Russell Long, Democrat from Louisiana, was so angry at the mothers' conduct that when adjourning the meeting he banged the gavel so hard its head flew off. Long became enraged at the black recipient protestors and referred to them, in a revealingly racial manner, as "brood mares."[49] The welfare recipients only left when District police threatened to fine and arrest them for unlawful entry.[50]

Despite NWRO's intense lobbying, WIN was enacted into law. The passage of WIN was a clear loss for the welfare rights movement. In practice, however, WIN did little to move recipients into the labor market. Congress provided limited funding for job training or child care and welfare administrators focused their attention on finding employment for poor fathers on welfare rather than mothers.[51] Nevertheless, the 1967 Amendments signaled an important shift in federal welfare policy. It enacted the first federal mandatory work requirement for AFDC recipients.

Debating WIN

Although NWRO had vehemently opposed WIN, the NWRO national office, under Wiley's leadership, signed in December 1968 a $434,000 contract with the

Department of Labor to educate and train participants in the WIN program.[52] Carl Rachlin, general counsel for NWRO, proposed the contract. He suggested that NWRO devise its own voluntary work program, demonstrating that with training and support recipients were eager to work.[53] For Wiley and his staff, the Department of Labor contract was not inconsistent with their opposition to the Work Incentive Program. They wrote in the national newsletter:

> We are still opposed to forcing mothers to work and the other terrible features of the anti-welfare law. We have applied for and are operating this contract because we feel that since this law is on the books, we must see to it that the rights of recipients are protected.[54]

Thus, middle-class staff members believed that mitigating the punitive components of the law would make it palatable and implicitly assumed that women on welfare should work.

Staff members opposed mandatory work programs, but argued that recipients wanted to work and would work if good jobs and appropriate training were available. So, strategically, as Tim Sampson explained, the organization favored employment: "Whenever we tried to figure out how to ... [relate] ... to the public, obviously jobs, the work issue, was always a key issue around communication."[55] Wiley similarly felt that recipients' willingness to work dispelled the racist stereotype that women on AFDC were lazy.[56] NWRO's grant proposal stated that WIN "can provide new opportunities for training of welfare recipients for meaningful jobs which could lift them out of poverty."[57] Most of the NWRO staff concurred with the popular belief that employment was the best route out of poverty.[58]

Female leaders of the organization, primarily black, did not see employment for women on AFDC as a prescription for poverty. Some welfare recipients preferred work or took jobs while on welfare. Majorie Caesar of the Pittsfield Association of Adequate Welfare in western Massachusetts worked in a bar, as a nurse, in a bank and as a bookkeeper: "I've always been a person, independent, very independent. And so I always looked for a job."[59] Catherine Jermany, as well, believed employment allowed recipients to reach their "maximum potential."[60] While recipients like Caesar and Jermany valued work, most recipients favored choice. The Department of Labor contract troubled many of them, especially at the grassroots level precisely because of the lack of choice in WIN. The Philadelphia Welfare Rights Organization lambasted Wiley and the other staff in Washington for "selling out" to the establishment. Roxanne Jones and Alice Jackson of Philadelphia perceived the national office's Department of Labor contract as an endorsement of the "WIP program," as they preferred to call it, which would help implement "the most reactionary program in decades. It is designed to remove mothers from the home and place them into 'slave labor' jobs."[61] The Pennsylvania leadership was so disturbed by the WIN contract that in May 1969 they disrupted the NCC meeting in New York City and issued a press release outlining their grievances and threatening to secede from NWRO.[62] Rather than taking the criticism seriously one national staff person framed the conflict as a power struggle; "Roxanne Jones was still 'turn-oriented' rather than 'change-oriented.' She was seeking, he thought, to retain a secure position of local domination to the detriment of the ideological goals of the movement."[63]

Welfare Recipients on the Work of Mothering

Contrary to staff opinion, the women opposing the contract were not concerned primarily about "local domination" but had an ideological position rooted in their experiences and identity as mothers. Women in the welfare rights movement resisted WIN and NWRO's WIN contract because they valued motherhood and opposed forcing women into the workforce. Welfare rights activists often referred to themselves as "mothers" or "mother-recipients," and sought to bring dignity and respect to their work as mothers.[64]

Welfare recipients challenged the artificial dichotomy between work and welfare. In 1968 Mothers for Adequate Welfare, a Boston group, said that "motherhood—whether the mother is married or not—is a role which should be fully supported, as fully rewarded, as fully honored, as any other."[65] A Massachusetts welfare advocacy organization argued "This means that a mother with school-age children will be forced (if they do not volunteer) to accept the same old inferior training or jobs that have always been left for poor people."[66] They believed that mothers and poor people had a right to welfare, regardless of the availability of jobs, and that as mothers they *did* work. For the women in the movement, challenging society's assumptions about poor mothers, putting forth a morally defensible position, and protecting their dignity and worth as mothers was the most important task.[67]

Welfare recipients' insistence that the work of mothering served an important function in society resonated with the maternalist movement of the early twentieth century. Maternalist reformers in the 1910s and 1920s pushed for state pensions for poor single mothers—also called mothers' pensions—the precursor of AFDC. Like women in the welfare rights movement, they justified assistance for poor single mothers based on their mothering responsibilities.[68] But the maternalist movement of the progressive era differed qualitatively from the struggle of women in the welfare rights movement. Most maternalists were prosperous white women as concerned with social disorder as helping the poor. For them, maintaining social stability and improving the lives of the poor meant requiring poor women to adapt to middle-class standards of respectability.[69] These included class, and culturally defined ideas of how to keep house and properly raise children. Maternalists' reforms reinforced women's socially defined role as homemakers. Women in the welfare rights movement, on the other hand, ultimately sought to give women autonomy to make choices for themselves. Because black women, who were often expected to work, did not have a primary identity as mothers, valuing black women's work as mothers challenged social norms. It did not conform to dominant expectations.[70] For many black women in the welfare rights movement, their work as mothers had never been valued as much as their participation in waged labor.

Historians Linda Gordon and Nancy Fraser argue that historical constructions of notions of dependency shaped the discourse around welfare. In the early twentieth century policymakers considered recipients of AFDC "dependent," in contrast to recipients of Social Security and unemployment compensation. Originally defined by social relations, the term dependency did not necessarily have a negative connotation. They argue that in the postindustrial period, however, notions of dependency changed. Social problems were defined as individual and psychological and recipients of AFDC became stigmatized.[71] However, it seems that in the postwar period, as welfare increasingly came to be seen as a problem of race more than individual failure, dependency was defined culturally rather than psychologically. In the 1960s, the poor became a culturally distinct group and poverty was more closely identified with African Americans.[72] The changing views of AFDC reflected the emerging culture of poverty thesis and long-standing perceptions and stereotypes of black women. These stereotypes fueled the argument that black women, rather than being on welfare, ought to take paid employment.

This view of black women on welfare contrasted sharply with the situation of white women. In the 1960s, middle-class feminists had begun to demand greater opportunities for employment outside the home.[73] Psychologists and policymakers, however, discouraged the employment of middle-class mothers, arguing that employment would impair the emotional and psychological development of their children. For poor women, however, especially AFDC recipients, the story was quite different. An official HEW publication exposed the disjuncture between what was considered appropriate for middle-class white women and what was considered appropriate for women on welfare. Concluding that children on AFDC have more behavioral problems than other poor families, a study found that problems worsened when the mother stayed at home with the children. Welfare children "seem to have a higher incidence of serious disorders such as psychosis and appear to be more isolated, mistrustful, and anxious than the non-welfare children. ... The employment status of the welfare mothers also seems to affect impairment: children of working mothers have less impairment."[74]

Women in the welfare rights movement analyzed and scrutinized the different social expectations of white middle-class women and poor women of color, who had never been seen primarily as mothers and had never approximated the domestic ideal. One welfare recipient cleverly contrasted her situation with the reigning symbol of womanhood of the time, when she asked, "Jackie Kennedy gets a government check. Is anyone making her go to work?"[75] Welfare activists insisted that society value their work as mothers, illustrating the very different perceptions and realities of gender across racial and class lines. For African American women, gender had not been shaped primarily by their roles as mothers and housewives, but instead by wage work. So, while many white middle-class women in the 1960s sought to be unshackled from the burdens of domesticity, black women on welfare wanted to be recognized as mothers.[76] This ideological front constituted part of their struggle for welfare rights.

Although welfare rights activists valued motherhood, they did not encourage mothers to stay home with their children, believing that women should have the opportunity to choose whether to work outside the home or not. To assist mothers wanting paid employment, welfare recipients supported the creation of child-care centers. This was "one of the first priorities" of Johnnie Tillmon's welfare rights organization in California.[77] Mothers entering the workforce needed child care, but recipients cautioned that poor women employed at day-care centers might also be exploited. The image of the "Mammy" was a powerful one for African American women. Since slavery, black women had been forced, because of lack of employment options, to care for other people's children.[78] Usually paid meager sums, they left their own children to create a comfortable home and environment for middle-class or wealthy families. Therefore, day-care centers freed some women from the constraints of child care, but could just as likely exploit other women.

So, "mothering is work" became a rallying cry of the welfare rights movement. It was the basis upon which women in the movement opposed mandatory work requirements. It also enabled them to confront the stigma and widespread disdain for welfare recipients. In their engagement with policy debates, this argument reflected one important political position of welfare rights activists.

Conclusion

Both middle-class staff and grassroots activists in the welfare rights movement participated in the debates about the black family, single motherhood, rising welfare rolls, and employment of women on welfare. The organization opposed the 1967 welfare amendments, but men and women in NWRO had somewhat different approaches. The male staff did not believe that welfare recipients should be forced to work. Their long-term solution, in fact, included providing well-paying jobs for men in order to re-establish the two-parent black family. But to counter racist images of black women as lazy, they publicly took a position that women on AFDC wanted to work, and given the opportunity, they would do so. On this, they were not that far from the women, who also believed that AFDC recipients should have the opportunity to work. But the female recipients defended their status as single mothers and justified public assistance by their work as mothers rather than simply the lack of employment opportunities. In doing so, they sought not just to transform the welfare system but the public's perception of black women as well.

Despite the internal differences, influencing legislation and policy empowered recipients and helped them overcome the dehumanization and stigma associated with AFDC. By publicly identifying as welfare recipients, demanding participation in the making of welfare policy, and claiming their rights, they challenged the welfare status quo. Intelligent recipients articulating why they deserved assistance contrasted sharply with the stereotype of lazy, promiscuous, and ignorant single mothers on AFDC. By participating in the policymaking process, welfare rights activists helped demystify welfare and challenged a hierarchical, bureaucratic system that functioned to keep them passive and silent. In addition to their strategies of lobbying and participation, welfare rights activists also waged grassroots campaigns to ensure an adequate income, dignity, and respect from caseworkers. Their claims to motherhood were premised not just on the right to stay home, but required economic resources to enable them to properly raise their children.

4

WE DEMAND A RIGHT TO WELFARE

In conjunction with NWRO's national lobbying effort, welfare rights activists around the country waged grassroots campaigns to ensure their dignity, an adequate income, and the right to welfare. They pursued a multi-pronged strategy that combined legal campaigns with building takeovers; the development of welfare rights handbooks with organized boycotts; marches and rallies with public testimony. They organized to increase monthly benefits, guarantee protection of their civil rights, and raise public awareness about the difficulties of living on an AFDC budget. Their campaigns constituted a demand for a "right" to welfare that sought to revamp a program that had historically designated those on AFDC as recipients of charity. They argued that a decent income, based on the living standards of those around them, was a right that should not be tied to waged work, that the poor were not responsible for their own poverty, and that the nation could and should provide for them. Women on welfare claimed assistance based on their work as mothers who were raising the next generation of citizens. By justifying state assistance as mothers, welfare rights activists redefined the meaning of work to take into account the unpaid labor of social reproduction. Their arguments that mothering was productive and meaningful work that ought to be supported by the state also challenged racial and gendered characterizations of women on welfare as unproductive, "lazy," and unworthy of support.

The Fight for Special Grants

One of the most successful campaigns waged by the welfare rights movement was to request special grants from the welfare department. Welfare departments provided special one-time grants for things such as furniture, school clothing, and household items that were not included in the regular monthly allowance and which recipients could apply for as needed. In assessing what items warranted special grants, local welfare departments developed formulas for determining the minimum living standards for recipients. It might have included, for example, one bed per person, a new winter coat every three years, or costs associated with high-school graduation. Prior to joining a welfare rights groups, many recipients did not know about special grants. Even when they did, welfare departments often refused to award them.

Across the country, welfare rights organizations mobilized women on welfare to apply for special grants, assisted them in filing applications for the grants, and encouraged them to demand a prompt response from the welfare department. Some groups mimeographed checklists of "minimum standards," which they distributed to friends and neighbors. They organized groups of recipients—anywhere from ten to several hundred—to collectively request special grants and sat in or disrupted welfare offices until caseworkers fulfilled all of the requests.

One of the first special-grant campaigns took place in New York City in 1964. Members of the Committee of Welfare Families and the Welfare Recipients League sent letters to the welfare department asking for allowances for winter clothes for their children. The department granted eighty out of the 100 requests.[1] Over the next couple of years, the special-grant campaign spread rapidly throughout the country.[2] The Welfare Grievance Committee in Cleveland, Ohio campaigned in June 1966 for telephones for clients.[3] The Ohio Steering Committee for Adequate Welfare (OSCAW) staged a two-and-a-half week vigil at the governor's office in October 1966 to pressure him to grant a $100 a year clothing allowance for school children.[4] And in Detroit in late 1967 the Westside ADC Mothers refused to send their children to school until the department increased the $5 per month clothing allotment for their children.[5]

The special-grant drive peaked in New York City in the spring of 1968, when dozens of local welfare rights organizations simultaneously engaged in protest, nearly overwhelming city officials. The Citywide Coordinating Committee of Welfare Rights Groups (Citywide) coordinated activity and provided support for local groups demanding money for spring and Easter clothing, Mother's Day clothing, graduation clothing, camp supplies, and telephones. The sheer magnitude of the protests, the persistence of welfare recipients, as well as their knowledge of department regulations, left many welfare officials with little option but to agree to the demands of welfare rights activists. In 1968, over 100 people sat in at the Melrose welfare office in the Bronx for three days and two nights until the department granted recipients $35,000 for Easter clothing. In upper Manhattan a small group of nine mothers, members of Langston Hughes Welfare Rights, met with the administrator of the Dyckman Welfare Center and walked out with over $4,500. At the same time, 200 mothers and their children spent four nights at the Tremont Welfare Center in the Bronx requesting money for "beds, lamp-shades, dust mops and clothes pins." The staff worked into the evening for two days screening applications and issuing checks.[6] Sit-ins and blockades of welfare center entrances sometimes prompted caseworkers to walk off the job and welfare directors to shut down the centers.[7] When welfare officials could not approve special-grant applications immediately, activists demanded emergency checks.[8] Regulations required caseworkers to visit a client's home before issuing a check, but welfare recipients insisted that caseworkers bypass standard procedure and grant money on the spot. On the Lower East Side groups were given checks for graduation clothing without the usual mandatory verification from the school.[9] At the Jamaica Welfare Center in Queens, the director appointed a task force to process application forms for new cases and provide emergency cash grants the same day.[10] The threat of protest and disruption convinced many welfare officials to circumvent bureaucratic regulations and meet the demands of irate welfare recipients.

Welfare rights organizations relied on nonviolent direct action, a tactic popularized by southern-based civil rights activists who disrupted business as usual, but did so in a peaceful manner. But welfare rights activists didn't limit their strategies in this way. They sometimes engaged in violence or threatened violence. The welfare rights movement's use of multiple tactics complicates the simplistic violent/nonviolent trajectory that has framed popular understandings of the black freedom movement. Welfare rights activists, as historian Rhonda Y. Williams argues, had a "tactical flexibility" and "enacted divergent strategies and verbal postures," including self-defense and threats of violence, to win concessions and counter state violence.[11] In many public demonstrations, welfare rights activists adopted a militant posture. With their children in tow, they marched in downtown centers and in front of city halls, "shopped-in" at department stores, blocked entrances to public welfare buildings, and sat in the offices of high-ranking politicians. In one incident welfare recipients took over a welfare office in the Bronx, overturned furniture and ripped telephones off the walls.[12]

At first glance, it might seem that the occasional turn to violence or threat of violence was born of frustration and anger. That is, welfare recipients simply lashed out. But more often than not, activists consciously deliberated over the most fruitful strategy and turned to violence only when more tame protests seemed ineffective. The Bronx protest occurred after welfare officials eliminated the special-grant system, which had yielded countless victories for activists. When welfare officials dug in their heels and refused to negotiate with protesters, organizers began to contemplate more radical alternatives. Welfare rights activists had also learned through observation that violence or the threat of violence can actually be quite effective. Tillmon expressed this sentiment:

> It is true that when we're not heard we have to make people hear us. We do whatever becomes necessary. We're not a violent group…even sometimes we might have to throw a rock to get attention. We don't want to throw rocks to hit anybody. But just to make a noise…People don't seem to hear us if we don't demonstrate.[13]

So while most welfare rights activists preferred nonviolence, they were not beyond employing violence if they felt it was necessary, appropriate, or more likely to win concessions. Welfare rights activists' thoughtful and intentional use of violence, in fact, parallels other Black Power activists who didn't seek out confrontational violence but held it in a strategic reserve arsenal.[14]

Special Grants Go National

At NWRO's August 1968 annual convention in Chicago, dubbed an "Action Conference," participants decided to wage a national campaign for school and winter clothing and Christmas grants. The campaign for More Money Now! coordinated special-grant protests already in progress. Staff members in Washington sent out packets of literature to affiliated local groups, instructing organizers to develop minimum standards checklists.[15] Over the next year welfare rights activists employed direct-action tactics, including rallies, pickets, and sit-ins to force concessions from local welfare centers. The national office gave direction and support to local struggles, reinvigorating the local movements. In Ohio in early 1969 welfare recipients demanded a Thanksgiving and Christmas bonus so "welfare children may attach the same significance to traditional American holidays as other children."[16] In Detroit, Westside Mothers ADC Group requested $25 per person for the Christmas holidays in 1968. When their request was not granted they sat in for two weeks at the Department of Social Service.[17] Similar campaigns occurred in Toledo, Boston, Philadelphia, Providence, Washington, D.C., Newark, and Youngstown, Ohio.[18]

The special-grant campaign was premised on the notion that welfare was a right and that recipients were entitled to a basic standard of living. Welfare rights activists refused, for example, to accept material items at the expense of their "dignity." Maintaining dignity meant being treated with respect, not being stigmatized, protecting their individual civil rights, and, ultimately, deciding for themselves what was in their best interest. They rejected anything that smacked of charity:

> In Washington, The District government has responded to the drive for winter clothing grants with appeals for private donations…The mothers do not want private charity…Mrs. Etta Horn, the President of the Citywide Welfare Alliance, put private donations in the right perspective when she returned a $500 donation and said, "From slavery on, it's been tokenism. The day of tokenism is over. The $500 is nothing but hush money."[19]

In Columbus, Ohio, recipients refused second-hand clothing because it did not include items they needed and much of the clothing was out of style.[20] In Worcester, Massachusetts, MAW refused vouchers for new furniture and insisted on cash so they could shop anywhere they wanted.[21] Similarly, just before

Christmas recipients in Columbus picketed the local "Toys for Tots" program. Their leaflets read, in part:

> Christmas is perhaps the only time every year when almost everybody wants to help someone else. And so we are given Christmas baskets, Christmas clothing and Christmas toys. This is maybe nice but people need food, clothing and a place to live the whole year round—not just at Christmas time.[22]

Thus, recipients believed they were entitled not just to hand-me-downs, but to fashionable clothing; not just to what others did not want, but to items of their own choice. They wanted assistance not only when others were in the spirit of giving, but when they needed particular items. So, the needs and desires of the recipient, not the generosity and excesses of the giver, they believed, should be the deciding factor. This, in a nutshell, is what they meant by a right to welfare. Claiming welfare as a right would diminish the stigma of charity historically tied to receipt of welfare. Welfare recipients wanted to live their lives no differently from the non-poor around them. In this way, they subscribed to the politics of respectability that had historically informed so many poor people's struggles.[23]

The special-grant campaign sought to acquire for recipients basic necessities, such as clothing, furniture, and appliances. But more significantly, welfare rights activists turned to the state for an assurance of a minimum standard of living. They sought to leverage state power and state resources. In making demands upon the state, welfare rights activists confronted a bureaucratic system theoretically unaccountable to them. Welfare recipients desperately needed welfare services, but they wielded little power over the program. Protests against the state were hardly new, but welfare rights activists in the 1960s forged a new road—consciously trying to make the AFDC program more responsive to its clients and consequently fashioning a new relationship between the state bureaucracy and the people it served. In many ways, the model of leveraging the state flowed from Wiley's strategy of creating a power bloc of poor people who could influence policy.

George Wiley and many NWRO staff members used the special-grant campaign as a way to bolster the power of the national organization and build the membership of welfare rights groups. Tim Sampson, the point person for the campaign in the national office, said "I was very interested in … creating a membership organization … So, we set up a membership system."[24] They required recipients to join the organization and pay the yearly dues of $1 in order to participate in the special-grant campaign. The NWRO information packet on the special-grant winter action campaign in 1968 reflected the aim of recruiting recipients: "The main idea of action is to win benefits—*MONEY and BUILD MEMBERSHIP*."[25] This brought into welfare rights organizations thousands of recipients who wanted additional money from the welfare department.

Between 1968 and 1969, at the peak of the special-grant tactic, NWRO membership more than doubled from 10,000 to 22,500.[26] And while recipients eagerly participated in the strategy of membership-building, they had a different understanding of its importance.

Many welfare recipients justified special grants by their status as mothers, believing that material benefits would improve their living standards and enable them to properly care for their children. Most of the special-grant campaigns were for school clothing, winter clothing, summer-camp items, or other things for recipients' children. The Philadelphia WRO believed special grants could vastly improve the quality of life for children. In an internal document the organization argued:

> The frequent inability of children on assistance to participate in the more formal events of community life (such as graduation ceremonies) because of lack of appropriate clothing sets these youngsters apart from their friends...The careful use of special grants would go far toward helping such deprived children take part in the more constructive experiences society offers.[27]

In Ann Arbor, Michigan, welfare recipients campaigned for school clothing for their children. Throughout the summer of 1968, women on welfare in Ann Arbor requested money for school clothing from their caseworkers. They argued that the allotted amount of $9 a month, based on 1960 cost of living estimates, was not enough and their children had only shorts and sandals to wear to school. In September, they took over a meeting of the County Social Services Board for nine hours to get $100 for school clothing. With school beginning the next day, the mothers threatened an all-night sit-in at the welfare office unless the Board issued the grant immediately.[28] The following day, after a late-night meeting, the Board of Supervisors agreed to give $40 to all mothers for school clothing. When protestors rejected this offer, the county promised to determine needs individually and award up to $60 for each recipient. Sticking to their original demand of $100, welfare rights activists sat in at the County Building.[29] Garnering support from University of Michigan students, the sit-in grew to 800 after the county began to process the $60 grant requests. On the third day of the sit-in, frustrated by the impasse, the Director of the Social Service Department declared, "We aren't going to put up with this anymore" and ordered the arrest of 200 people.[30]

The protest in Ann Arbor is one example of how welfare mothers organized on behalf of their children's needs. The special-grant protest empowered them as mothers and enabled them to publicly place value on motherhood. Welfare recipients believed special grants provided items or opportunities that would foster in their children the self-esteem and self-confidence necessary for success. For example, at a 1966 meeting in New York City, welfare mothers stressed the psychological impact of the lack of adequate clothing on the well-being of their children. Appropriate clothes and participation in social activities, they believed, were critical for healthy development. "Our children always have to feel an inferiority complex because they can't participate in some social programs, because they can't dress properly and we can't afford to buy their outfits."[31] A group in Rhode Island argued that more money for school clothing "will improve children's attendance, attitudes, and performance at school ... Authoritative studies show that children do poorly in school if they don't have proper clothing. Clothing is an essential ingredient in a child's self-image."[32] Some recipients claimed that poverty was not just an obstacle to success, but the source of damaging and potentially dangerous behavior. Stark poverty may alienate children, profoundly affecting their psyche. A Philadelphia welfare rights organizer quoted one mother:

> "Children who feel different, act different." Habitual "differentness" of this kind tends to lessen a child's respect for his parents and for the society from which he feels estranged. It may lead to destructive behavior or to illegal acts that will finance special items or activities enabling such a child "to be like his friends for once."[33]

Thus, these mothers justified special grants for school clothes, graduation clothes, and summer camp as mothers concerned about the future of their children, rather than just as welfare recipients.

By framing special grants as necessary to enable them to raise emotionally stable and successful children, welfare rights activists did several things at once. First, they tapped into popular discussions about psychological health and emotional well-being. Since World War II psychologists, sociologists, intellectuals, social workers, educators, and even economists had stressed the importance of emotional health.[34] The heightened concern about mental health led President Kennedy in 1963 to convince Congress to allocate money for community mental-health centers. The number of mental-health clinics in this period increased dramatically. Thus, psychological health became a topic of public concern, woven into discussions of medical care, workplace issues, family status, public policy, and civil rights.

The connection between mental health and civil rights was most obvious in the 1954 *Brown vs. Board of Education* Supreme Court decision, which argued that Jim Crow segregation damaged black children psychologically and stigmatized them as inferior. The Supreme Court based its decision in part on research by psychologists Kenneth Clark and Mamie Clark. The Clarks tested children in segregated settings to determine if they would identify with black or white dolls and which ones they would describe as good, beautiful, and nice. The Clarks found that most black children living in the segregated South associated negative traits with the black doll and positive traits with the white doll. Moreover, many of these black children represented themselves as white or identified with the white doll.[35] This, the Clarks concluded, indicated self-hate and was evidence that segregation destroyed the emotional health and self-esteem of black children. This argument helped convince the Supreme Court Justices to declare school segregation unconstitutional in the landmark 1954 Brown decision.[36]

Welfare mothers crafted similar arguments—about the psychological well-being of their children and how the stigma of poverty created in them an inferiority complex—to demand greater allowances for clothing and other necessities. For them, equal opportunity meant not only access to school, but an emotional and psychological mindset that allowed them to take full advantage of educational opportunities. Along the lines of Brown, welfare recipients analyzed the way society categorized people as different—especially based on economic status—and how this negatively influenced their self-esteem or translated into a form of discrimination.

Recipients' attention to children dressing properly also points to the social significance of clothes. Clothing reflects identity and status. Members of the countercultural movement in the 1960s often rejected their own middle-class or privileged background by shedding conventional outward appearances. They grew their hair and wore tattered t-shirts and ripped jeans. These cultural rebels challenged social norms by dispensing with the accoutrements that others expected of them. Welfare recipients and other poor people who sought to dress their children in new clothing also defied the social norms of someone of their class background and, especially, welfare status. They believed that an individual's dress shaped self-respect, affected personal behavior, and influenced success. By dressing fashionably and neatly welfare recipients could begin to break down the class and cultural barriers distinguishing them as inferior.

The special-grant campaign brought thousands of recipients into the welfare rights movement, collectively won millions of dollars for women on welfare, and legitimated the welfare rights movement as a force to be reckoned with. The national coordination and shared sense of purpose soldered bonds among local groups. Moiece Palladino, who worked with the San Francisco WRO, explained the importance of this connection: "A lot of our campaign activity was focused as a result of … national campaigns. And that's what we pushed. We pushed the national campaigns … I think [our local work] would have been very difficult if we hadn't … felt that we were part of a larger scheme."[37]

The Decline of Special Grants

Although the special-grant campaign won concessions and brought thousands of women into the welfare rights movement, it was short-lived. Officials clamped down on demonstrations by replacing special grants with flat grants. The flat grant gave recipients a set amount of money each year, rather than permitting them to request money for specific items. The abolition of special grants meant the elimination of a crucial organizing tool for the welfare rights movement. The special-grant campaign pressured local welfare departments, brought visibility to the movement, and demonstrated the power of welfare rights organizations. Implementation of the flat grant undermined a tactic that had won millions of dollars' worth of items in the previous months and helped activists build membership. The flat grant took power away from welfare rights activists and placed it in the hands of welfare administrators. It was a bureaucratic solution to a political problem. Hugh Jones, Chairman of the Board of Social Welfare in New York, indicated in the summer of 1968 that the "volume of [special-grant] applications has come close to breaking down the system." Special grants strained the budgets of local welfare departments, fueling the concern that municipalities spent too much money on welfare. Mitchell Ginsberg, Director of the New York Human Resources Administration, warned that special grants cost the city an enormous amount and that it "desperately needed" a flat-grant system. The *New York Times* editorialized: "'Flat grants, used virtually everywhere else in this country, will not cure this situation, but they are an immediate necessity to help meet the city's current welfare crisis."[38]

New York City adopted the flat grant in August 1968. Under the new system, AFDC recipients received $100 a year per person to buy household items, furniture, and clothing not covered in the monthly grant. The city rationalized that all recipients, not only those requesting special grants, benefited from flat grants. In addition, clients could plan for their own needs, without the indignity of investigations, which were routine for special grants.[39] The city expected to save close to $40 million a year. Other states adopted flat grants as well. The Massachusetts State Welfare Department in April 1969 froze special grants for furniture and household items in order "to meet the basic budgetary needs of recipients in the period ahead."[40] A few months later, in December 1969, the Massachusetts governor announced he would implement a flat grant.[41] A flat grant was also proposed in Washington, D.C. in 1972.

Welfare rights activists vigorously organized against the flat grant to sustain the political life of the movement. In New York, Citywide's massive protests in response to the new system achieved few tangible gains.[42] The city's response was intransigence, and usually, arrest. Cops and welfare recipients often clashed violently. During a two-week period of nearly continuous demonstrations in 1968 after the adoption of the flat grant, police arrested hundreds of people and dozens of injured were taken to the hospital. At one demonstration at City Hall, 200 foot patrolmen and nine mounted police, in the words of one journalist, "herded" the group of 600–700 mostly black women away as they attempted to enter the building. One recipient caught up in the melee screamed as she ran from mounted officers that they "wouldn't do this to white people!" Police arrested other participants for blocking traffic and crossing police barricades.[43] Simultaneous protests occurred in Brooklyn, Queens, Manhattan, and the Bronx, tying up nearly two-thirds of the city's thirty-eight welfare centers during two weeks of protest.

Anywhere from fifty to 500 demonstrators usually took over a building and sat in until arrested or threatened with arrest.[44] Although a number of welfare centers were effectively shut down, the protests yielded little. The flat-grant system remained in effect.

Knowledge, Empowerment, and a Right to Welfare

In addition to special-grant protests, NWRO also campaigned to make welfare a right in law and policy. This included procedural rights (to be treated equally and informed of one's rights) as well as substantive rights (the right to a basic minimum standard of living). The organization worked to achieve these through legal campaigns, by mobilizing welfare recipients, and by raising public awareness. They succeeded in establishing procedural rights for recipients, but were unable to guarantee substantive rights.[45]

Ensuring procedural rights meant, in part, informing recipients of their rights and enforcing them. Welfare rights activists studied the complex maze of ever-changing welfare regulations and used this knowledge to transform power relations within the welfare system. They demanded access to welfare manuals and put together easy-to-use handbooks to educate other recipients about the rules of welfare. In many cases, however, local welfare departments refused to share copies of the AFDC manual with recipients. In the spring of 1967, members of the Minneapolis Community Union Project Welfare Committee wrote letters to the assistant welfare director requesting copies of the county welfare manual so they could draft a welfare rights handbook. After a series of protests, the county welfare board finally invited them to a meeting only to tell them the manual was not for public use and offered to write its own welfare rights handbook. As a last resort, the organization tried unsuccessfully to take the welfare department to court.[46] The blatant refusal to share manuals indicated that welfare officials had a vested interest in keeping recipients uninformed and powerless.

Because of the difficulty of obtaining welfare manuals, local groups often relied on other sources. The NWRO national office, the ACLU's Welfare Civil Liberties Project, the Center on Social Welfare Policy and Law at Columbia University, and other middle-class allies aided local welfare rights organizations around the country in developing and distributing handbooks.[47] In Long Beach, California, Citizens for Creative Welfare circulated a ten-page booklet called "Poor Man's Bible: A Welfare Rights Handbook."[48] "Your Welfare Rights Manual," produced by Mothers for Adequate Welfare (MAW) in Boston, addressed topics such as "What do I Get on AFDC?" "What about Sheets and Furniture?" "Can my Children go to College?" and "How to Appeal a Decision by Your Caseworker."[49] The Hinds County Welfare Rights Movement in Mississippi developed a handbook called "Your Welfare Rights," counseling recipients: "Welfare is not charity. If you are in need and meet the other standards, you have a *right* to welfare help."[50]

The handbook also advised recipients on how to deal with predicaments with caseworkers:

YOU: My children need help.

WELFARE WORKER: Where is the father?

YOU: I don't know. Last I heard he was in Chicago.

WORKER: You won't get any help until you find him and bring him to court. He's got to support your children.

DISCUSSION: The worker is wrong. You do not have to find him and take him to court. To get help from the Welfare, you must sign a form against the deserting father. This tells where he is now, or where he was the last you knew. Then they may try to find him and get him to give some support to his children, if he can. They may take him to court for the support, and ask you to testify.[51]

In addition to producing manuals, activists found other methods to educate recipients about their rights. In Virginia, the Fayette County WRO and the Raleigh County WRO, with the help of Mount Hope Baptist Church, held a training session for low-income people and welfare recipients.[52] Other groups started newsletters, handed out fliers, set up information tables in welfare waiting rooms, or wrote pamphlets and brochures to keep recipients informed. The Los Angeles County WRO, for example, published a regular newsletter updating recipients on current legislation and advising them how to seek help when they had a problem.[53] Welfare recipients' newfound knowledge gave them a foothold to question caseworkers and thus transform the patron–client relationship so characteristic of AFDC.

Recipients also used group power as leverage in their battles with welfare caseworkers. In many cases, welfare officials treated recipients better or resolved grievances more quickly because of recipients' association with a welfare rights organization. In Washington, D.C., the United Welfare Rights Organization explained: "NWRO buttons are well known at the welfare department. Our members find that when they go down to the department with buttons on, they receive prompter and better service. Everyone there seemed a little scared of NWRO."[54] In Boston a mother of ten called a member of MAW about getting Easter clothing for her children. The MAW member, aware of departmental regulations, insisted that the caseworker give the mother the money.[55] This kind of mutual support when dealing with the welfare department and the legal backing welfare recipients had was an important component of welfare rights work. In the words of one historian, lawyers gave welfare rights activists "considerable status" and caseworkers were often aware when dealing with welfare rights activists that the legal buttressing for their claims was "only a phone call away."[56] This legal backing helped shift the balance of power between caseworker and client.

In this way knowledge and group association empowered recipients. Well-educated recipients limited the power of caseworkers, questioned decisions, and checked subjective and unfair treatment. In some instances, welfare activists were better apprised of complex, ill-defined, and ever-changing rules than caseworkers.[57] Activists sometimes corrected caseworkers at their own jobs because they had access to the latest regulations, high-ranking welfare officials, and poverty lawyers. Welfare rights activists' familiarity with the welfare system potentially reversed the power dynamic between recipient and caseworker. Caseworkers were no longer the lone experts and were more often on the defensive about their decisions and actions.

The Struggle for Fair Hearings

Another important welfare rights strategy in shifting the balance of power between caseworker and client was the fair hearing, a formal non-judicial hearing before a state board of welfare to overturn a caseworker's decision. In 1950 federal legislation guaranteed AFDC recipients the right to a hearing to contest decisions about their case. Clients could appeal decisions by the local welfare center to the state welfare department. This grievance procedure was designed to protect clients from unfair rulings by caseworkers or their supervisors. Few welfare recipients, however, knew about this right or took advantage of it.

Welfare rights organizations waged a mass campaign to inform recipients about fair hearings and assisted them in the appeals process. The most extensive fair-hearing campaign occurred in New York City, which had a history of violations and extended waiting periods in the state welfare appeal system. The Citywide Coordinating Committee for Welfare Rights Groups used fair hearings in conjunction with other campaigns, such as the demand for special grants, as a way to overload the welfare system. If caseworkers denied special grants, recipients immediately appealed the decision and requested a fair hearing. By inundating welfare officials, Citywide members hoped to pressure the welfare department to grant concessions to welfare rights activists. According to Executive Director Hulbert James, Citywide sponsored 3,000 fair hearing cases from August through October of 1967, a huge increase over the usual 50 cases a year. James estimated that each fair hearing case cost the state $300 a day.[58]

Welfare rights activists in other states conducted similar fair-hearing struggles, encouraging recipients to challenge unfair or seemingly arbitrary decisions through the appeals process. In Ohio, OSCAW asked HEW to investigate the Ohio Department of Welfare because it failed to grant fair hearings after recipients were denied special grants.[59] In Massachusetts, MAW worked to ensure recipients' right to a fair hearing. Prior to MAWs involvement, "to get recipients to try for a fair hearing, or a hearing of any sort, before the welfare department … was almost unheard of."[60] The organization "successfully fought to bring about a citywide policy to the effect that no recipient's aid will be cut off without an investigation in which she will be able to see the evidence brought against her."[61] The Englewood WRO in New Jersey demanded that the Director of the Bergen County Welfare Board in May 1968 ensure "that clients be made aware of their right to question all decisions of the department and to be advised of the right to a fair hearing if they are not satisfied."[62]

Despite the potential benefits of fair-hearing trials, many local groups encountered problems. Some organizations simply did not have the time or resources to accompany clients to fair hearings. In Mississippi, welfare departments scheduled hearings in many different locations, making it hard for recipients and their lawyers to attend. Even when aware of their right to appeal a decision, they often did not have access to legal counsel to present a compelling case. In other instances, local officials illegally denied recipients the right to a fair hearing by giving them inaccurate information about whether they were entitled to an appeal. Recipients also complained that welfare rights attorneys dominated fair hearings and inhibited recipients from speaking for themselves. In these cases, recipients believed that the scrutiny and disempowerment they experienced with caseworkers was replayed in the hearings.[63] This discontent points to patterns of domination between the educated middle class and the poor—a problem that would resurface in the welfare rights movement.

NWRO also pursued a more systematic legal strategy of test cases to ensure recipients' procedural rights, especially the right to a fair hearing. One of the most important legal victories was the 1970 *Goldberg v. Kelly* Supreme Court decision. Justices ruled that recipients were protected by due process and welfare benefits could not be terminated without a hearing. Waged in conjunction with the campaign for fair hearings, the case demonstrated how lawyers and welfare rights organizations could work together. Fair hearings were a useful political tactic, but they did not prevent unfair decisions. Rather, they gave recipients the power, after considerable time, energy, and argument, to reverse such decisions. In other words, recipients could challenge the decision to cut them off assistance, but only after the fact. The caseworker's decision would stand until it was overturned. The Goldberg case sought to guarantee recipients a fair hearing before caseworkers cut off benefits.

The first plaintiff in the case was New York City resident John Kelly, a twenty-nine year-old homeless black man. Disabled by a hit-and-run driver in 1966, Kelly went on home relief. In December 1967, his caseworker told him to move from the Broadway Central Hotel, where he resided, to the dangerous and drug-infested Barbara Hotel. Kelly stayed with a friend but used the Barbara Hotel's address to receive his welfare check. When his caseworker learned he was not living at the hotel, she cut off his assistance and refused to see him. In late January 1968, Kelly and five other welfare clients, represented by lawyers from Mobilization for Youth, the Legal Aid Society, the Roger Baldwin Foundation, and the Columbia University Center on Social Welfare Policy and Law, filed a suit in federal district court against the New York State and City Commissioners of Social Service and the State Board of Social Welfare. Lawyers argued that a recipient's right to a hearing before termination of benefits was guaranteed under the due process clause of the fourteenth amendment of the Constitution. Recipients won the case in November, when a three-judge U.S. district court ruled that welfare recipients should expect to receive benefits and plan their life accordingly without arbitrary changes. The court argued, "Under all the circumstances, we hold that due process requires an adequate hearing before termination of welfare benefits." Although the city appealed, the Supreme Court in 1970 affirmed the ruling of the lower court.[64] The case won procedural rights for welfare recipients. That is, a right to welfare was not guaranteed, but everyone would be ensured equal access and equal treatment once on welfare.

The Goldberg decision set an important legal precedent by successfully establishing the right to due process for welfare recipients and restraining bureaucratic discretion. It recognized that AFDC benefits should be treated and protected as any other form of property and assured recipients that welfare would not be regarded as charity, but a right.[65] This was important because welfare had historically been considered charity and thus the property of the state—to be disbursed and taken away at will. The Goldberg decision made welfare an entitlement, not just in theory, but in practice, and gave recipients a measure of protection from having benefits terminated unexpectedly. Although the Goldberg decision did not guarantee receipt of welfare—recipients could still be cut off welfare after a hearing or their application for assistance might be denied altogether—it, nevertheless, protected the civil rights of welfare recipients. Moreover, the welfare rights movement could—and later did—use this legal decision as ammunition to oppose state policies designed to reduce the welfare rolls. By demanding protection of their due process rights, questioning the discretionary powers of caseworkers, and advocating public and formal procedures in the welfare system, recipients addressed a key source of their oppression and gained a measure of dignity and respect. They also brought the organization one step closer to the notion that welfare was a right.

The other component of the right to welfare was the question of whether welfare grants provided a decent standard of living. Although the Goldberg decision was important, it also revealed the limitations of the Court. By guaranteeing procedural rather than substantive rights, the Court's decisions did not address whether the grant was large enough to support a family, whether AFDC's lower benefit levels compared with other programs constituted discrimination, or whether a state could implement stringent eligibility criteria. NWRO's legal test case to guarantee welfare recipients a basic minimum income originated with Governor Nelson Rockefeller's plan to tighten welfare eligibility and eliminate the special-grant system in New York in 1969. The Center on Social Welfare Policy and Law and NWRO filed a lawsuit which made it to the Supreme Court.[66] The case, *Rosado v. Wyman*, sought to establish the right to live—that a basic minimum income was a protected right that could not be compromised or violated because of budgetary constraints. The Center argued before the U.S. Supreme Court that the reduction of benefits left recipients in a situation that fell far short of the "health and decency" required by the 1967 Social Security Amendments. Moreover, they claimed that the cuts violated the equal protection clause because a minimum standard of living was necessary to protect other Constitutional rights. That is, denial of basic human necessities, such as food and shelter, jeopardized freedom of speech or assembly since an individual consumed with the work of sheer survival could not adequately exercise these rights. The Supreme Court decided in April 1970 that the 1967 Amendments required states to determine a standard of need, but this was a guide, not a mandated minimum. So, states may set benefits lower than their established standard of need. The Court ruled that New York State had haphazardly eliminated special grants, but that after re-computing the standard of need, it had the right to reduce grants to accommodate its budget.

In another case, *Dandridge v. Williams*, welfare rights lawyers argued that Maryland's practice of setting maximum public assistance grants violated the equal protection clause because the state denied to poor children in large families the same level of assistance available to poor children in small families. In 1970, the Supreme Court upheld Maryland's right to set family maximum grants and decide how to distribute its scarce resources. In both cases, the court dismissed the notion that the equal protection clause guaranteed a minimum income or a "right to live" as welfare rights lawyers argued. The justices were unwilling to move from a discussion of equality in procedure and process to one of endorsing the idea that poor people had a right to a basic minimum standard of living. As long as states applied the law equally, they could reduce grants and reject as many applicants as they saw fit.[67]

Poverty and Inequality

In the 1960s, welfare officials and policymakers were intent on reducing the welfare rolls and encouraging or requiring welfare recipients to accept paid employment rather than providing permanent income support. The economic prosperity of the time bolstered the notion that ample opportunity was available for all. The welfare rights movement—both staff and recipients—had a different view. They believed that welfare recipients were blameless for their economic situation, good jobs were unavailable, and that expanding public assistance was a necessary solution. In claiming a right to welfare, recipients in Washington, D.C. explained their poverty as a result of larger structural forces: "We are forced into poverty because of circumstances beyond our immediate control. We are kept in poverty because of a pitiful inadequate allowance … We are living like dogs because you all will not give us enough to live decent lives."[68] The claim to a right to welfare questioned the long-standing assumptions that the poor were responsible for their own poverty, that public assistance was charity, or that in order to qualify for assistance recipients needed to conform to an established set of behavioral or moral standards.

In addition, through their various campaigns, welfare recipients asserted that AFDC ought to provide a basic level of economic security that included household items, clothing, and participation in social and cultural activities. They challenged the accepted definition of poverty and urged policymakers, social workers, and the public to raise the minimum standard of living. Based on their understanding of what constituted a modern-day level of health and decency, they argued that they needed specific items or services. They analyzed how a poor diet led to poor health, how improper clothing impeded their children's education, how the lack of a telephone could endanger their lives and safety. A higher standard of living provided them greater self-respect, a better quality of life, and expanded opportunities for their children. Many of the campaigns reflected their concerns for their children's well-being and they justified state assistance based on their work as mothers.

Welfare rights organizations addressed the relative poverty of welfare recipients and pointed to the fundamental problem of inequality: that they had so little while others had so much. Recipients' desires for new furniture, a better diet, and more household appliances were a product of the ostentatious wealth and affluence surrounding them. They wanted to participate fully in postwar consumer culture and be brought up to par with the American standard of living. As Mothers for Adequate Welfare in Boston explained, "The MAWs view is that recipients need to live in a way which approaches the average for the society around them."[69] They also believed that the nation was capable of providing a higher standard of living for them. As welfare recipients in Cleveland argued in 1966, "Nobody argues whether there is enough money in this nation to clothe and feed everyone decently. Everyone agrees that there is enough. If this is true, then WHO decides that some people get their share and other people don't? WHO makes the decisions that some people can have enough and others just can't?"[70]

Certainly many welfare recipients in the 1960s would have been defined as poor by objective as well as relative standards. In 1960, 28 percent of AFDC households had no flush toilets or hot water and 17 percent had no running water at all.[71] Most women on AFDC struggled to put food on the table and buy clothes for their children. Welfare recipient Esther Washington explained, "Sometimes a child only gets one meal a day. He usually has to go without breakfast because there's nothing available, he has to go without lunch because there's no money to pay for lunch at school, and the only meal he gets is dinner and that is often inadequate."[72] Recipients lucky enough to have a roof over their heads often lived in dilapidated and neglected spaces that fell far short of national standards of health and decency. In 1968, a hearing officer for the D.C. Department of Public Welfare confirmed "the inadequacy of the existing shelter and food allowances."[73]

Yet the definition of poverty in the 1960s was a relative and arbitrary concept, as it has always been. Since the late nineteenth century, officials defined poverty in relation to the general standard of living. In calculating a minimum standard of living, social scientists assumed that the poor needed less than middle- or working-class Americans. The standard of living for average Americans fluctuated as well. Thus, the criteria bringing a family above the poverty line changed over time, and might have included indoor plumbing, electricity, a refrigerator, a telephone, or two pairs of shoes for every child. This variability in the meaning of poverty and its relation to general living standards suggests that what constituted a minimum standard of living was open to interpretation.[74] Rather than an objective measurement, the term poverty described how the living conditions of people at the bottom of the economic ladder differed from those in the middle and on the top. Inherent in this analysis was the logic that efforts to eliminate poverty will make little headway, unless the problem of inequality is rectified. In addition to raising the standard of living of the poor, the gap between the rich and the poor had to be narrowed.

Conclusion

Welfare recipients' struggle for dignity, equality, and protection of civil rights was a product of their experiences as poor black women on welfare. The welfare system silenced, marginalized, and disempowered women on AFDC. They found most unbearable the arbitrary nature of AFDC and worked to formalize and educate recipients about welfare procedures.[75] The concentration of power in the hands of caseworkers left recipients with few avenues to contest decisions. Although caseworkers could be sympathetic and supportive, they were subject to the same stereotypes and biases about black welfare recipients that dominated the public discussions about welfare in the 1960s. Since its inception, AFDC relied on casework investigation, premised on caseworkers evaluating recipients' worthiness and moral standing as a condition of aid. Welfare rights activists sought to abolish such subjective judgments, suggesting that economic need was the only legitimate measure of qualification. They diminished the power of caseworkers, modified rules and regulations, and ended some dehumanizing welfare practices. In this way, welfare rights campaigns chipped away at a cornerstone of the welfare state: the idea that relief should be discouraged and recipients should meet a behavioral and moral litmus test in order to qualify for aid. Arguing that AFDC was a right eroded the building blocks that made the welfare system punitive and repressive. It transformed the very meaning of AFDC assistance: from a form of public charity to an entitlement with little cause for stigma or shame.

Partly a battle for the public mind, these campaigns shifted the political debate about welfare in a direction that recognized the relative deprivation of women on welfare. Whether an additional fifteen cents a day for food or an extra blanket on a cold night, these concrete improvements meant a lot to people with very little. They attempted to refashion the public image of welfare recipients as consumers, mothers, and citizens rather than dependants on the welfare state. Through their association with welfare rights organizations women on welfare brought dignity to their lives and asserted their right to assistance. They struggled for basic rights and privileges ostensibly available to everyone in a liberal democratic political system. But because they were black women on welfare, whose race, sex, and status as welfare recipients disempowered and stigmatized them, their demands for dignity, due process, and the right to motherhood did not legitimate but challenged the gendered and racialized assumptions about work, welfare, and citizenship. In this way, the demands and goals of the women in the welfare rights movement were an important departure from the perception and standard disbursement policies of AFDC.

By 1969, after several years of campaigning for special grants, educating clients about the current AFDC program, and pursuing legal protection for their privacy and civil rights, activists began to ponder a more fundamental transformation in the welfare program that would take the concept of welfare as a right to a whole new level. In that year, the organization launched a national campaign to replace AFDC with a federally guaranteed minimum income for all poor people.

5

THE FIGHT FOR A GUARANTEED ANNUAL INCOME

In the summer of 1969, the welfare rights movement reached its peak. It had initiated several successful campaigns to establish welfare recipients' civil rights, raise monthly benefits, and demand that caseworkers treat them with dignity. It won thousands of dollars in special grants and assisted countless women on AFDC in their day-to-day struggles with the welfare department. Amassing a respectable following, the national organization had a membership of 30,000, but, according to some estimates, participation in the movement reached 100,000.[1] The largest local chapters, Boston and New York City, counted 1,600[2] and 4,000 members.[3] Attendance at the annual convention in Detroit in 1969, the largest ever, drew between 3,000 and 5,000 people, exceeding by ten times the 350 people at the 1967 convention in Washington.[4] The number of affiliated locals increased as well, from 130 groups in December 1966 to 800 in 1971.[5]

During its first few years on the national stage, the most ubiquitous slogan of the welfare rights movement was "welfare is a right." T-shirts, banners, buttons, and posters were emblazoned with that short but provocative phrase. Welfare activists believed, as New York City welfare recipient Jennette Washington succinctly stated, that they "have a right to [welfare] because the Constitution says that everyone has a right to life. Life includes everything necessary to maintain life."[6] The movement's early campaigns to bring AFDC under constitutional protection and raise the standard of living for welfare recipients contributed to this goal. The right to welfare, however, was most clearly embodied in the movement's demand for a guaranteed annual income, which would make economic status the only criterion for eligibility and sever the link between employment and income. Since the 1966 founding convention, a guaranteed income had been NWRO's long-term goal, but little had been done to explicitly organize for it.

By 1969, NWRO made the guaranteed annual income its main strategy. In that year, the organization entered the national political debate about income maintenance when Richard Nixon proposed his own version of a guaranteed income, the Family Assistance Plan (FAP). NWRO seized the moment to influence the direction of legislative reform and implement its nascent long-term goal. Welfare organizers demanded that the federal government replace the current welfare system with a guaranteed minimum income, which would bring all people who fell below that, working or not, up to a decent standard of living. They believed that the guaranteed annual income ought to be a targeted grant, with money going to the poor to lift them above the poverty line, rather than a universal grant given to everyone, regardless of income. This demand was in many ways a culmination of many of their earlier struggles. A guaranteed minimum income for all poor people, regardless of sex, family status, personal behavior, or employment promised to eliminate investigations by caseworkers and to standardize and simplify the administration of welfare. Raising the living standard of all poor Americans to an adequate level could also ameliorate racial and economic inequality. Moreover, divorcing economic security from paid employment challenged age-old American traditions, which tied income to work.

Although men and women in NWRO had different rationales for wanting a guaranteed income—the male staff emphasized the lack of employment opportunities and the female constituency framed the guaranteed income as necessary because of their work as mothers—they united around this goal. Nationwide debate about the merits of a guaranteed income enabled NWRO to push its agenda, bringing it to the zenith of its influence. Nixon introduced FAP in part because of NWRO's agitation and political pressure, which contributed to the momentum to reform the welfare system. In addition, NWRO leaders met frequently with members of the Nixon administration, introduced their own guaranteed income bill into Congress, and helped shape the debate about a guaranteed income.

After pushing for a guaranteed income from 1969 to 1972, members of the welfare rights movement realized that revamping the welfare system was a bigger political battle than simply getting a place at the bargaining table. The guaranteed income debates illustrated the degree of consensus among liberals and conservatives that the poor needed income support. Although they disagreed bitterly on where to establish the minimum income, the nature of the work requirement, and the expansiveness of the program, people across the political spectrum agreed on the need for an income floor. Ideologies of race and gender circumscribed this consensus, however. If the public believed that income maintenance would benefit African American women on welfare, political support diminished. Support was more widespread for two-parent, male-headed families. In the end the racial and gender stereotypes long associated with AFDC doomed the passage of any guaranteed income legislation.

NWRO and the Guaranteed Income

The guaranteed annual income was perhaps the best example of NWRO's campaign to secure for AFDC recipients a basic standard of living. In the late 1960s, NWRO demanded a yearly income of $5500 for a family of four administered by the federal government. The guaranteed income would have rectified problems of arbitrary caseworker decisions, variations in AFDC payments among states, and the susceptibility of welfare to the changing winds of local politics. The guaranteed annual income had the potential to radically transform not only welfare, but the meaning of citizenship and government responsibility. It would have established the principle of social citizenship—that everyone was entitled to a basic standard of living. The welfare rights movement found its niche in this mold, pushing the boundaries of the discussion by insisting that a guaranteed income provide a level of security without obligation to work outside the home. Men in the movement emphasized the lack of jobs and women sought to redefine mothering as work.

The welfare rights movement's demands for a guaranteed income originated with the two social scientists who had been long-time supporters of welfare rights organizing. In 1966, prior to the formation of NWRO, Frances Fox Piven and Richard Cloward outlined in an article a strategy for welfare rights activists to achieve a guaranteed annual income. They encouraged welfare rights organizers to add to the welfare rolls people qualifying for, but not receiving, assistance. This would precipitate a "profound financial and political crisis," and city governments, unable to deal with the crisis, would pressure the national government to implement a guaranteed annual income.[7] Although NWRO never adopted Piven's and Cloward's crisis strategy, most welfare rights activists came to see the guaranteed income as the most obvious solution to a system that not only provided an inadequate amount of money, but also demeaned its recipients.[8] Loretta Domencich, a Native American organizer of a WRO in Milwaukee, explained, "A lot of things that Welfare Rights is going after are Indian ideas—Guaranteed Adequate Income is really an Indian concept. It is the way the Indians themselves ran their early communities … The dignity of the individual says that no matter what a person's capabilities are, whether he is the leader or whether he is a person who is crippled or elderly or can't do anything, he still has a place in the tribe."[9] In 1968, Catherine Jermany of the California WRO explained that "the most important [long-range goal] would repeal all welfare laws and replace them with an annual guaranteed income fixed at about $4,000 per family unit."[10] The guaranteed annual income was, as the Philadelphia WRO explained in an internal document, "the out-growth of the concept of welfare as a right."[11]

In 1969, after failing to raise AFDC benefits, the Ohio Steering Committee for Adequate Welfare (OSCAW) argued:

> Each person in this country has a right to life. Our society must *subsidize life*. We call upon this nation to eliminate the inadequate, humiliating hodge

podge of programs like food stamps, welfare and the others that perpetuate poverty. This country must get down to business with a Guaranteed Adequate Income for all.[12]

In the same year, a MAW member explained that they "are not interested in the public welfare system as it exists now" but instead worked towards "some kind of income maintenance program."[13] The Los Angeles County WRO, which called in 1966 for a "decent standard of living," demanded in 1969 a "guaranteed adequate income."[14]

Gender and the Guaranteed Income

By 1969 activists in the welfare rights movement agreed on the need for a guaranteed annual income, but the predominantly middle-class male staff and the black female members differed about why one should be implemented. Staff members usually rationalized a guaranteed income by the lack of available paid employment. George Wiley explained in 1970:

> We agree that there must be an economic incentive to work. But we know there aren't enough jobs to go around *now*, that there is 5.5% unemployment. In New York 70% of the welfare recipients who answered a survey said they would rather work, but there were no jobs available to them at their skill level, or there was no day care for their children.[15]

Wiley and many staff members did not challenge the traditional notion of the work ethic or the trend requiring welfare recipients to take paid employment. For them, the guaranteed income was a practical solution to support people who could not find jobs. Wiley and other national office staff also believed the guaranteed income could reduce the number of female-headed families and reestablish traditional nuclear families. They blamed the welfare system, not individuals, for the rise in single-parent families. One staff person said, AFDC "does undermine the family structure because in most states a family headed by an able-bodied man cannot get welfare no matter how poor it is. So to get help for his family the father has to leave."[16] The guaranteed income, available to two-parent and single-parent families, would resolve this problem.

Women in the welfare rights movement, on the other hand, believed that a guaranteed income would acknowledge and compensate them for the work they performed as mothers. Johnnie Tillmon summarized the position formulated by many welfare rights activists at the grassroots level when she proposed in 1971 that we could resolve the "welfare crisis" and "go a long way toward liberating every woman" in the country if the president issued "a proclamation that women's work is *real* work" and paid women "a living wage for doing the work we are already doing—childraising and housekeeping."[17] A welfare rights group in Ohio advocating a guaranteed income argued that "raising five kids is a full time job" and mothers should have a choice about taking paid employment.[18] Cassie Downer, Chair of the Milwaukee County WRO, explained:

> A guaranteed adequate income will recognize work that is not now paid for by society. I think that the greatest thing that a woman can do is to raise her own children, and our society should recognize it as a job. A person should be paid an adequate income to do that.[19]

For women in the welfare rights movement the guaranteed annual income was both an avenue to achieve women's economic independence and compensation for their work as mothers. These women sought self-determination and autonomy to decide whether to work inside or outside their home.

Many political activists in the 1960s called for self-determination and personal autonomy. Women's liberationists, for example, touted women's right to choose to take paid employment or to have an abortion. But these demands rang hollow if a woman couldn't pay for an abortion or had to work out of necessity. Black community organizations demanded control over the schools in their neighborhood. But community control would only marginally improve the education of poor children in inner-city schools without resources to purchase textbooks, pay teachers adequately, improve facilities, or decrease class size. Similarly, poor women needed financial support to allow them to make choices that middle-class and wealthy women could make. By advocating a guaranteed annual income, welfare rights activists hoped to enable poor women to make choices about work, motherhood, and personal relationships, and realize autonomy in less abstract and more concrete terms.

For women in the welfare rights movement, a guaranteed annual income served several purposes at once. It forced the state to recognize housework and child care as legitimate work, freed women from dependence on men, debunked the racial characterizations of black women as lazy by acknowledging their work as mothers, and gave women a viable option to degrading labor market conditions. By redefining "work" to include mothering, or parenting, they hoped to challenge the notion that mothers on welfare didn't work, were lazy, and contributed little to society. The Philadelphia WRO suggested that a guaranteed income "would eliminate the stigma of being a special class or more accurately caste within our society since it is for all families."[20] By improving the economic status of poor people and women, it ameliorated racial and gender oppression and potentially made women's and children's security a national priority. The Philadelphia WRO produced a document on a "Federal Family Investment Program" that insisted: "The federal government must now invest in families to assist them economically to raise their children. Families produce this country's most important natural resource: CHILDREN."[21]

Despite the differences between men and women in NWRO, they found common ground in the demand for a guaranteed annual income. In June 1969 the organization officially launched its campaign for a guaranteed income of $5,500 for a family of four without any other income.[22] To maintain a work incentive, it proposed a tax of 66 percent on the earned income of recipients. Under the plan a family of four would be entitled to some level of assistance until their income reached just under $10,000. Table 5.1 is taken from a brochure outlining the plan.

NWRO's guaranteed income plan would have replaced all existing public assistance programs. Administered by a single federal agency, it determined eligibility by a person's declaration of need, with spot checks. NWRO's plan offered fair hearings, free medical care, legal services, day care, as well as emergency grants to "take care of critical or unusual situations" and to bring recipients up to standard at the grant's inception.[23]

In establishing a minimum standard of living, NWRO rejected the federal government's official poverty line, which was based on the Department of Agriculture's "economy food plan." NWRO claimed that government surveys show that families living at the poverty line have "nutritionally inadequate diets."[24] NWRO based its figure of $5,500 for a family of four on the Department of Labor's Bureau of Labor Statistics' low budget for an urban family of four.[25] Although NWRO's basic minimum income exceeded the poverty line and provided for a slightly more comfortable lifestyle, it did not include money for items such as a car, cigarettes, out of town travel, use of a laundromat, long-distance phone calls, or life insurance.[26]

On June 30, 1969, the third anniversary of the Ohio march that launched NWRO, 20,000 people demonstrated nationwide in support of a $5,500 minimum income. The movement's internal developments, as well as a national dialogue about the merits of a basic minimum income, created a political opening and pushed the guaranteed income to the forefront of NWRO's agenda.

TABLE 5.1 NWRO'S Guaranteed Adequate Income Plan, 1969

Earnings	Final income under the NWRO Adequate Income Plan	Final income under the 1966 Tax Law
$ 0	$5500	$2460 (avg. AFDC grant)
$2000	$6166	$2000
$3000	$6499	$3000
$4000	$6832	$3860
$5000	$7165	$4710
$7500	$7998	$6814
$8246	$8246	$7432
$9000	$8497	$8057
$9887	$8792	$8792

Consensus on Income Maintenance

In many ways, the late 1960s was an unusual moment in the history of this nation. It has long been recognized as a period of political polarization—when the left and right were locked in battle to define, or redefine, the core values of the nation. Lost in this discussion, however, is the extent to which there was consensus around certain issues, such as a basic minimum income. In the 1960s, people from vastly different political places supported a version of income-maintenance plans. The plans varied by scope, administration, and level of assistance. The guaranteed income advocated by NWRO allocated direct cash assistance to any poor person whose income fell below a basic minimum. The Negative Income Tax, administered through the Internal Revenue Service, functioned in the same way to subsidize individuals whose income was too low to pay taxes. These IRS payments brought recipients up to a minimum standard and, as with the NWRO plan, payments decreased as income rose. Children's allowances subsidized families with children, regardless of family income, with cash payments. Other proponents linked a guaranteed income to employment through government job creation and wage subsidies. Despite the many differences, all of these plans established a minimum standard of living for recipients and simplified and standardized payments across the country.

In the 1960s, republicans, conservatives, liberals, and radicals proposed or endorsed income-maintenance plans. The Ripon Society, a Republican youth group, endorsed in 1967 the Negative Income Tax as an alternative to the War on Poverty and as a way "to help the poor."[27] The National Council of Churches wanted to make a guaranteed income "available to all as a matter of right ... with need as the only eligibility criterion and adequate standards of assistance."[28] In 1966 the Southern Christian Leadership Conference called for the government to "ensure all American families an income of at least $4000 a year."[29] The Black Panther Party's Ten Point Program demanded full employment or a guaranteed annual income. In 1968, 1,200 economists lobbied Congress "to adopt this year a national system of income guarantees and supplements."[30] And in the same year, the National Association of Social Workers presented petitions to the Democratic and Republican Party Conventions "For the Elimination of Poverty in the U.S.A.," calling for "an assurance of job opportunity for those able to work and, for all Americans, a guaranteed minimum income."[31]

Although the War on Poverty rejected income maintenance in favor of education, job training, and expanded social services, President Johnson formed several task forces and a Presidential Commission on Income Maintenance, made up of economists, community leaders, and businessmen, to study the benefits and viability of an income-maintenance plan. In its final report, released in 1969 just two months after Nixon proposed his Family Assistance Plan, the Presidential Commission, also known as the Heineman Commission, after its head Ben W. Heineman, president of North West Industries, endorsed a guaranteed income with a floor of $2,400 a year for a family of four.

The political discussions about economic security were part of the intellectual project in the postwar period of rethinking the meaning of citizenship. Citizenship in the U.S. has historically been defined by civil and political rights: freedom of mobility, the right to vote, the right to own property, freedom of speech, and the right to due process. The welfare rights movement's inclusion of a minimum standard of living as a "right" of citizenship was both radical and very much a product of its time. Numerous economists and scholars took similar positions in the 1960s. British sociologist T. H. Marshall, for example, made a case for expanding public services, such as health care and education, and implementing a guaranteed income to provide a "modicum of economic welfare and security." He argued that after granting political and civil rights, the state should extend social rights to ameliorate differences in status and foster a level of social stability. For him, citizenship rights also required duties and obligations such as work.[32]

Similarly, in 1962 conservative economist Milton Friedman argued for "governmental action to alleviate poverty; to set, as it were a floor under the standard of life of every person in the community."[33] Friedman hoped to abolish the hodgepodge of government programs, such as public housing, food stamps, welfare, and social security, and replace them with a federal cash grant—a Negative Income Tax—allowing individuals to purchase what they needed in the free market.[34] John Kenneth Galbraith, the liberal counterpoint to Friedman, also endorsed the idea of a Negative Income Tax in his influential book *The Affluent Society*: "For those who are unemployable, employable only with difficulty or who should not be working, the immediate solution is a source of income unrelated to production" which was "a matter of general right and related in amount to family size but not otherwise to need."[35] Galbraith went on to say that "an affluent society" that is "compassionate and rational" would provide for all people a basic minimum income to ensure "decency and comfort."[36]

Theorists discussing social rights in the 1960s came to similar conclusions for different reasons. Their justifications varied from concerns about a growing government bureaucracy to problems of unemployment in an age of automation, but they all grappled with how the nation might provide a basic level of economic security for its citizens. The most radical economists suggested divorcing income from employment, past and present, and basing it only upon need. They envisioned a future in which human toil was minimal or obsolete.[37]

The relatively widespread support for the guaranteed income in the 1960s represented a common understanding among economists, policymakers, activists, and politicians about how best to address problems of poverty. First, they assumed that poverty and unemployment were anomalies in postwar America and needed to be explained, understood, and addressed. They argued that everyone could be brought up to a minimum standard of living through economic growth, job training, or a more generous welfare state. Second, fewer people contended that giving money to the poor was detrimental to their character, a long-standing belief shaping the American welfare state from poorhouses of the colonial era to

Roosevelt's New Deal. As Galbraith argued in 1958, "The corrupting effect on the human spirit of unearned revenue has unquestionably been exaggerated as, indeed, have the character-building values of hunger and privation."[38] In a similar vein, Friedman preferred cash assistance to government-run services because it would shrink the bureaucracy of the federal government and strengthen the market economy. Finally, many people in the 1960s favored an activist federal government that could stabilize the economy and meet the basic economic needs of its citizens. Liberal, conservative, and some radical promoters of a guaranteed annual income ultimately had faith that American capitalism could create profit for the wealthy, satisfy the middle class, and ameliorate the problems of the poor at the same time.

Nixon Proposes a Guaranteed Annual Income

The policies of Richard Nixon, the first president to propose a guaranteed income, reflected most clearly the consensus around poverty and welfare in the 1960s. In 1968 Nixon ran on a platform of law and order as well as his "secret plan" to end the war in Vietnam, distancing himself from the previous Democratic administration and catering to conservatives. It seemed that 1968 was a moment of crisis, testing the limits of U.S. international power and the strength of cherished American political and economic ideals. In response, Nixon crafted an image as someone who would clamp down on disruptive protests and advocate for the "silent majority," the large number of Americans disdainful of political activism. Nixon promised to restore order to a country shaken by urban rebellions, military setbacks in Vietnam, violent confrontations between demon-strators and police, assassinations of several national figures, and threats of violent insurrection, however feeble those threats might have been. He successfully linked his Democratic and liberal opponents with the dissenters and promised a different political course.

Upon taking office, however, Nixon seemed to extend, rather than reverse, the Democratic liberal agenda. He appointed both Democrats and Republicans to his administration, instituted cost-of-living adjustments for social security recipients, expanded the food-stamp program, and excluded the poorest Americans from paying income tax. He repealed a freeze on federal AFDC payments to states for women who had children out-of-wedlock, which passed as part of the 1967 Social Security Amendments under President Johnson. He formed the Urban Affairs Council and chose as its head Democrat Daniel Patrick Moynihan.[39]

Nixon's attempts to restructure welfare also belied his conservative rhetoric. In August 1969 he proposed replacing AFDC with a new federal program, the Family Assistance Plan (FAP). Nixon sought to simplify AFDC, reinforce the work ethic, and provide a basic level of financial support for poor male- and female-headed families. FAP assured a minimum annual income of $500 for the first two household members and $300 for each additional family member, which worked out to $1,600 for a family of four, plus $864 in food stamps. Even this low-base income significantly improved the living standard for families in the South, where both welfare payments and wages were below the rest of the country. Mississippi, the state with the lowest benefits, paid the average AFDC family $396 per year in 1965.[40] FAP required states with higher welfare payments to supplement the federal income until recipients reached their current standard, ensuring no reduction in benefits. Designed to assist single-parent and two-parent families with children, FAP included both a work requirement and a work incentive. Able-bodied adults and parents of school-age children had to register for work or training. If they refused, their monthly allowance was withheld, but their children continued to receive assistance. Working heads of households could keep the first $60 a month they earned and anything beyond that was taxed at a rate of 50 percent. A working family of four received assistance until their total income reached $3,920. Nixon also allotted $600 million for job training and child care.[41] Under FAP, the federal government, not states, determined eligibility standards and spot-checked income to verify eligibility.[42] Whatever problems were inherent in FAP, it was a dramatic move for a Republican in the 1960s. As one HEW staff member explained: "I couldn't believe that I was sitting there talking to a Republican administration that seemed eager for this new solution [Negative Income Tax] that six months before I hadn't been able to convince [Democrat] Wilbur Cohen was the right thing to do."[43]

Similarities in liberal and conservative positions notwithstanding, partisan politics greatly influenced the contours of the debate. Although support for income-maintenance plans crossed political boundaries, over the course of the decade, the term guaranteed annual income became associated with leftists and liberals. Indeed some historians have erroneously attributed income maintenance proposals exclusively to the Democratic Party.[44] Democrats eagerly embraced phrases like income maintenance and guaranteed income to champion the needs of the poor and underprivileged. Conservatives framed their proposals differently, using terms and language such as work ethic and a reduction in the welfare rolls. In keeping with his conservative image, Nixon distanced himself, at least rhetorically, from those on the left and argued that his proposal was not a guaranteed income.[45]

Despite Nixon's insistence that FAP was not a guaranteed income, it looked very much like a guaranteed income proposal. In his 1969 televised speech he proposed "that the Federal Government build a foundation under the income of every American family with dependent children that cannot care for itself."[46] FAP provided a minimum income for all American families and federalized and standardized welfare payments. Potentially costing the federal treasury between $4 billion and $6 billion a year, it extended benefits to more than ten million people in poor working families with children and tripled the number of children aided by the federal government.[47] Nixon's welfare reform proposal reinforced the work ethic and attempted to placate the working poor, but his plan also spoke to the needs of the welfare poor. He justified his reforms by arguing that "the tragedy [of the current welfare system] is not only that it is bringing states and cities to the brink of financial disaster, but also that it is failing to meet the elementary human, social, and financial needs of the poor."[48]

Why the Family Assistance Plan?

So why did Nixon support a guaranteed annual income? The welfare system had been severely criticized since the early 1960s because of rising costs, a tug-of-war between federal and state officials about both funding and regulations, the perceived inefficiency of the system, ongoing political protest, and the belief that AFDC did little to bring people out of poverty—and may even exacerbate it. The racial and gender composition of the welfare rolls and assumptions about recipients' immorality and lack of work ethic undoubtedly contributed to negative characterizations of AFDC. And the stigma attached to welfare was roundly criticized by welfare recipients and their advocates. In short, by the end of the 1960s few people were happy with the welfare system. A scholar at the time noted that "general dissatisfaction with the failure of Public Welfare to deal adequately with the massive problems of poverty" resulted in "far-reaching proposals" by economists, social scientists, and politicians.[49]

The increases in the welfare rolls in the late 1960s fueled criticism. The number of families on AFDC rose dramatically from one million in 1965 to over two-and-a-half million in 1970.[50] Escalating costs burdened state and local officials most heavily. In regions with high AFDC payments, such as the Northeast, state governments bore a greater portion of the AFDC budget. For example, in 1965 the federal government gave Alabama, Mississippi, Georgia, and South Carolina between 75 and 78 percent of their public assistance budgets. But California, New York, Massachusetts, and New Jersey received between 41 and 48 percent of their public assistance budgets from federal funds.[51] These states more acutely felt the burden of higher costs and experienced most of the increase in the welfare rolls.

The rising caseload and skyrocketing expense led state officials to demand greater federal funding and responsibility. New York Governor Nelson Rockefeller, for example, favored federalizing welfare to address the rising costs.[52] In 1971 New York City Mayor John Lindsay filed suit in federal court contending that federal and state mandates of welfare payments were unconstitutional because of the city's ultimate responsibility for the expense. The court ruled against the city arguing that states opted to participate in the welfare system. These examples illustrate that the issue of funding seemed to pivot, in some cases, on local versus federal responsibility. The 1969 Supreme Court decision declaring residency requirements unconstitutional also increased pressure for a federalized system. Local officials feared the decision would encourage welfare recipients to move from states with low monthly payments to states with higher monthly payments. Thus, rising welfare rolls created a crisis of major proportions for local and state officials, particularly in a few key areas such as New York, increasing the momentum to replace AFDC with a new program such as FAP.

Politicians in the late 1960s were also confronted with massive, sometimes violent, rebellions in urban centers, where local officials seemed unable to control looting, arson, and general mayhem. In addition, radical groups such as the Republic of New Afrika and the Black Panther Party threatened instability, while also articulating a critique of the political and economic system. The Panthers, for example, organized free breakfast programs for poor children and SCLC launched "Operation Breadbasket" in Chicago to highlight problems of poverty and unemployment. The specter of welfare mothers protesting and demanding more money and better treatment contributed to a sense of crisis of the welfare system. The politically explosive climate and social disorder undoubtedly forced Nixon to consider addressing the inadequacies of the nation's economic policy.[53] In 1968, the National Advisory Commission on Civil Disorder appointed by President Johnson published its report. The Commission traced the deep-seated causes of urban turmoil to the high rates of poverty and unemployment. But it singled out the welfare system: "The Commission believes that our present system of public assistance contributes materially to the tension and social disorganization that have led to civil disorders."[54] It called for an expansion of the welfare program, less restrictive rules, and more generous welfare benefits. The report contributed to political pressure to dismantle an inefficient welfare system, and replace it with something that could provide basic support as a way to mollify inner-city malcontents. Whether observers were sympathetic, scared, or fed up with the demonstrations, they nearly all concluded that something had to be done.

Concerns about the working poor and apprehension about undermining the work ethic also guided welfare reform. Most proposals expanded public assistance to include two-parent families to prevent fathers in poor families from leaving home so the mother and children qualify for aid. Proposals also included assistance to the working poor to encourage employment and avoid penalizing those who worked. But including the working poor and two-parent families also greatly enlarged the number of people eligible for assistance and increased costs. Administration officials grappled with how to justify more people on welfare and keep costs low yet have an effective work incentive. Robert Finch, secretary of HEW, suggested a conservative argument about the benefits of aiding the working poor:

> To include the working poor is not basically a "leftish" or liberal initiative, but rather an essentially conservative move which, while appealing to liberals, is rooted in the concept of making work as rewarding as welfare in a system which in many cases has reversed the incentives.[55]

The Nixon administration worried less about cost than reducing the number of single-parent families and reinforcing the work ethic. Although politicians preferred to contain the costs of any reform, most proposals, including FAP, would have cost more than the present AFDC program.

FAP seemed to address the concerns of people across the political spectrum: conservatives and liberals troubled about single parenthood, the working poor who felt left out of the Great Society, local politicians burdened with paying for welfare, taxpayers frustrated about supporting a system they believed was inefficient, free-market advocates who favored cash assistance over government services, and radicals demanding a more dignified welfare system. Nixon and his aides had little doubt about the need to completely revamp the current welfare system. At a cabinet meeting to discuss FAP, Nixon's Urban Affairs advisor, Moynihan, urged: "We now have terror in our cities. ... We've got to move on this issue or we will be recorded as the people who sat by."[56] At a private meeting on welfare reform, Nixon articulated the overwhelming pressure to reform AFDC: "We're doing it because we can't go on with the present system ... I am not for improving the present system ... We don't know whether [FAP] will work, but we can't go on with the present system."[57] Hoping to stave off political protest and pacify the inner-city poor, Nixon and his advisors intended to abolish welfare as they knew it and replace it with a comprehensive system that more adequately met the needs of the poor.

Not all administration officials were on board with the guaranteed income. Commerce Secretary Maurice Stans, for example, opposed FAP and suggested that instead of relying on federally supported income maintenance, the poor and unemployed "reduce their living costs by self-help means such as growing gardens, fishing and hunting."[58] Aside from the lone dissenters, however, the parameters of debate reveal an astonishing level of agreement among administration officials committed to expanding and raising welfare benefits and enlarging the role of the federal government. Nearly everyone in the administration concurred on the need for national minimum standards for welfare recipients.[59]

Nixon's support for a guaranteed income was less an indication of his own political orientation—he was still to the right of most public figures of the time—than a reflection of the political climate. The political instability and urban protests instilled fear in many Americans about the future of the nation. Nixon's far-reaching welfare proposal attempted to either placate the poor or co-opt radical protest. While heralding black capitalism as Black Power, Nixon at the same time felt pressure to offer palliatives to constituencies he likely perceived as his enemies. Political volatility in an era of expanding social programs led to an unlikely moment when Nixon and some radical groups spoke the same language and battled for control of the same playing field. People on both the right and left worked to establish new priorities and meet the needs of the underprivileged within the framework of the existing economic system, albeit they were motivated by different reasons and feuded fiercely about exactly how to define those priorities.

Both liberals and conservatives lauded Nixon's Family Assistance Plan. The weekend after the announcement of FAP, the White House was flooded with phone calls and telegrams, the overwhelming majority supporting the proposal.[60] In an October 1969 Harris Survey 47 percent of Americans favored FAP and only 17 percent opposed it.[61] James Reston, a columnist for the *New York Times*, wrote:

> A Republican President had condemned the word "welfare," emphasized "work" and "training" as conditions of public assistance...but still comes out in the end with a policy of spending more money for relief of more poor people than the welfare state Democrats ever dared to propose in the past...He has cloaked a remarkably progressive welfare policy in a conservative language...He has insisted that poverty in a prosperous country must be eliminated.[62]

The administration prided itself on the cross-section of support for FAP. Robert Finch, secretary of HEW, believed this reflected "the fact that Family Assistance is a sensible though revolutionary plan—that it commends itself to persons of all persuasions who seek a workable solution to the crisis in our current welfare system."[63]

NWRO Opposes FAP

Although the Family Assistance Plan may have been viewed as a radical step, especially for a Republican president, after a close reading of Nixon's proposal and some internal deliberation, NWRO eventually launched a nationwide campaign to "ZAP FAP," submitting instead its own legislative bill for a guaranteed income.[64] Objecting vociferously to FAP's low monthly payment and the work requirement, NWRO also denounced FAP for its lack of provision for cost-of-living increases, emergency grants, Medicaid, guarantees of due process, or assistance to families without children.[65] The organization threw its energy into influencing legislation as well as shaping the parameters of discussion about income maintenance.

Criticisms of FAP reflected the divisions within NWRO between the middle-class male staff and female recipients about the guaranteed income.[66] Recipients opposed the work requirement because they believed it impeded women's ability to properly raise their children. In a 1969 statement to the House Ways and Means Committee, which was considering Nixon's proposal, Beulah Sanders explained:

> Surely the mother is in the best position to know what effect her taking a particular job would have on her young school child, but now we are told that for welfare mothers the choice will be made for them, work for the mother, government centers for the children, the government decides.[67]

They adamantly believed a mother should choose whether or not to work outside the home. Sanders continued:

> NWRO is for adequate jobs for all men who are able to work. We are for adequate jobs for all mothers who freely decide that it is in their own and their children's best interest for them to work in addition to their primary job as mother and homemaker.[68]

The men in the movement did not object as strenuously to the work requirement as did the women. Wiley and other staff members opposed forcing mothers of small children to work, but as Nixon stated quite clearly in his speech proposing FAP before Congress in 1969: "It is not our intent that mothers of preschool children must accept work."[69] Wiley supported a work incentive, however, arguing that any guaranteed income plan should have

> a certain degree of reverence for the Protestant ethic, which infuses all of us in and out of the welfare system, and therefore should provide economic incentive so that recipients who try to improve their economic situation by work can actually do so, and hopefully work their way off the welfare system.[70]

Moreover, Wiley advocated assisting the working poor, believing this would blunt the sharp distinction in the public mind between people on welfare and people who work. In other literature produced by the National Office, the staff wanted FAP to provide *"guaranteed adequate jobs!"* Further down the list, it stated much less forthrightly, FAP should ensure "that no mother is forced to work at times when she is needed in the home to care for her children."[71] In his critique, Wiley emphasized the lack of jobs and methods of encouraging people to work. As with NWRO's own guaranteed income proposal, women and men in the welfare rights movement had different approaches to the meaning of work. Women wanted their work as mothers to be recognized while men continued to speak primarily in terms of employment outside the home.

Despite these differences, both men and women in the organization shared the view that FAP failed "to provide *adequate* income to meet basic human needs."[72] Arguing that $1,600 a year for a family of four was not enough for a nutritionally adequate diet or a decent standard of living, NWRO advocated a higher minimum income. Nixon and NWRO did not disagree about the principle of a minimum income standard, but about where to set that standard.

In 1970, NWRO drafted its own guaranteed income legislation for debate in Congress.[73] Introduced by Senator Eugene McCarthy, Democrat from Minnesota, and endorsed by twenty-one members of the House of Representatives, the Adequate Income Act of 1970 called for $5,500 for a family of four. The bill had no work requirement, but included a work incentive so recipients' earnings were not taxed at 100 percent. The basic minimum income for nonworking heads of households was $5,500, and the working poor received federal subsidies until their income reached $10,000. In February 1971, taking into account inflation, NWRO's National Coordinating Committee raised the minimum income to $6,500.[74]

NWRO, as always, combined a strategy of confrontational protest with peaceful negotiation. They threatened disruption of the legislative process while working within the system to ensure their political influence. NWRO members testified before Congressional committees, developed position papers, met with representatives, and encouraged local welfare rights chapters to send letters to Washington.[75] Wiley outlined to numerous congressmen his specific criticisms of FAP and urged them to support amendments.[76] After FAP passed the House of Representatives, NWRO lobbied the Senate in the spring of 1970, demanding that "the Senate Finance Committee hear from organized poor people."[77]

In addition to lobbying, NWRO organized militant actions. In one interview, Wiley threatened a "violent revolution" if the nation failed to respond to the needs of poor people.[78] Welfare rights activists planned demonstrations and marches across the country in the spring of 1970 as the Senate debated FAP. One hundred and twenty-five people attended a rally in front of the White House. In May, Wiley and a group of NWRO members held a seven-and-a-half-hour sit-in at the office of Robert Finch, Secretary of Health, Education and Welfare (HEW). The next day they seized an auditorium at HEW and held hearings on their adequate income proposal. Calling FAP "an attack on poor people," NWRO organized nationwide demonstrations on June 30 in support of the $5,500 plan.[79] In the fall, it encouraged groups around the country to plan "People's Hearings" with social workers, politicians, labor unions, welfare recipients, welfare officials, and community leaders.[80] In November 1970, Senator Eugene McCarthy sponsored unofficial Senate hearings, attended by 350 NWRO members, twenty-three of whom spoke passionately about the drawbacks of FAP and called on the eleven Senators present to oppose it. Shortly after that, on November 20, 1970, the Senate Finance Committee voted down the first version of Nixon's Family Assistance Plan.

After the Senate Committee voted FAP down, a revised version, known as HR1, was introduced into the House of Representatives in early 1971. Even less acceptable to NWRO, HR1 guaranteed an annual income of $2,400, but eliminated food stamps, resulting in less money for families than under FAP. Unlike FAP, HR1 expected mothers with preschoolers to register for work and did not require states whose current benefit exceeded the minimum income to maintain those levels.[81] Throughout 1971 NWRO lobbied to defeat the new version of FAP. It encouraged local affiliates to meet with representatives, send telegrams, and write letters.[82] In September, groups across the country, in places as diverse as Maine, Nevada, Washington, Illinois, and Missouri, planned anti-FAP protests.

Neil Downey, an NWRO volunteer, wrote a protest song to the tune of Battle Hymn of the Republic:

> Oh, they've got a bill in Congress
> that they're calling H.R.1;
> And it's coming to destroy us,
> every single mother's son
> F-A-P is what they call it,
> and you'd better understand
> The letters stand for Family Annihilation Plan.
> Gory, gory, what a helluva way to die!
> Gory, gory, what a helluva way to die!
> Gory, gory, what a helluva way to die!
> Kill FAP instead of me![83]

HR1 passed the House of Representatives in June 1971, but the Senate voted it down in October 1972.[84]

The new version of FAP failed, in part, because Nixon did not actively back the legislation. Although Nixon publicly reaffirmed his support for FAP in 1972 and two years later promised again to reform welfare, he no longer prioritized this kind of legislation.[85] Nixon had abandoned his strategy of placating the left and liberal community. Counseling a new political course, his chief of staff suggested the:

> need to reexamine all our appointments and start to play to *our* group, without shame or concern or apology. Should feel our way, *appear* to be listening to critics, but we have now learned we have gained nothing by turning to the other side. [The President] has changed his mind, reached a new conclusion. Is convinced policy of sucking after left won't work, not only can't win them, can't even defuse them.[86]

During the 1972 election, NWRO and local welfare rights groups petitioned other presidential candidates, including Eugene McCarthy and George McGovern, to endorse the $6,500 guaranteed annual income proposal in exchange for the organization's support. Despite the persistence of NWRO, this last-ditch effort to push for its guaranteed income proposal in the national electoral arena proved futile.

NWRO's Influence on the Welfare Debates

NWRO's involvement in national deliberations about a guaranteed income reveals the parameters of political debate in the 1970s. Both NWRO and Nixon concurred that the poor ought to participate in policymaking. During the Nixon administration, NWRO had access to the most powerful political offices and believed that as representatives of the poor they could influence federal welfare policy. More strikingly, they relied on Nixon to provide them with the opportunity. Johnnie Tillmon and George Wiley wrote to Nixon during his first year in office: "When you were elected you promised to 'bring us all together.' You asked that we lower our voices and listen to one another. Poor people have tried to give you the chance to hear our concerns and to show that you respect our needs and want to include us *in*—in your new consensus, *in* this country."[87]

During the first month of Nixon's presidency, NWRO representatives met regularly with members of the administration to discuss welfare reform. In January 1969 the NWRO Executive Committee met Moynihan, Nixon's director of Urban Affairs, at the White House. According to Tim Sampson, NWRO staff member, the meeting indicated NWRO's rising stature: "Moynihan wanted to show George that he was interested in George's movement and that he was concerned." In February they met with Robert Finch, Secretary of HEW, to discuss state compliance with federal AFDC regulations. Members of the welfare rights movement also participated on the FAP recipients' advisory committee.[88] In a 1969 press release, Wiley said "The meetings represent a recognition by the Administration of the growing power of NWRO's grass-root membership."[89] The Nixon administration may or may not have recognized NWRO's "growing power": it nevertheless maintained close contact with the organization.

NWRO also submitted proposals and made recommendations. When dissatisfied with the pace of change, it passed on to HEW a list of grievances:

> NWRO began serious negotiations with HEW at the outset of your administration. We brought specific complaints of illegal practices and regulation counter to Federal Law to Secretary Finch's attention in February and March. There has been no forthright response to these complaints and although discussion has continued, HEW officials have not yet taken action to enforce federal welfare regulations guaranteeing due process to welfare recipients and those in need who apply for aid.[90]

In response, HEW presented to NWRO a seven-page, single-spaced letter addressing their list of demands.[91] Shortly after that, Elliot Richardson, the new secretary of HEW, assured George Wiley in a telegram that "the department is eager to continue its discussion with the NWRO and other similar organizations."[92] The Nixon administration and NWRO fashioned together a democratic process that acknowledged poor people's participation in shaping policies affecting them. They were considered an indispensable part of policy discussions about poverty. Input and dialogue were the catchwords cementing the new consensus on policymaking and the new vision for democracy in America.

NWRO leaders' participation in the policymaking process—their frequent meetings with members of the Nixon administration, their representation on local welfare boards, the introduction of their proposal into Congress—indicated a change in the role and status of NWRO. On one level, the organization reached its pinnacle of influence. NWRO had argued for many years to include the poor in the decision-making process. During the Nixon administration, for the first time, they had access to the highest echelons of power in the country. AFDC recipients discussed, debated, and voiced their opinions about social welfare policy on a national level. Although Nixon and NWRO differed on the meaning of representation, both agreed that input of the poor was imperative when reforming social and welfare policy. Rather than excluding poor people, Nixon presented himself as committed to open lines of communication, dialogue, and mutual decision-making. It is unlikely that Nixon had truly been won over to this new vision of politics, as his abrupt reversal in 1972 indicates. He probably felt political pressure and saw few other avenues to placate the protesters. But this ostensible agreement, while falling short of full-fledged commitment, might make its mark on the historical record as well. In other moments politicians did not hesitate to silence and ostracize their opponents. These meetings between NWRO and federal officials reflected the administration's attempt, however meager, to pay lip service to needs of welfare recipients, and in the process they legitimated the articulated needs of people on welfare. Never before had the poor felt such entitlement to government assistance or participation in the policymaking process. Never before or since has there been such consensus on including welfare recipients in the making of social policy.

It is unclear if NWRO altered the policies and practices of HEW. In hindsight, looking at the administration's turn away from concern about the poor after 1972, it is doubtful that NWRO had any direct, lasting impact. But NWRO's influence on welfare policy has to be measured in broader terms than simply the failure or passage of a legislative bill or whether HEW implemented NWRO's specific recommendations. NWRO helped shape the political climate, making welfare a public issue and establishing the terms of the debate. It raised awareness about the inadequacy of welfare benefits and the need to increase recipients' standard of living. Organizations otherwise unconcerned about welfare took positions because of NWRO. In the 1960s few elected officials or political organizations could stand on the sidelines as the debate about welfare raged around them.

NWRO's lobbying and mobilization presented a concrete alternative and compelled many organizations to take a position for or against FAP.[93] The National Federation of Social Service Employees, the National Association of Laymen, an organization of 12,000 Catholic laymen, twenty-one congressmen, including the Black Caucus, and the National Women's Political Caucus, all endorsed NWRO's guaranteed income plan.[94] Vincent and Vee Burke argue that NWRO mothers had political influence "far beyond their numbers" and that many liberals refused to support FAP "unless at the same time Congress acceded to the demands of leaders of the National Welfare Rights Organization."[95]

NWRO's political positions also became a yardstick to measure other proposals. During the legislative debate, moderates in Congress formulated compromise bills between FAP and NWRO's Adequate Income Bill. Senator Abraham Ribicoff, in 1971, introduced amendments to FAP calling for a minimum income of $3,000 a year for a family of four, to be increased to $4,000 a year within three years. Congressman Donald Fraser proposed $3,600 a year. These compromise bills suggest that NWRO's political position, in effect, helped set the terms of the debate. Their proposal of $5,500 made the Nixon proposal seem inadequate and prompted liberals and moderates to search for middle ground. Thus, Nixon and NWRO, in effect, became the two poles of the debate about welfare.

Race, Sex and Social Policy

Despite the unprecedented level of consensus about the need for some kind of income support, no minimum income proposal for AFDC recipients passed in the 1960s or 1970s. That failure cannot be attributed solely to the economic troubles of the early 1970s. Tight economic circumstances decreased support for massive new federal programs and most people were reluctant to expand assistance to the poor. But simple ideological beliefs to enlarge or reduce the welfare state based on economic growth did not drive social reform. In fact, the public and policymakers did not oppose expansion of all assistance programs, only those tainted by racial and gender stereotypes that branded certain recipients undeserving. For example, in October 1972 Congress implemented Supplemental Security Income (SSI), a need-based federal income guarantee for the elderly, blind, and disabled. It made Old Age Assistance, Aid to the Blind, and Aid to the Disabled, which were previously state-run programs and considered part of "public assistance," federally funded and administered programs. SSI passed with little discussion or fanfare and federalized part of the welfare state, leaving the portion serving poor women and children—AFDC—in the hands of state and local officials. In addition, unlike AFDC, SSI and social security were pegged to inflation with automatic cost-of-living-adjustments (COLAs). In addition, in December 1970 the federal government expanded the food-stamp program and raised benefits. And in 1972 it increased social security benefits across the board by 20 percent. Between 1969 and 1973 social security benefits rose by 52 percent, adding $25 billion to the cost of the welfare state.[96] Thus, public assistance expanded for some people, but not for others. Social welfare legislation in the early 1970s widened the gulf between the deserving and undeserving poor, further stigmatizing single mothers.

Political mobilization and electoral power might explain the growth of the welfare state for the elderly. Older citizens had pushed for government assistance as early as the New Deal. In the 1960s and 1970s, groups such as the Gray Panthers and the National Council of Senior Citizens (NCSC) formed. Started by Maggie Kuhn and other retirees, the Gray Panthers, an intergenerational, multi-issue group, tackled the war in Vietnam, health care, and racism.[97] The NCSC, established in 1961, lobbied for expanded cash benefits, health care, and services for the elderly. With a dues-paying membership of around 250,000 in the mid-1970s, the NCSC more than likely had close to three million people in its senior citizen clubs nationwide.[98] This surely influenced the vote of some political officials. A staff member to Representative Wilbur Mills said of the 1972 Social Security bill: "Mills knew the increase was a good thing for the aged and, accordingly, a good thing for him at the polls … there are a lot of organized senior citizens in this country and their voting turnout is relatively high."[99] While important, this single factor of electoral power cannot explain the complex unfolding of government policy and public opinion in the 1970s. It doesn't account for the expansion of benefits for the blind and disabled or the increases in funding for food stamps. Political mobilization, moreover, does not necessarily reap positive political results. Public perceptions that a politician caters to a particular constituency might hinder his or her chances of re-election. Had there been strong public sentiment opposing benefits for the elderly, politicians would have had to weigh the potential loss of those votes with the gain of elderly votes. Thus, while voting power might have influenced the allocation of resources in the early 1970s, equally important was the composition of the constituency. Many Americans considered the elderly, disabled, and working poor worthy of assistance; and they considered poor black single mothers unworthy.[100]

Further evidence of the disparity in how recipients of the welfare state fared in the early 1970s was the unanimous passage of the 1971 Talmadge Amendments, which strengthened the coercive features of the Work Incentive Program. Rather than allow states to determine which recipients to refer to the work program, the Talmadge Amendments required all recipients with school-age children to register for work. Recipients without jobs were placed in a public service employment program in exchange for their welfare check. The Talmadge Amendments remained in effect until superseded by the 1988 Family Support Act. Politicians passed SSI and the Talmadge Amendments within a year of one another, demonstrating the influence of race on shaping social policy in U.S. history.[101] As the welfare state expanded for certain sectors of the population, it became more constricted and punitive for one group in particular: poor women on AFDC. The pitfalls of big government and the availability of funding seemed less important in guiding reforms in the early 1970s than racial/gendered assumptions about who deserved support and under what circumstances.[102]

The political fate of income-maintenance plans also depended in large part on the intended beneficiaries. Guaranteed income proposals not tied to reform of AFDC and that did not see AFDC recipients as the primary beneficiaries received the most support. Negative Income Tax Experiments conducted by OEO and Friedman's and Galbraith's proposals relied on a model of a two-parent family with a working father. These economists and policymakers formulated a guaranteed income to benefit a typical two-parent, male-headed and, implicitly, white, family; people they believed were impoverished because of circumstances beyond their control, such as regional economic depression, technological advancements, or low wages. OEO organized a controlled experiment of two-parent families with a working male in New Jersey to test the feasibility of a Negative Income Tax.[103]

Similarly, proponents packaged FAP as a plan with a strong work incentive to assist two-parent households.[104] In his opening statement to Congress, Representative Wilbur Mills endorsed FAP as "a supplement to the income of the individual who is working and not making enough to supply his family with the ordinary needs of life, but who is not now on welfare." Furthermore, to disassociate FAP beneficiaries from the stereotypical welfare recipient, he claimed that over half the working poor lived in the south, many in rural areas, and 70 percent were white.[105] By and large, Congressional conservatives who believed FAP contained an effective work incentive and would benefit the working poor supported it. But, in reality, FAP could not be disentangled from welfare or the politics of race. NWRO's activism helped identify the program in the public mind with welfare and militant black women. In addition, FAP was billed, in part, as welfare reform; as a solution to the multiple problems plaguing AFDC. Liberals and conservatives, favoring or opposing FAP, connected FAP to AFDC.

The stereotypes and snapshot images of black single mothers on AFDC, who many assumed were lazy and promiscuous, dominated the FAP debate. Concern abounded that FAP would encourage the dependency that many people believed characterized the current welfare rolls. Using scare tactics, conservatives charged that FAP would add millions to the welfare rolls.[106] In addition, some people were concerned that FAP would discourage people (black women in particular) from paid employment. In Senate Finance Committee hearings on FAP in 1972, Senator Russell Long of Louisiana argued that FAP's work incentive was ineffective because current work training programs gave mothers "absolute veto over whether she will agree to the provision of day care for her children."[107] Most important here is the use of the pronoun "she." Thus, in his analysis of FAP, Long focused, not on two-parent families, but on single mothers, whom he believed didn't want to work. Equally revealing was Long's declaration: "I can't get anybody to iron my shirts," suggesting that any guaranteed income plan would exacerbate the shortage of domestic laborers—an occupation dominated by African American women.[108] Long's reference to black women as domestic servants illustrates how central African American single mothers remained to discussions of welfare and income support. During the hearings Long also publicly expressed concern about the racially tainted issues of "illegitimacy and fraud."[109] Long's opinions dominated the Senate debate about FAP and, according to the *New York Times*, he served as a "one-man blockade" for FAP because he refused to report the bill out of committee.[110] The stereotypical African American woman on welfare had become the pivot around which the FAP debate revolved.

Conclusion

After Nixon took office in 1969, NWRO devoted its energies to national political reforms and lobbying. The rapid legislative changes on the national level and the possibility of input propelled NWRO onto the national stage. NWRO's demand for a guaranteed annual income addressed many problems with the current welfare system that the organization identified: the work disincentive, meager monthly grants, the discretionary power of caseworkers, and extensive application procedures. Ensuring everyone a basic minimum income, through either work, an allowance from the government, or a combination of the two, it would have attained their goal that "welfare is a right." NWRO seized the moment of opportunity to enact its own legislation and influence policy.

The guaranteed income debate reflected a seldom acknowledged level of consensus in the late 1960s. People across the political spectrum, with exceptions such as Ronald Reagan and George Wallace, embraced the belief in a guaranteed minimum standard of living. Nixon's and NWRO's welfare reform proposals are the most striking examples of the level of consensus. Avowed public enemies on opposite sides of the battle lines, Nixon and NWRO adopted militant postures, obscuring the agreement in the political debate. Yet, the two found common ground on liberal ideas of government intervention in the economy, work opportunities as a strategy to end poverty, and political representation of the poor in the policymaking process. There was also widespread support for a work incentive or requirement among many economists, the Nixon administration, and much of the NWRO staff. NWRO staff and progressives in Congress argued for a work incentive, rather than a work requirement, because women on welfare, they suggested, were willing to work and did not need to be forced. But they all believed in the principle of the work ethic. Finally, NWRO attended meetings with the administration and conferences about welfare reform, was recognized as a legitimate representative of the poor, and influenced the outcome of social policy. Nixon, NWRO, and other advocates of a guaranteed income operated under a set of assumptions that had come to define liberalism in this period.

Women in the welfare rights movement were an exception to the consensus around the guaranteed income. Although they concurred on the need for a minimum standard of living and wanted the poor to be recognized as a political force, they differed with others about how to define work. They challenged the assumption by many on the right and the left that women at home with their children did not work and they wanted society to recognize women's work as mothers. Thus, men and women in the welfare rights movement disagreed, not about whether poor black women deserved assistance, but why they deserved assistance.

After FAP failed, many welfare rights activists believed that they needed to wage an ideological battle dismantling the racial and gender stereotypes linked to AFDC in order to convince the public, the press, and political officials of the need for a system of income support. Negotiating with welfare officials and meeting with the politically powerful was not enough. By the early 1970s, welfare rights activists accepted the improbability of legislatively implementing a guaranteed income. As the public climate became more hostile, NWRO considered new political strategies. NWRO fought to maintain the ground it won, but the differences within the welfare rights movement, some of which had existed since the outset, began to take its toll. The transitions the movement underwent in the previous five years strengthened the movement in some ways, but also divided it irreparably.

6

RECKONING WITH INTERNAL TENSIONS

Throughout the history of the welfare rights movement, grassroots women activists, who were the heart and soul of the movement, articulated political positions that reflected their multiple identities as women, poor people, mothers, community members, tenants, and people of various colors. Because of growing internal conflicts within NWRO, as well as their own experiences as poor women, during the late 1960s these women developed a more coherent political philosophy. Although racial identity was important for welfare rights activists, as the question of race began to fracture the movement, women activists reasserted their commitment to an interracial alliance based on common concerns about motherhood. They resisted attempts by middle-class staff members to control their movement and more frequently began to identify as proponents of women's liberation and Black Power and fought for greater autonomy for poor women. Their campaign for autonomy included the right to choose whether to take paid employment or stay home with their children and whether or not to have an intimate relationship. For some women in the welfare rights movement these ideas formed the basis of a radical black feminist politics that was rooted in their day-to-day experiences as welfare recipients. Their philosophy emerged slowly and haltingly within the welfare rights movement. It was nurtured by ongoing differences with staff members and by the women's own political evolution. Reflecting on both the organizational development as well as the women's intellectual positions helps us understand how they came to embrace a distinctive black feminism that spoke to the needs of poor women on welfare.

Who's in Charge?

The predominantly white, middle-class male staff and the overwhelmingly poor black female constituency had wrestled since the movement's inception over control of the organization and the strategies and goals of the movement. These divisions were not rigid, however. Some recipients were more in tune with staff members. And some staff members allied closely with recipients. Staff members in the national office often clashed with each other, as did recipients on the national and local level. The conflicts were not constant or predictable, but always in flux, with battle lines redrawn frequently and personal animosity sometimes overshadowing political differences. Nevertheless, over the course of the movement some basic divisions emerged that affected both the structure and politics of NWRO.

One of the most pressing issues was who held the reins of power and would make decisions in the organization. In 1966, when a white organizer in California called a statewide meeting of welfare activists, Johnnie Tillmon tore up the constitution the organizer had written and pointedly instructed him, "You don't just come into somebody's neighborhood and run it."[1] Tillmon's position that welfare rights organizing took place in "her" neighborhood was a common one. Staff domination within the national organization and in local groups was an ongoing problem for welfare recipients who viewed staff members as "outsiders." George Wiley hired and supervised the NWRO staff in Washington and field organizers working with state and local groups. And the people he drew on to fill these positions, were, by and large, not welfare recipients, but seasoned middle-class organizers. In theory, the National Coordinating Committee and the Executive Committee, both comprised of welfare recipients elected by the general membership at the annual conferences, were responsible for policymaking. In practice, however, staff members wielded disproportionate power because they managed the budget, wrote the newsletter, maintained contact with local groups, and spoke for the organization. They were available on a day-to-day basis, while recipient leaders only came together periodically. The National Coordinating Committee met four times a year and the Executive Committee met eight times a year. Middle-class organizers in Washington, not welfare recipients, mapped out many of the earliest national campaigns. George Wiley, Tim Sampson, Hulbert James, and other key staff members regularly attended Executive Committee meetings. While meeting minutes suggest that Executive Committee members participated actively in discussions, it also seems that staff members influenced the outcome of many decisions.[2]

In some cases, staff members designated leaders and set the agenda of welfare rights meetings. At a 1967 National Coordinating Committee meeting in Washington, D.C., amidst chaos and confusion, the staff, in the words of one staff member, "hand-picked" a recipient leader to "pull things together."[3] In another case, some Virginia Welfare Rights Organization (VWRO) staff members rigged an election. They chose the winners in advance and failed to notify local groups about the election or give them time to nominate candidates. Recipients and other staff members objected vociferously, some even resigning. Dora Bonfanti, a recipient leader, labeled VWRO "a crooked organization."[4] Staff member Sally

Ylitalo suggested in a six-page letter to Wiley that Virginia staff "do a great deal of manipulating and lying." According to Ylitalo, other organizers told her "'yes, this was a farce, yes, this was predetermined' but that 'these people *think* this is democracy, that this is the closest thing they have *seen* to democracy.'" When Ylitalo asked why recipients could not be nominated, she was told that they "did not have cars, that they had children, and that a community leader should not be an 'organizer' because it makes for personality conflicts and competition." Yet, she suggested, "community leaders do as much as the organizers but get no money for it." Ylitalo questioned the impact of these policies:

> Does NWRO merely replace *one* system with *another*? Here in Virginia the organizers talk about the people as something less than them. The organizers are mainly middle class and live in the suburbs far away from the people. Some of the organizers write statements for the people to be made at city council and letters to be sent to the welfare department when the *people* are capable of doing this.

Pleading for a democratic organization, she suggested that only when middle-class domination has ended will recipients gain their rights, dignity, and equality.[5] Bonfanti and other recipient leaders ultimately appealed to Tillmon about their right to hire recipients as organizers.[6]

Different Organizing Strategies

Compounding the problems of democracy and decision-making were differences between staff and recipients about how to organize. Many staff members—fluent in formal political theory—advocated mobilization strategies to build the membership of the organization for welfare recipients. They usually measured success by membership rolls and recipients' ability to extract concessions from welfare officials. So, if organizers could bring out 200 welfare recipients to a demonstration, regardless of why or how they got there, that might be a sign of success. Some staff members followed political theorist Saul Alinsky who argued that poor people wielded power through mobilization. In this tradition, Wiley hoped to build a national organization of poor people, a union of welfare recipients, to gain political and electoral leverage.[7] He believed that civil disorders, such as riots and rebellions, gave marginalized groups such as African Americans or welfare recipients "substantial … power" to "have a major impact on the country."[8] Consequently, he sought to organize a mass base, exploiting the public fear of urban uprisings and threatening more such violence if NWRO's demands were not met.[9]

Staff members' familiarity with theories of mobilization and social change created an artificial divide between staff and recipients; a divide that some staff members saw as insurmountable. They assumed that black welfare recipients needed political guidance and were unable to make their own decisions or run their own organization. At a training session for VISTA volunteers, Hulbert James explained that he was far more sophisticated politically than the women recipients:

> One of the greatest difficulties I have as an organizer is that often I recognize the gap between where I am politically … and where the ladies are. I think that your success as an organizer is to be able to live with that gap, and to some extent to help to close that gap.[10]

Bill Pastreich of MWRO was even more blunt in his assessment of women's leadership abilities. Speaking to a student group in 1969, Pastreich said, "I would discourage their picking a lady [as an organizer], because she doesn't have the time to put in the hours on that kind of stuff. I also think that women in general are bad leaders. They have to take a week off to have emotions."[11] Welfare recipients' added responsibility of maintaining their home and caring for their children was another obstacle to their potential leadership roles. Their needs were sometimes trivialized by male staff members. In a letter to the national office, Pastreich suggested that the national office should guarantee organizers a car and insurance, whereas national officers (who were welfare recipients) "should be people who can take care of their own babysitting problems and they should look to neither their local WRO or [the] National [office] for babysitting money."[12] These attitudes contributed to the marginalization of poor women on welfare, reinforcing the dominant idea that black women needed the guidance and supervision of the white or black middle class.

Welfare recipients, on the other hand, had less formal training and were unfamiliar with classic organizing texts. Their theories of social change were rooted in their daily experiences as poor black women. Many valued the process of organizing as much as the result. They were interested not just in the victories, but in the decision-making behind the victories. They had come to believe, as did many other political activists in the 1960s, that day-to-day interactions between people reinforced and recreated racism, sexism, and class oppression; patterns manifested in their own organization.[13] They also believed that the stigma associated with AFDC could best be overcome by empowering welfare recipients and making a moral claim for assistance. Although middle-class support aided the movement immensely by providing office space, money, and legal assistance, many welfare recipients, ultimately, wanted to stand up for themselves. For them, stigma, isolation, and mistreatment characterized the problem of welfare as much as allocation of resources. An ideology of black mothers as undeserving of assistance, lazy, and promiscuous was embedded in the postwar AFDC program and justified cutbacks and other punitive welfare policies. So, they worked not just to build the organization, but to transform public perceptions of welfare recipients by making claims as mothers.

These differences between staff and recipients were reflected in the special-grant campaign which promised an immediate material benefit to recipients who became members. While this strategy was successful for a short period of time, when the material rewards disappeared, membership rolls shrank. Organizers were less successful at developing long-term participation in the movement. A member of the Columbus WRO explained:

> The prime method for organizing [used by WRO staff] has been a union-type model in which benefits (or gains) are used as ways to draw people into the organization. The difficulty of such organizing is that goals and ideology are often ignored. Therefore people often fail to establish a commitment for ongoing change based on his understanding of social change.[14]

A member of a non NWRO affiliated welfare rights organization in Chicago similarly argued that NWRO's "crisis orientation works against a sustained organizing effort. With NWRO groups get started and are coordinated around local crises. There is no follow-up after the crisis is over—no real nitty-gritty organizing is done at all."[15] Women in the organization, instead of relying solely on mobilization and pressure tactics, were also interested in education and politicization. They looked at long-term goals, not just short-term concessions.

The situation of Dovie Coleman, a recipient organizer in Chicago, illustrates some differences between grassroots recipients and national leaders and staff. In 1948 Coleman moved from St. Louis to Chicago, where she worked as a hair-dresser until 1952 when she applied for public assistance after a near-fatal auto accident. In 1964, she started working with the Jobs or Income Now (JOIN) organization, which was one of SDS's Economic Research and Action Projects.[16] She and other recipients broke away from JOIN and formed Welfare Recipients Demand Action (WRDA) in 1967, an interracial group that included African Americans, poor whites, Puerto Ricans and Native Americans. Run out of Coleman's apartment, WRDA was a resource-poor, but recipient-led, organization that refused "outside" staff.[17] In 1966 Coleman represented Illinois on the NCC and served as NWRO financial secretary. Reputedly an effective city-wide organizer since 1968, according to the local Friends group, she "knows welfare regulations better than most caseworkers."[18] After criticism by the NWRO Executive Committee for not signing up enough members, Coleman resigned, explaining that numbers alone could not measure her organizing success. There was a difference, she argued, between "deeply organizing" people and simply "getting a lot of people together." She continued:

> People will give up easy unless they are really organized and determined to keep fighting; as soon as the system fights back or refuses to change they will give up. Then the movement will fall apart. We have to stop somewhere

along the line to teach people what this system is all about. This is what I have done. This is what I think the key to organizing is.[19]

As an organizer, Coleman never intruded where she was not welcome or imposed her views on the poor people with whom she worked. She always waited until invited to a meeting: "It takes a long time and the work is very slow to build up trust between you and other organizations." Recipients such as Coleman formulated political theory from their daily experience, from their involvement with the poor, and from a sensibility of how to empower and create a better society for the disenfranchised. Loretta Johnson of Richmond, the Virginia representative to the NCC, helped kick off a Hunger Campaign in 1970 to inform people of the food-stamp program.[20] She eloquently explained her commitment to social justice:

> WRO has been the backbone and the power I've needed to make my voice heard, to get action and bring to light the ill-treatment and lies the people in power have given the poor, voiceless, helpless, elderly, the blacks, and the oppressed people in this country ... I will never, can never, shall never give up this fight for human dignity, equal rights plus Bread and Justice which will put an end to hunger in this country.[21]

For many welfare recipients, confidence was nurtured because of their intimate knowledge of how welfare functioned and their experiences with poverty. As they became more self-assured over time, as the organization encountered bigger external obstacles, and as staff control became more glaring, clashes with staff members became frequent and acrimonious. Women welfare rights activists examined how racial, gender, and class oppression—the patterns of structural domination they sought to eradicate—permeated everyday interactions among individuals. Transforming these personal relations—or seeking autonomy—became part of their agenda for social change.

The Black Caucus and Divisions of Race

Many of the divisions within NWRO exploded in a very public way at the 1969 convention in Detroit. The most visible conflict was over racial control of NWRO. Since NWRO's formation, middle-class white men dominated the administrative and organizing positions. According to white organizer Rhoda Linton who began working in the national office in 1968, "There were a lot of white people involved in making decisions about what the organization was going to do. And there were a lot of people of color doing the 'do,' doing the work."[22] Compounding this was resentment that a large portion of the organizers hired by Wiley to work with local groups were also white. A MAW member explained at a training conference in 1969 that black communities in Boston did not want "to be involved with white organizers."[23] Many black staff members and welfare recipients both inside and outside NWRO had come to believe, as Doris Bland of MAW put it, that the organization was "not oriented to black people" because most of the staff and organizers were white.[24]

The festering racial tensions in the welfare rights movement were exacerbated by the shifting terrain of social movement politics in the late 1960s—in particular the gaining currency of black nationalism. In the early 1960s, the civil rights movement modeled an interracial politics. This was best exemplified by Martin Luther King's speech at the 1963 March on Washington, where he conveyed his dream of black and white harmony, and the Student Nonviolent Coordinating Committee's (SNCC) notion of a beloved community. Although the civil rights movement was more complicated than this—some activists, even in the early years, advocated Black Power—the interracial components of the movement were elevated to heroic status. Over the course of the 1960s, however, these interracial alliances became increasingly tenuous. Conflict emerged between blacks and whites and many black activists began to question the viability of an interracial movement and called for organizing separately along racial lines in one's own community. Some organizations such as SNCC and the Congress of Racial Equality expelled white members. The rising tide of nationalism was also evident in demands for black pride and Black Power. Consequently, the insistence on black leadership in organizations dedicated to black issues became imperative.

Black staff members working in the NWRO national office criticized and publicly exposed white middle-class control within the organization. In 1969, they formed a caucus. John Lewis, an African American who headed NWRO's printing division, wrote in an article in the *Washington Afro-American* that black staff members, feeling "manipulated by white people," believed that "at national headquarters, professionals have a paternalistic frequently racist attitude about recipients, consistently making policy decisions the recipients themselves should have made."[25] Lewis also expressed concerns about lack of recipient control. He explained, "The main issue is—do the recipients control the organization. And they don't…As [NWRO] grew, it became very clear that most of the policy-making positions were going to whites." He pointed out that only one recipient out of a total of forty staff members worked for NWRO:

> Recipients should have been brought in from the beginning to learn the administrative jobs, but they weren't. The issue is not just race, but whether a recipient should be executive director … and have a person like Dr. Wiley to give him assistance if he needs it.[26]

Members of the Black Caucus, with Lewis at the helm, attended the NWRO conference in Detroit in 1969 armed with evidence of white domination and control in the organization. They circulated leaflets charging that important staff positions, such as executive director, should not be filled by "middle-class professionals"—clearly a swipe at Wiley—and demanded that the staff "reflect the racial constituency of NWRO members."[27] The actions of the Black Caucus struck a cord with some recipients critical of staff domination and the operation of the national office; others simply wanted more information about the discontent. A white delegate from Milwaukee took the stage during the opening session of the convention and asked Wiley to respond to accusations in the leaflet. Five or six members of the NCC forcibly escorted the woman off the stage and out of the auditorium.[28] While the national officers and staff prevented a debilitating disruption in this instance, in the long run their actions fostered unease and intensified concerns about democracy and dissent.

Many women in the welfare rights movement shared the concern about recipient control and repeatedly demanded that NWRO hire black AFDC recipients as organizers. The Pennsylvania contingent, led by Roxanne Jones of PWRO and Frankie Mae Jeter, chair of the Welfare Rights Organization of Allegheny County, pushed NWRO to "spend its money to hire welfare mothers to organize their own communities instead of professional organizers." In Massachusetts, ongoing conflict plagued relations between white organizers in the Massachusetts WRO and Mothers for Adequate Welfare (MAW), which was independent of NWRO. MAW members resented Bill Pastreich, hired by NWRO to work with the Massachusetts WRO.[29] According to researcher Mary Davidson, MAW member Doris Bland criticized Pastreich because he "is a white organizer who was not invited, not wanted and who is using the mothers for his own ends."[30] She wanted, instead, "to reconstruct, reorient, and have welfare mothers themselves implement the welfare system."[31]

One of the most rancorous conflicts took place in Michigan. In November 1969 Pamela Blair resigned as organizer because the state WRO wanted a recipient in the job and had already selected one prior to her appointment. Hired by Wiley in June 1969, Blair had worked with MWRO as a student volunteer since late 1967. Although Wiley notified the Michigan WRO of his decision to hire Blair and asked if they objected, he did not seek prior input.[32] The following month, in a letter to Wiley, NCC delegate and MWRO member Mamie Blakely expressed unequivocal opposition to the hiring of Blair. MWRO had decided that only the State Executive Committee should hire staff and that members and their children should fill jobs.[33] Recipients, especially those in the Detroit area, commonly complained that staff in Michigan held disproportionate power, pushed recipients to demonstrate when they weren't interested, kept speaking engagements away from mothers, and discredited recipient activists who disagreed with them.[34] Attempts by the national office to resolve the crisis in Michigan had little impact. Blair resigned because of the discontent and her conviction that the organization needed "a strong and *united* front against the terrible welfare system in Michigan."[35]

By late 1969, it was clear that action had to be taken to address the growing criticism. National leaders sought to remedy some of the problems by designating regional representatives on the Executive Committee to facilitate communication between national officers, staff, and local groups.[36] They barred staff members from business meetings and divided national meetings into a conference for non welfare recipient organizers and a convention for welfare recipient delegates to minimize control by the staff. In the summer of 1970 Wiley hired eight black field organizers as well as two recipients and a larger number of middle-class black men to work in the national office.[37] But by this time, morale and trust seem to have eroded. A white welfare recipient working in the national office resigned towards the end of 1970 because she was "so discouraged at the way in which people in this organization deal with each other." She could not continue to work for NWRO or with "the racist people I have met here, who despite the fact that poor white people are just as oppressed as poor black people and are greater in number, still feel that white people don't belong here."[38] Catherine Jermany worked in the national office and recalled that the staff

> questioned our decision-making ability ... [They] placated the ladies. They would buy them a hamburger rather than taking into consideration what they had to say ... The ladies felt that disrespect. And they made suggestions that never got acted on. And not only didn't they get acted on. They didn't even get discussed.[39]

Despite the token hiring of two recipients, the overwhelming power remained with the middle-class staff, black and white, most of whom were men. Wiley still retained power to hire and fire the staff, delegate responsibilities, and control the budget. In December 1970 a member of the National Office in an "Evaluation of NWRO and Affiliates" pointed out ongoing problems of staff domination: "The policies approved by the Executive Committee tend to be ignored or half heartedly carried out."[40] Moreover, these changes failed to address the fundamental problem of different organizing styles of recipients and their middle-class counterparts. Many recipient leaders argued that the means of organizing and the process of politicization, empowering one of the most oppressed sectors of society, was as important as demanding adequate state assistance for the poor.

Although the Black Caucus and grassroots recipient leaders may have agreed on the need for a recipient-led organization, in many ways, women in the movement had views on organizing that diverged from members of the Black Caucus, who seemed to conflate racial control with recipient control. Tillmon professed support for Wiley, who not only had important contacts and brought invaluable fundraising skills to the movement, but had proven his ongoing commitment to the welfare rights struggle. Throughout the entire brouhaha, she recounted, "I believed in George." The welfare recipient leadership generally and Tillmon specifically refused to align themselves fully with the black staff members who they saw as calling for racial exclusion. Recipients had a slightly different take—one that centered race, but in a racially inclusive way.

Recipients and Racial Identity

Although racial divisions threatened to tear apart the unity of the NWRO, women welfare rights activists concerned about recipient control and autonomy generally did not want NWRO to simply hire more African American men to work in the national office or as organizers. They subscribed to a strain of politics that took class, gender, and race seriously and also invited the participation of men and women of all racial backgrounds who respected the autonomy of poor women on welfare. Some welfare rights activists were proponents of black nationalism, but they advocated a variant of black nationalism that spoke to the needs of poor black women while also embracing the struggles of poor white women. These women found common ground in their work as mothers and their efforts to clothe, feed, and adequately house their children. Recipients, however, never transcended race. Race was always present, mediating their relationships, their encounters with the welfare department and their self-definition.[41] For both recipients of color and white recipients their racial identity was inextricably interwoven with their gender and class identities.

Catherine Jermany, of the Los Angeles County WRO and NCC representative, was an advocate of black nationalism and had a family history of black activism. Born and raised in Los Angeles, Jermany was an outspoken, confident, and articulate woman who questioned unfair policies and practices when employed by General Hospital and the Police Department in LA.[42] Jermany came from a politically active family, with one uncle who ran for governor of California in the 1960s and another uncle who worked with the Dodge Revolutionary Union Movement in Detroit. Jermany was involved with the Southern Christian Leadership Conference and Maulana Ron Karenga's cultural nationalist US organization in southern California.[43] She went on welfare after the birth of her third child when the county refused to give her job back because she was "too heavy." She helped organize a city-wide welfare rights group in Los Angeles long before the formation of NWRO and quickly rose up the ranks of welfare rights leadership.[44] Jermany acknowledged that most welfare recipients were white, yet underscored her own black identity as an organizer.[45] Speaking before the Association of Black Social Workers, she counseled them, "to think Black is revolutionary" they should therefore "Think Black" and "Talk Black."[46] Using language that echoed Black Power slogans, she clearly hoped to build support for the welfare rights movement through an appeal to racial solidarity. Thus, race was central to both understanding the welfare system and in building a movement to change it. Racial politics became more central to the welfare rights movement as internal tension heightened and as the Black Power movement grew in visibility. This was reflected in some local groups as well. In Ohio, welfare recipients had a training session in 1968, run with the help of black cultural nationalist Maulana Ron Karenga, "to wed the skills of massive community organization for self-determination to the black movement of self-identity."[47]

Even welfare recipients who were not black recognized that racial politics informed the welfare system. Loretta Domencich, a Native American organizer in Milwaukee explained, "I think Welfare Rights has also given me a clearer idea of racism. The Welfare Department has a way of lumping people together; whether you're black, white, red, or brown, you're all a bunch of niggers when you go into the Welfare Department."[48] Domencich glosses over the complex and varying ways women of different racial and cultural backgrounds encountered the welfare system. But Domencich's statement points to a common social stigma that all women on welfare experienced—one that she equates to a form of racism. Receipt of welfare, she is suggesting, is a social marker leading to patterns of mistreatment akin to the pervasive racism experienced by African Americans. The widespread discussion of racism generated by the civil rights and Black Power movements created a framework and provided a language for recipients of all colors to make sense of their marginalization. These welfare recipients articulated their problem with the welfare system as one of racial discrimination as well as poverty. From this perspective, racism is understood in broader terms than skin color, but was a larger pattern of social, political, and economic exclusion. For non black recipients of color such as Domencich, the black experience became a trope to understand their oppression.

The Black Freedom Movement's articulation of racial oppression also resonated with poor white recipients in important ways. Despite being relatively privileged within the welfare bureaucracy, they too could identify with the experience of marginalization. Particularly in the Midwest, white migration from Appalachia accounted for much of the increase in welfare in the postwar period. Cleveland was a destination of many white southern migrants. Over 80,000 moved to the city and most settled in the West Side in an area that came to be known as "Hillbilly Heaven," an area characterized by concentrated poverty, high rates of welfare receipt, and dilapidated housing.[49] Jennifer Frost recounts the divisions between white student organizers and poor white residents, "revealing not only class but also ethnic and racial differences within whiteness."[50] In her memoir, white welfare recipient activist Lillian Craig explained that her impoverished upbringing negatively affected her self-esteem: "If you're white and poor, the main thing you are taught every year in school is that you are dumb."[51] But she felt empowered as she gained respect through welfare rights activity: "At first it was important that I was in the spotlight … the spokesperson, with my picture in the papers and on TV. That came out of my past … I needed to feel that I was *somebody*. I hadn't been sure I was anybody."[52] In Chicago, Peggy Terry was also victimized by an ideology that looked down upon and marginalized poor white people. She referred to some of the white women in Chicago's Jobs or Income Now (JOIN) who harbored racist attitudes as "hillbilly women" (a term she had previously identified with).[53] Once when she was participating in a civil rights demonstration, a well-dressed white woman asked why she was picketing for civil rights. Terry replied: "Well, where else could I go and be treated with this respect that I've been treated with by Reverend King, the Nobel Prize Peace winner? No white Nobel Prize winner would pay poor white trash like me the slightest attention. Reverend King does."[54] Although recipients of color and white recipients did not experience poverty or the social stigma of welfare in quite the same way, these cases illustrate that the shared experiences of marginalization and "outsider" status enabled some poor whites to sympathize with the plight of African Americans, fueling the commitment to interracial organizing.[55]

Maintaining an Interracial Movement

While committed to integrating an analysis of race into their organizing, the NWRO Executive Committee and most welfare recipients also attempted to maintain the interracial unity that had characterized NWRO since its inception. In the words of one staff member, the Executive Committee argued that NWRO was about "poverty and poor people, not just black people."[56] Because of the association in the public mind between welfare and race, many people in the movement highlighted the fact that more white people than black people received welfare and that economics, not cultural or racial traits drove people into the AFDC program. Mrs. Rosie Hudson of Milwaukee explained, "Too many people are saying welfare's a black problem, when it's really a green problem. Why don't we have decent food, clothing, or shelter? It's simple. We don't have enough money."[57] Many white AFDC recipients had joined the movement because they saw welfare as a fundamentally economic problem. Moiece Palladino worked with the Sunnydale Projects Mothers Group, joined the San Francisco City Wide WRO, and became the first vice president of the statewide California WRO. She believed that "economic freedom is the only real freedom in this society." Raised in a white working-class family in San Francisco, Palladino married young, divorced her husband because of physical abuse, and went on welfare to support herself and her three children. She went to her first welfare rights meeting "looking for ... sociability." Palladino remembers intense conflicts around race in the racially mixed San Francisco City Wide group. "Whites," she said, "didn't want to be identified with the movement or with them blacks." And many African American activists discussed "white privilege," sometimes targeting Palladino, one of the few white people in the movement: "I understand why people would attack me because ... they perceive me to be the representative of a majority class, culture for which they perceive got benefits they didn't get." She believed ultimately, however, that race was just an "excuse" and that the conflicts were at the core about economics.[58] Catherine Jermany, a member of the Los Angeles County WRO and proponent of Black Power, reflected on the racial conflict plaguing the Northern California group and, interestingly, supported Moiece's involvement: "I don't think that the black women within the movement understood the relevance of having Moiece's participation. ... People got involved in personalities and didn't necessarily look at what the contribution of a person could be."[59] So, for Jermany, there was no contradiction between advocating Black Power and black pride and working closely with white welfare recipients.

Similarly, Johnnie Tillmon, who subscribed to a variant of Black Power politics, was perhaps one of the most ardent defenders of NWRO's interracial status. She explained in a 1971 interview:

> NWRO is not a black organization, not a white organization. … We are all here together and we are fighting the people who are responsible for our predicament … We can't afford racial separateness. I'm told by the poor white girls on welfare how they feel when they're hungry, and I feel the same way when I'm hungry.[60]

For Tillmon addressing race and racism and the way in which black women bore the brunt of AFDC's punitive policies did not mean disregarding the reality of white poverty. Empowering poor black women did not necessarily require erecting racially exclusive boundaries. Tillmon often referred to one of her visits to Appalachia where she met poor white women on welfare who implored her "not to leave them out." She never wavered from her belief in an inclusive movement: "One thing I want to say about our organization is there is no color line. We don't look at the color of skin when a person needs help. We don't look at religious background."[61]

Most recipients were committed to interracial organizing, as long as NWRO was not dominated by whites or non recipients. Roxanne Jones, a vehement critic of the middle-class domination within NWRO, wrote in the PWRO newsletter in 1969:

> 'I am proud that our poor white brothers and sisters in other parts of Pennsylvania are requesting and getting their money and other benefits under welfare…We must never forget that until all poor people begin working together rather than fighting each other and hating each other we will never fully achieve our basic goals.'[62]

The Kansas WRO expressed its commitment to developing "alliances across barriers of race, neighborhood, and family income."[63] Similarly, the Baltimore Welfare Rights Organization (BWRO) actively recruited white recipients. According to BRWO activist Rudell Martin, "I don't care what color you are. Everybody gets treated the same way—nasty."[64]

The welfare rights movement sought to bring together women of different cultural and racial backgrounds around a political platform that fought for autonomy for the most marginalized and oppressed group of women. They developed a solidarity that was premised on their common concerns about motherhood and economic justice. By building a broad-based movement they were better able to enhance their leverage with the welfare department. They recognized the racialized and gendered way in which the welfare system silenced and disempowered poor black women in particular. Peggy Terry, a white welfare rights activist in Chicago had an extremely sympathetic understanding of the appeal of Black Power: "Sure, there's an antiwhite feeling among blacks. Not in everyone, but in a lot. To me, that's understandable. It's unspeakable what black people have gone through since they were first brought to this country ... Whites [have] always been given better treatment."[65] Many welfare rights members believed that addressing the plight of poor women of color would ultimately benefit all women.

The Seeds of Radical Black Feminism

Through their ongoing battles with welfare officials and their involvement in the welfare rights movement, recipients sowed the seeds of a nascent radical black feminism. Their lived experience illustrated for them the way in which economic deprivation, racial discrimination, gender oppression, and social norms about sexuality were intertwined. And this became the basis for an intersectional analysis that combined race, class, gender, and sexuality. They rejected notions of essentialism: that all men of color or women, simply by virtue of being women, could ally with them. Instead their political solidarities were premised on a platform of liberation and autonomy for poor women on welfare. They had come to believe in the importance of defending their status as single mothers, demanding greater economic security, speaking for themselves, and transforming the racial and gendered ideology that underpinned the welfare system.

Many welfare recipients acutely felt the power of social stigma tied to their status as welfare recipients. In addition to making demands upon the state for more money or the elimination of specific regulations, they sought to change the public's perception of black women as well. For example, Catherine Jermany, in a speech before the State Welfare Finance Officers in Nevada in 1969, addressed the stigma and stereotypes associated with receipt of welfare. She attempted to turn the notion of fraud on its head by suggesting that welfare recipients rarely committed fraud. She argued that the inefficiency, inhumanity, and deception of welfare department administrators more often made recipients and taxpayers the victims of fraud. She debunked the popular stereotype that recipients cheated the system and attempted to expose the inconsistencies and unfairness of welfare policy and practices.[66] For recipients like Jermany, the "welfare problem" was complex and as much about ideology as facts and figures. Ideology shaped public policy and, in this case, bolstered popular support for more punitive and repressive policies.[67] The welfare rights movement's claims to motherhood, work and autonomy were all the more important in the 1960s when questions of illegitimacy employment outside the home, and black cultural traits helped define welfare as a black issue.

Women in the welfare rights movement insisted that the battle for public assistance was only partly about power, making demands upon the state, holding demonstrations, and having sit-ins. They believed that an argument for a welfare state based on economic efficiency or self-interest—that everyone would benefit if no one lived in dire poverty—would not be long-standing. Once the costs outweighed the benefits, then concessions would be revoked. By making demands upon the state as mothers, welfare rights activists questioned the popular belief that welfare recipients did not work and the dominant assumption that black women were not primarily mothers. Their emerging views on black feminism, which would only sprout in the early 1970s, advocated autonomy and self-determination for poor black women. It differed from staff members' view of forming a power bloc of poor people who could leverage the state for concessions. They posited a radically different conception of freedom and liberation from what other feminist or Black Power activists of the 1960s articulated. They crafted an expansive vision of black feminism—one that defied easy categorization and called into question the binary opposition of integration/nationalism and self-defense/nonviolence. Their vision challenged the masculine posture that had become so closely identified with Black Power as well as the middle-class orientation of many feminist groups, and expands our understanding of self-determination.[68] Welfare recipients fought for their right to stay home and care for their children, enter or reject intimate relationships, and embraced their status as single mothers. This distinctive ideology was rooted in their multiple identities as mothers, poor people, women of color, welfare recipients and community members. Fertilized in their day-to-day experiences and nurtured through political struggle, it promised autonomy for poor women on welfare.

Conclusion

Within any cross-race, cross-class, and cross-gender organization, the issues of racism, sexism, and classism operate both between the organization and society and within the organization itself—on both a personal and a public level. The welfare rights movement was not sheltered from the politics of the dominant culture but recreated those politics in the constant battles over goals, aspirations, and organizational style. Whatever good intentions motivated the staff, through their sexist and racist behavior, they ended up replicating the very power relations they sought to eradicate. The popular perception of welfare recipients as unworthy and undeserving was only reinforced when the central organization formed to remedy their situation continued to marginalize recipients and belittle their ideas and input. Thus, black women on welfare waged a struggle not only against mainstream American society, but their radical allies as well. This process of seeking empowerment within their organization helped nurture their black feminist outlook.

In the late 1960s, the radical black feminism of welfare rights activists was still in its infancy. Welfare rights activists worked hard to articulate their own views about race, motherhood, and economic autonomy, as the struggles over WIN, special grants, and the guaranteed income illustrated. They battled to become the dominant voice within the welfare rights movement, and to influence the larger debate about welfare. As the ideological perspective of welfare rights activists evolved, the external pressures on the movement mounted. Conservative forces that were gaining ascendency blamed the nation's economic troubles on welfare spending and linked social instability to radical political organizing. Pointed attacks on welfare recipients in combination with greater isolation of social movement activists created hurdles for advocates of welfare rights. Differences between staff and recipients were exacerbated by the external backlash and may have hindered the movement's ability to effectively respond to the growing welfare crisis. By the end of the 1960s, the costs of rising internal tensions and escalating pressures from outside had seriously tattered the organizational fabric of NWRO. As movement leaders pondered, and sometimes disagreed, about how to move forward, it became increasingly clear that welfare had assumed a prominent place in American political discourse. Welfare recipients were even more fiercely demonized and much of the country's ills were laid at their doorstep.

7

RESISTING EXTERNAL BACKLASH

By the early 1970s, NWRO was floundering. The internal conflicts, the failure of the guaranteed annual income, and a harsher political and cultural climate put the organization on the defensive. A rising mood of conservatism gripped the nation as much of middle America became tired of confrontational politics as well as a federal government that they believed kowtowed to special minority interests. State officials and welfare administrators—responding to and fueling a white backlash—slashed AFDC payments and winnowed down welfare rolls. NWRO launched two major national campaigns in the early 1970s to address this new political landscape—Operation Nevada and a Children's March for Survival. Both were designed to reverse the trend toward more punitive welfare policies. While Nevada brought short-term success, neither campaign halted the deepening antagonism toward AFDC recipients. Moreover, the ongoing attention to national struggles further weakened local welfare rights groups which fought bitterly to avoid losing ground. Paid membership declined nationally from 22,500 in 1969 to 11,500 in 1971.[1] The future of NWRO seemed bleak. The staff and recipients engaged in intense debates about the direction of the movement. They were unable to establish common ground, however, and found themselves further apart in an increasingly hostile climate.

Public Backlash Against Welfare

Since the welfare rights movement's inception, it had encountered public hostility. Welfare was never a popular issue. Even in the early twentieth century, recipients were stigmatized and viewed with suspicion. As welfare became racialized during the 1950s and 1960s, distrust only deepened. The white working class became resentful that its hard-earned tax dollars supported supposedly lazy and undeserving black welfare mothers. In the early 1970s these attitudes became more firmly implanted in the public mind and laced the dialogue and discourse about welfare. Many people had come to believe that welfare recipients were sexually promiscuous, could not control their childbearing, did not want to work, and collected hefty government checks enabling them to live a comfortable lifestyle on someone else's dime. Guy Drake's popular song "Welfare Cadillac," on the charts for six weeks in 1970, was emblematic of these stereotypes:

> Some folks say I'm crazy
> And I've even been called a fool
> But my kids get free books and
> All them there free lunches at school
> We get peanut butter and cheese
> And man, they give us flour by the sack
> ' Course them Welfare Checks
> They meet the payments on this new Cadillac.
> Now the way that I see it
> These other folk are the fools
> They're working and paying taxes
> Just to send my young'uns through school.[2]

The lyrics reflect a sentiment that the working class paid taxes and footed the bill for welfare recipients living the high life. People on welfare were characterized as free-loaders who milked the system and made fools of "hard-working" Americans.

These perceptions intensified in the 1970s for many reasons. Ricki Solinger suggests that the postwar discussion of reproductive rights framed as "women's choice" to bear children reinforced the notion of poor women on welfare as bad choice makers for having children they could not afford to raise and making them more culpable for their situation.[3] Consequently, assertions of individual freedom and personal choice by the mainstream women's movement may have exacerbated the political fallout experienced by women on welfare. One woman from Flushing, New York, referring to herself as a "hardworking taxpayer," seemed to provide evidence for this view in a letter to the editor of the New York Times: "There is no longer any excuse for illegitimacy to be supported by our welfare laws. Now that we have effective birth control methods and legal abortion, no child should be born to become a burden to society."[4] In addition, images of angry welfare mothers demanding their rights loudly and without shame undoubtedly fueled the resentment towards welfare recipients brewing since the late 1950s.[5] The welfare protests may have hardened the popular perception of the lazy, ungrateful woman on welfare looking for a handout. Opposition to welfare and the welfare rights movement encouraged people already disdainful of welfare to vocally oppose AFDC.

Anger about welfare was also fed by economic hard times. In 1973 a world-wide oil crisis led to skyrocketing prices. This was coupled with long-term shifts in the U.S. economy away from well-paying factory jobs to a new service economy that tended to offer jobs with lower pay and fewer benefits. The closing of industrial plants, slowing of the economy, and further decline of urban centers spread economic deprivation. High unemployment, spiraling inflation, and a greater tax burden characterized the early 1970s. The overall unemployment rate increased from 3.5 percent in 1969 to 8.6 percent in 1975. For blue-collar work-ers, unemployment rose from 3.9 percent in 1969 to 13.4 percent in 1975.[6] At the same time, consumer food prices rose by 20 percent in 1973 and 12 percent in 1974, and fuel prices by 11 percent in 1973 and almost 17 percent in 1974.[7] These economic realities burst the bubble of prosperity and deflated the optimism of the 1960s. Many Americans caught in the quagmire of stagflation—a new economic term that referred to the rather unusual combination of high unemployment and high inflation—began to rethink their own, as well as their government's, political priorities. The seventies ushered in a new political alignment and a new set of assumptions about political reform. Electoral power shifted from the Rustbelt states of the Midwest to the Sunbelt states of the Southwest. Belief in the benefits of expansive government—a regulatory state that ameliorates social problems of poverty, a weak economy, and housing shortages—faded quickly.[8] In this political climate welfare recipients, although they were particularly hard hit by galloping inflation which made their welfare checks worth even less, became convenient scapegoats for economic distress and helped justify a conservative political turn.

Some of the anti-welfare sentiment rested on the assumption that public assist-ance consumed the lion's share of taxes paid by the working poor and middle class. For example, a Pennsylvania woman wrote a letter to the Blair County WRO advocating public assistance for the elderly and disabled, but not for single mothers. The working class, she said, was "tired of seeing all of their hard earned money go to people who do not deserve it or who could be working and sup-porting their own families." Families on welfare, she argued, received dental care, hospital care, food stamps, "yet, the working man has to pay taxes, which are increasing by leaps and bounds, in order to provide these 'poor' people with such privileges." She contended that welfare programs "undermin[e] the very basis on which this country was founded—free enterprise and the right to work to obtain what you want."[9]

This woman's views were not extreme. During the late 1960s and early 1970s local taxpayer groups emerged around the country and a National Taxpayers Union, founded in 1969, dedicated itself to "lower taxes, less wasteful spending, and the principles of rational and limited government."[10] Taxpayers' organizations crossed political boundaries and addressed such issues as property tax assessment, tax distribution, and government spending. In the early 1970s people on the left mobilized around taxes, calling on corporations and the wealthy to bear a greater share of the tax burden. By the mid-1970s, however, the anti-tax position had become a prime conservative issue. One recurring theme among tax protesters throughout the 1970s was spending on welfare and the employment status of welfare recipients. Conservatives latched onto this issue to discredit AFDC and government spending. In 1971, Roger Freeman of the Hoover Institution, for example, blamed the welfare state for "imposing an excessive and lopsided tax burden" and thus "sap[ping] the natural growth potential of our economy."[11] Conservatives successfully linked rising taxes and economic straits of the middle and working classes to the expansion of the welfare state by capitalizing on racist and sexist stereotypes about welfare recipients and mistaken beliefs about the welfare budget. Many people incorrectly assumed that most of their taxes went to support mothers on AFDC. Between 1970 and 1973, the costs of public aid—which included Old Age Assistance, Aid to the Blind and Disabled, and AFDC—increased from $16.5 billion to $28.7 billion. Yet, during the same time period, social insurance costs increased from $54.7 billion to $86.1 billion. Even though public aid rose at a slightly faster rate than social insurance, it represented a much smaller portion of the budget. In 1974 public aid represented 13.9 percent of the total social welfare budget and social insurance 40.6 percent.[12]

Apart from taxation and social welfare spending, opposition to welfare centered on assumptions about recipients' needs. Many people believed that a vast majority of welfare recipients could, but refused to, work and simply took advantage of government handouts. In a 1971 Gallup poll two-thirds of respondents supported a program requiring welfare recipients to take jobs in private industry with the government paying most of their salary for the first year.[13] In addition, in a 1972 Boston-area survey, people of all social classes believed that welfare recipients were idle and dishonest, and had more children than they did.[14] In most cases, the negative images were racially inscribed, portraying the "typical" welfare recipient as an African American woman. Much of the news coverage, for example, reinforced the connection between race and welfare. From 1972 to 1973, the peak years of discussion of the welfare controversy in popular news magazines, 75 percent of the photographs were of African Americans, even though they constituted only 46 percent of welfare recipients.[15] Both the racial and gender encoded images and the articulated concerns about tax dollars echoed the long-standing belief that African American women, considered workers primarily and mothers only secondarily, should be employed—not on relief.

In addition, for a variety of reasons, including opportunism on the part of politicians and sensationalized news coverage, the public blamed increases in the welfare rolls on the purportedly liberal Democratic policies of the 1960s. Even though during the 1960s Democratic and Republican positions on welfare did not differ drastically, in the 1970s Republicans and conservatives successfully tied welfare to Great Society programs, and the Democratic Party became the culprit of the "welfare mess." Welfare, liberalism, and the Democratic Party converged in the popular discourse with the politics of race. Americans opposed welfare because of the racial images associated with it; and bolted the Democratic Party because of its association with welfare.[16] They correspondingly concluded that government bureaucracy was inefficient and wasteful. An article in *Newsweek* in 1972, for example, suggested that a bigger problem than individual cases of welfare fraud was the "ineptitude, sloth, mismanagement" of the "welfare establishment."[17] This dialogue laid the basis for a right-wing resurgence that differed from the solutions to the "welfare problem" in the late 1960s when policymakers sought to discipline welfare recipients through greater monitoring and work requirements—more expensive programs that expanded the welfare bureaucracy. In the 1970s, charges of systemic fraud and government mismanagement suggested one conclusion: shrinking the public sector.

The welfare debate was dominated, not by facts, figures, and rational argument, but by stereotypes, snapshot images, and ideology. In the 1970s, journalistic accounts, government reports, political rhetoric, and academic studies highlighted cases of welfare fraud, portraying recipients as lazy and dishonest, and characterizing the welfare bureaucracy as inefficient. A 1975 *New Yorker* article by Susan Sheehan is a good example. Sheehan tells the tale of a Puerto Rican mother of nine on welfare, recounting multiple sexual partners, carefree men, out-of-wedlock births, poor housekeeping, drug use, and indifferent attitudes about paid employment, school, and personal morality.[18] The widely read article reinforced popular misconceptions of welfare recipients as irresponsible and lacking discipline. Sheehan portrayed a welfare system supporting a dysfunctional, multigenerational culture of poverty and dishonest recipients who took advantage of the AFDC program. Based on anecdote, rather than scientific study or statistical analysis, studies such as Sheehan's created enduring images repeated and retold when convenient—images of a lazy recipient purchasing steak with food stamps and dressing in the latest fashion with little regard for money or budgeting. This type of coverage reinforced the idea that welfare recipients were not needy and made poor lifestyle choices, and fostered negative public perceptions of people on AFDC. So, the terms of the debate had shifted dramatically from concerns about establishing a basic minimum standard of living in the 1960s to an assessment in the 1970s that very few people on welfare deserved assistance, and that welfare, in fact, damaged recipients. This new political climate contributed to the reversal of many of the successes of the welfare rights movement in the early 1970s, putting welfare recipients on the defensive and providing a rationale for reducing the welfare rolls.

Operation Nevada

Nevada became ground zero in the battle between welfare officials and welfare rights activists—a case that tested the tenacity of both sides. In September 1970, after a random sampling audit, the state of Nevada enacted massive cuts in welfare, claiming that one-half of all welfare recipients earned additional, unauthorized income. It reduced the budgets of 4,500 women and children and cut

3,000 recipients off welfare completely, eliminating nearly one-quarter of the caseload. The state did not give recipients prior notice of termination nor did it inform them of their right to a fair hearing. This action was a blatant violation of the recent Supreme Court Goldberg ruling that assured recipients would be notified and informed of the right to a fair hearing prior to the termination or reduction of benefits. In one situation, a caseworker told a welfare recipient from Reno, Joanna "Cookie" Bustamonte, on three different occasions to work as a prostitute to support her children.[19] Democratic Governor Mike O'Callahan, who had won a narrow victory with poor and black support, enacted the Nevada cuts, illustrating that the campaign to cut welfare crossed party lines.

The local NWRO chapter in Nevada, the Clark County Welfare Rights Organization, responded immediately to the state cutbacks.[20] A group of women on AFDC living in the Marble Manor housing project on the Westside of Las Vegas formed the Clark County WRO in 1967 when caseworkers assigned them to a mandatory sewing class as part of the federal government's WIN training program. The organization participated in the special-grants campaign, which sought increases in the shoes and clothing allowance for children on welfare and educated recipients about their rights. Rosie Seals served as president for the first two years, before Ruby Duncan was elected. Duncan was born in Tallulah, Louisiana. Her parents died when she was two-and-a-half years old, and by the age of eight she was plowing fields and chopping cotton. In the early 1950s, at the age of eighteen, she traveled from Louisiana to Nevada, leaving behind the racial violence of the Ku Klux Klan and low wages in search of better job opportunities. A mother of seven, Duncan worked for nearly fifteen years in hotels on the Las Vegas Strip in the low-paying service sector, only applying for welfare after a debilitating work-related accident.[21]

When Duncan joined the WRO, she had little political training. Despite her inexperience she spoke passionately before elected officials about the difficulties of single motherhood and living on a welfare budget. Inspired and emboldened by her contact with the men and women of NWRO, after the welfare cuts Duncan began to consider how to hit Las Vegas "in the pocketbook," a phrase she had heard women such as Johnnie Tillmon utter. Her idea to focus on the Las Vegas Strip culminated in a national campaign by NWRO to roll back the Nevada cuts.[22]

George Wiley believed the Nevada cuts were a pivotal turning point in welfare history—a moment politicians might exploit to repeal the gains of the previous years. He urged NWRO to make Nevada an organizational and political priority. At a retreat in January 1971, staff members adopted Wiley's suggestion to fight the cutbacks in Nevada, which they considered "a training ground for similar actions in other states."[23] The staff decided to launch the Nevada campaign without approval from the National Coordinating Committee. Although staff members got approval from Johnnie Tillmon and polled the Executive Committee, it had little input in formulating the campaign.[24] In fact, it seemed that the opinions of the recipient leaders mattered little. During the retreat, Hulbert James said, "Whether NCC approves or not is inconsequential, because the action is on anyway. If field members don't approve, they shouldn't expect support from National on local actions, which don't relate to this National campaign."[25] Although the NCC met the following month in Nevada because of the planned campaign, it did not discuss Operation Nevada, focusing instead on FAP and the floor for an adequate income.[26] The planning of Operation Nevada illustrated staff use of the purse strings to push a particular political agenda, regardless of the views of grassroots members or leaders who differed with them.

NWRO designed Operation Nevada to "meet the repression head-on" and alert other states that it would not tolerate such illegal and unjust actions. During the campaign, lawyers, national officers, organizers, recipients from the region, and other well-known personalities descended on Nevada to help recipients file fair hearings and mobilize for mass action to force the state of Nevada to reinstate women cut off welfare. A contingent of welfare recipients from Northern California spent two weeks in Nevada organizing and demonstrating against the cuts.[27] NWRO demanded restoration of benefits and removal of the head of the state welfare department.[28] After several failed attempts to meet with welfare officials the organization planned demonstrations at the welfare department and marches down the central casino and entertainment strip in Las Vegas.[29] At one demonstration in mid–March, 1,000 welfare recipients and supporters, including Dave Dellinger, Jane Fonda, George Wiley, and Ralph Abernathy, marched into the world-famous Caesar's Palace Hotel. As gamblers and tourists stopped to watch, protestors singing "we are into Caesar's Palace; we shall not be moved" paraded into the hotel lobby, downstairs to the casino, and then back out onto the street.[30] The following week, another march down the Las Vegas Strip drew 250 demonstrators. During this protest, in typical fashion, Wiley combined militance, political accommodation, and an attempt to creatively raise money by threatening civil disobedience, but exempted those hotels pledging financial support to NWRO. When security guards blocked the entrance to the Sands Hotel, protestors sat down in the middle of the street and impeded traffic for a half an hour before police arrested those refusing to disperse.[31] Just a few short weeks after NWRO began Operation Nevada, a federal district judge ordered Nevada to reinstate all recipients cut off welfare, arguing that welfare benefits were a statutory right, as ruled in the 1969 Supreme Court Goldberg decision, and that the state's action violated the constitutional rights of recipients.[32] Operation Nevada successfully brought together NWRO's legal and protest strategies, demonstrating how the two worked in tandem. It was one of NWRO's most visible and important victories.

NWRO's success in Nevada did not stop the overall trend toward more punitive and repressive welfare policies. Between 1970 and 1980, the median monthly AFDC benefit for a family of four fell from $739 to $552 in constant 1990 dollars. In addition states employed a number of alternate, albeit legal, strategies, including a cumbersome application process and higher rejection rates, to discourage recipients from applying for or continuing to receive welfare.[33] Nor did Operation Nevada diminish the public hostility towards welfare recipients. In fact, unfavorable and irresponsible news coverage of the campaign may have encouraged such attitudes. In the midst of the protest, the *Las Vegas Sun* reported in large headlines that Ruby Duncan, a leader of the Clark County WRO and organizer of the Nevada protests, had put her license plates, registered to a 1968 Chevrolet, on a 1971 Cadillac Eldorado. This report undoubtedly fed the popular stereotype that recipients lived "high on the hog" and drove Cadillacs. Two days later the newspaper printed in a small article that its earlier report about Duncan was incorrect.[34] Thus, the victory in Nevada proved to be bittersweet. Self-congratulatory celebration aside, Nevada was a harbinger of more punitive welfare measures, as the staff originally predicted, but one they had little power to thwart. Despite their success, welfare rights activists still faced the fundamental problems of a repressive welfare state and a hostile public.

New Directions

After Operation Nevada, movement leaders were at a crossroads and contemplated new strategies. The rising tide of conservatism, the economic crisis, and the welfare backlash dealt a severe blow to the welfare rights movement. Compounding this, the struggle for a guaranteed income bill had consumed NWRO for several years, draining it of resources and detracting from grassroots organizing. And internal divisions were widening. As they grappled with how to address the deep-seated negative popular attitudes, and, at times, downright hostility that the movement had encountered, the many undercurrents of tension and conflict were brought to the fore. The most glaring division remained that between the mostly male staff and female constituency.

Keenly aware that the battle for welfare rights would have to be fought not just in welfare offices and the halls of Congress, but in the arena of public opinion as well, both staff and recipients took notice of the derogatory and at times vile images of black women embedded in debates about welfare. Welfare rights activists pondered how to build popular support for their position. The staff wanted to expand the movement to include the working poor and unemployed men in order to shift the focus away from black women. The women, on the other hand, sought to demystify the stereotypes and misconceptions by remolding the image of AFDC recipients into one of women who worked and contributed to society.

Staff members proposed broadening the organization's constituency beyond single mothers on welfare as a way to build power. At a retreat in Romney, West Virginia in 1970, staff members resolved to mobilize unemployed fathers and the working poor to revive the floundering organization.[35] NWRO had already taken steps in this direction. At the Detroit convention in 1969, it voted to extend membership to any family earning less than $5500 a year.[36] Little came of this decision, however, and as they searched for a new approach the staff hoped to translate this into a concrete plan.

Including the working poor, the staff believed, would expand the base of the movement and appease the ire of the white working class against the "dependent" poor. The racist and sexist attacks on the welfare rights movement could be neutralized, they argued, if the constituency encompassed more men and white families. In addition, recruiting the working poor into the movement as beneficiaries of government programs might blur the distinction between the "dependent" and "independent" poor and diminish the stigma of welfare, thus forging a real alliance between welfare recipients and the working poor.

In Rhode Island, Massachusetts, and New York, welfare rights organizers had already begun to recruit the unemployed and working poor by encouraging them to apply for home relief or wage supplements, state-run programs giving poor working people a government subsidy if their incomes were very low.[37] Wage supplements, explained Hulbert James, enabled a working man to earn more than a welfare recipient. Predicting in 1969 that "this would start a whole new movement" he advised welfare organizers to recruit construction workers in unemployment centers because "the time may be coming in this movement when we will have to do some of our own labor organizing."[38]

In Massachusetts, Bill Pastreich, a long-time NWRO organizer, formed a wage supplement organization independent of the WRO. In mid-1969, predating the official expansion of NWRO's membership, he made a case in a letter to Tim Sampson for NWRO to get involved in other issues besides welfare and urged visible demonstrations with working men and old-age assistance recipients.[39] Frances Fox Piven and Richard Cloward, two academics who had played a critical role in the formation of NWRO, originally outlined the wage-supplement campaign, which they believed could build bridges between the labor movement and the poor.[40] Getting seed money from the two social scientists, Pastreich began door-knocking in New Bedford, a mostly white mill town in Massachusetts where men worked in sweatshop conditions for a minimum wage. Before the first meeting of the New Bedford Wage Supplement Organization (WSO) in August 1969, he worried the men would not show up. Revealing his interest not just in mobilizing masses, but in creating a new racial and gendered image of "the poor," he said, "A lot of guys will send their wives—we want the guys … I'll kill them if they send their wives."[41] More than a hundred people, mostly men, showed up to fill out forms for aid.[42] This laid the basis for a statewide wage supplement association.[43]

Organizing unemployed and low-income men dovetailed nicely with some staff members' goal of reestablishing the traditional two-parent family. James explained that wage supplements would keep "men and women together with their families."[44] But the staff also subscribed to a romantic male-centered notion of union organizing with all of its gendered connotations. They pictured "workers" not as employed women or mothers engaged in the work of social reproduction, but typical blue-collar, male-dominated, largely white construction or factory workers. The AFDC recipient was a woman, the wage supplement recipient, a man. As one journalist reported, they sought "a new constituency of tough men to support the struggle of the ADC mothers."[45]

These staff members' idealization of masculinity was fed by a broader social trend. Both within popular culture and activist circles, the dominant male image was one many people revered. Masculine representations permeated radical groups such as the Black Panther Party and the Weathermen, both of which adopted strategies, attitudes, and attire reflecting their male-centered politics. The "blaxploitation" films of the early 1970s conveyed the sensibility that masculine physical strength would ultimately subvert racism.[46] Even within more conservative and mainstream circles, traditional notions of manhood resurfaced in the early 1970s partly as a response to the perceived instability and disruption of traditional values. A reassertion of masculinity seemed both a militant antidote to racism and a cure for the radical protests that middle America hoped to quash.

Welfare recipient leaders, however, resisted the move toward organizing the working poor. The staff believed that recipients' hesitation was a product of self-interest and a desire to maintain power within the movement.[47] Some recipients may have been concerned about personal power, but others differed politically from the men in the movement—fearing the shift to the working poor would dilute the focus on the needs of women and children. They emphasized rather than retreated from their agenda as poor black women and countered the public sentiment that women on welfare were lazy and undeserving of support by arguing that as mothers they did work:

> The belief that welfare mothers can work assumes that they are not working now. The work of raising a family, of household tasks, is not considered worthy of even an unjust wage. Scrubbing floors, preparing meals, changing bed linens, sewing, caring for the sick, budgeting, and helping educate and discipline children—all this is very hard work, as every woman knows.[48]

Women in the welfare rights movement placed greater value on motherhood and worked to redefine welfare rights as women's rights. Redirecting the political focus to another constituency, they believed, would not debunk the racist and sexist stereotypes about them and thus would have only marginal impact on the ideology of welfare.

Despite the opposition by women recipients, staff members launched the working poor strategy to revive the organization and to challenge the power of recipient leaders. Wiley stated this explicitly:

> The staff will have to organize groups like the working poor without much help from the mothers, and then bring the organized groups into NWRO

to challenge the mothers. Through a challenge like this, some kind of accommodation will be worked out.[49]

The working poor strategy, however, never extended beyond a few isolated places, but the underlying differences between staff and recipients about whether to deflect attention from or direct it to welfare mothers never disappeared.

The Children's March

Although a full-fledged shift to organize the working poor never occurred within NWRO, the staff did attempt to cultivate sympathy for AFDC recipients by organizing a Children's March for Survival. The NWRO staff planned the Children's March on Washington to turn the spotlight away from black women on welfare and shore up public support by focusing on children. Although Wiley believed that the march might be "the beginning of a grassroots movement ... around issues affecting children," in reality, it was NWRO's last attempt at mass mobilization.[50] The staff hoped that the march would put the National Office "back meaningfully in touch with local WROs," but, instead, it exposed more vividly differences between staff and recipients, and local and national activists.[51] Designed by the male staff in part to protest Nixon's welfare agenda and to pressure Congress to defeat the Family Assistance Plan, both the planning and the organizing for the march was a top-down affair. Staff members clearly stated, "there is neither the time, nor interest on NWRO's part to develop, at this time, a truly participatory structure of supporting organization."[52] But equally important, as with organizing the working poor, staff member Bert De Leeuw outlined the campaign with the hope that the march would "change the focus away from welfare moms, work, etc ... to a much more politically and emotionally acceptable group, i.e. children."[53]

Women in the welfare rights movement refused to shift their focus or redefine their goals because it was politically unpopular. Soliciting charity or cultivating sympathy by relying on images of children was not an adequate response to welfare cutbacks, they argued, particularly when the reason for the cutbacks was the perceived inadequacies of poor women. Although they had often made claims for assistance as mothers and asked for items to benefit their children, they always emphasized the work they performed as mothers. Moreover, over time they came to view their struggle as one to assert their rights as women, not just as mothers. Minimizing the attention on women and focusing exclusively on children, they believed, could serve to further circumscribe women's rights. The internal conflict around the Children's March reinforced the belief among women in the welfare rights movement that welfare was a women's issue. It hardened the different visions and strategies of Wiley and the female leadership and ultimately contributed to the resignation of Wiley and many other staff members.

The Children's March on March 25, 1972 drew close to 40,000 people to the Washington Monument. A large proportion of participants were children from the Washington, D.C. area, who attended after the District school board, in a much-criticized decision, endorsed the march and encouraged students to attend. In a carnival-like atmosphere with games and activities for children, protestors chanted opposition to Nixon's FAP. They carried signs reading "Nixon Doesn't Care," and highlighted the particular problems of children in poverty. The list of speakers included Ralph Abernathy, Jesse Jackson, Coretta Scott King, Eugene McCarthy, Shirley MacLaine, and Gloria Steinem.[54] Despite the large turnout the march garnered little support from grassroots welfare recipients around the country. Moreover, it gained little publicity, drained NWRO of much-needed resources, and strained internal politics in the organization. The *New York Times* called the protest a "dubious venture on every ground."[55]

The conflict within the welfare rights movement—of whether or not to focus on the pariah class of recipients of government assistance—is indicative of a broader political tension between people supporting targeted programs and those supporting universal programs. Some scholars have argued that in the U.S., social programs serving "targeted" groups, like African Americans, are more vulnerable to cutbacks and repressive policies. They suggest that policymakers should instead develop universal programs, such as social security, benefiting everyone and, in the process, those needing help the most will be assisted.[56]

On the face of it, this argument seems plausible. But it fails to take into account that only some, not all, targeted programs encounter problems of public support. Historically, most Americans considered certain constituencies, such as the elderly, blind, disabled, and students, more worthy and deserving than other groups. In the early twentieth century, single mothers were deemed worthy of financial assistance. Although these programs for mothers were restrictive and paltry, they were not controversial.[57] When a higher proportion of black women began to receive assistance as poor mothers, those programs became less popular and even despised. In the postwar period, AFDC came under bipartisan attack, with benefit reductions, stricter eligibility standards, and the implementation of work requirements.

Within the US welfare state African Americans have always been categorized as undeserving. Regardless of the type of program—public housing is another example—when the constituency of a program shifted from predominantly white to predominantly nonwhite, the program also shifted from popular to despised. The real problem, therefore, is the way in which racism, sexism, and discrimination are embedded in American culture and reflected in the politics of welfare. Instead of camouflaging the truly needy in universal programs that give handouts to those who don't need help, an alternative solution may be to make a convincing political claim for those needing assistance. Such an approach would challenge popular myths and stereotypes and may decrease the stigma associated with particular groups. It will help construct a welfare state serving people unable to support themselves, regardless of societal prejudices, and will begin to close the racial and gender gap. Universal programs, benefiting everyone regardless of need, would not address the fundamental problem of inequality in society or in the welfare state. In addition, they would do little to present a moral case that some people need and should be given assistance because of structural inequalities.

The division within NWRO about the Children's March reflected this political divide between universal and targeted programs. Staff members favored a broader constituency to counteract the negative stereotypes associated with AFDC. Welfare recipients advocated claiming the mantle of motherhood for poor women on welfare as a way to highlight their work as mothers and defend their rights as women.

Conclusion

The early 1970s was a difficult period for the welfare rights movement. The political climate had shifted dramatically since the late 1960s, when the promise of ending poverty circulated among a range of political constituencies. Nixon's Family Assistance Plan was permanently defeated, middle- and working-class support for anti-poverty measures was dwindling, and states seemed to be on an unstoppable rampage to slash their welfare budgets. The welfare rights movement was fractured both because of its internal tensions and because of the costs of external backlash. Staff and recipients disagreed on whether to counter the racism and sexism directed at welfare recipients by trying to dispel the myths or by shifting attention away from recipients altogether. Operation Nevada and the Children's March were such top-down campaigns, however, that in both cases, professional organizers and celebrities subsumed the voices of local welfare recipients.[58] These campaigns sharpened differences between staff and recipients and laid bare the core conflicts about the future direction of the movement. In a context where welfare recipients were under attack by politicians, policymakers, journalists, and many sectors of the American public, these strains would lead to a permanent split within NWRO and ultimate control of the organization by welfare recipients.

8

A RADICAL BLACK FEMINIST MOVEMENT

The year 1972 proved to be a turning point for NWRO. The relentless attacks on welfare and growing public hostility, evidenced by the Nevada cuts and the response to the Children's March, in conjunction with underlying internal tensions, put enormous pressure on the organization. Activists had to develop an effective strategy to deal with the backlash. Many recipients had become even more dissatisfied in the interim about the internal politics of the organization. The issues revolved around sexism, power, and ideology, and culminated in a leadership change in NWRO that enabled black women recipients to take full control of the organization. It also crystallized more clearly their radical black feminist politics.

The Problem of Sexism

In some ways concerns about sexism within NWRO were not altogether distinct from earlier struggles about recipient control. Most recipients, after all, were women; and most staff members were men. But in the early 1970s women in the organization were increasingly aware of their social position as women and encountered a new language of sexism and women's autonomy to articulate their positions. Since NWRO's founding in 1966, the women's movement grew from pockets of activism to a powerful, mass-based movement. The National Organization for Women was formed that same year to push for gender equality and to open up job and educational opportunities for women. Radical women who had been involved in the civil rights and student movements began to organize consciousness-raising groups that looked not just at the barriers to equality, but at the way in which men and women were expected to conform to socially defined roles. The integral involvement of women in the struggle for black freedom didn't preclude the possibility of sexist behavior or the marginalization of women. Although black women were more likely to stake their claim to power within civil rights and Black Power organizations, some black women also established independent organizations.[1] Women in the Student Nonviolent Coordinating Committee (SNCC) and the National Black Feminist Organization developed an analysis that combined race and gender to speak to the experiences of black women. In addition, Chicana, Native American, and Asian American women organized as well. Although there were ideological and political differences among the many strains of women's activism, many women (and some men) outside the narrowly defined women's movement began to think more deeply about gender inequality and women's liberation.

Women in the welfare rights movement were undoubtedly influenced by the growth of women's activism. But even at the start of the welfare rights movement, before the women's movement was in full swing, women recipients had a gender consciousness that was rooted in their day-to-day experiences as mothers, welfare recipients, and poor people. Their gender identity and understanding of sexism was shaped by their interaction with the welfare system, their experiences with racism, and their struggles to feed and clothe their children. So, for welfare recipients, the question of gender was inseparable from race, class, culture, and power. But in the early 1970s, many of the internal struggles in the organization were framed as struggles over sexism. According to Tim Sampson, Wiley's policy of almost always hiring male organizers created a backlash.[2] Overt instances of sexism in the movement became a source of conflict between men and women in NWRO. As an internal report documented in 1972

> Attitudes of sexism on every level affect the way that programs are implemented. Major decision-making comes out of the national offices which is controlled by men. Because of this, membership at local, state and regional levels do not have the opportunity to participate in any meaningful way in their organization, and every time they attempt to participate they are ignored or regarded as emotional women. The problem then becomes not "how do we have an effective program guided by the membership," but "what do we do about the ladies" … Further, the program areas cannot be implemented properly as long as there is such wide range sexism. This is evidenced by the predominance of paid male organizers and how male staff dominate decision-making of a women's organization on every level.[3]

The report was a powerful indictment of the imbalance of power within NWRO, as well as the way in which women recipients were marginalized.

The subtle and not-so-subtle racism and sexism of mostly white, male organizers in NWRO reinforced the feminist orientation of women in the struggle for welfare rights. As women in the organization became increasingly aware of the sexism of staff members they asserted their right to control their own organization and determine its political direction. Paralleling the experiences of some women in the Student Nonviolent Coordinating Committee (SNCC), Students for a Democratic Society (SDS), and the Black Panther Party who encountered sexism when expected to perform menial tasks or were excluded from decision-making of the group, the day-to-day practices of sexism encouraged women in the welfare rights movement to question their secondary status within NWRO.

Change in Leadership and a New Agenda

In 1972, the organization's internal conflicts—instances of racism and sexism, control wielded by the predominantly middle-class staff, and conflicts over the direction of the organization—came to a head. Welfare recipients who had battled for years for autonomy and self-determination concluded that their goals could best be achieved by an organization run by welfare recipients. Johnnie Tillmon argued that the nonpoor should serve only in supportive, not leadership, roles and proposed that women on welfare "try and do something for ourselves and by ourselves to the extent that we could."[4] By the early 1970s Tillmon and many other welfare rights activists wanted autonomy in decision-making and, most immediately, sought control of NWRO.

As a result, George Wiley stepped down as executive director and left NWRO in late 1972. The resignation was voluntary but it had become obvious that the differences between recipients and staff were irreconcilable and Wiley's continuation as executive director was untenable. After his departure, Wiley launched the Movement for Economic Justice (MEJ), an organization dedicated to organizing all poor people rather than only welfare recipients. MEJ enabled him pursue unhindered his objective of developing a broader movement that included the working poor.[5] Most of the white organizers and volunteers loyal to Wiley also quit or resigned when black welfare recipients took the reins of power. Many staff members who left NWRO had become convinced that in order to be effective, the antipoverty movement needed to expand its base to include men and the working poor. Some chose to get involved in multi-issue community organizations such as the Association of Community Organizations for Reform Now (ACORN).[6] With Wiley's resignation, Johnnie Tillmon became Executive Director and moved to Washington to take charge of the national office. Despite the unease surrounding Wiley's departure, Tillmon tried to strike a conciliatory note: "George Wiley is not the problem of NWRO. We all played a major part in creating the present situation ..." Yet, she hoped he would "leave in a way that whatever he would be doing would not be detrimental to the organization."[7]

Once Wiley left black women took complete command of NWRO, both formally and informally. Although the organization remained interracial and open to men, the political focus shifted. Shortly after assuming her new position, Tillmon outlined to the Executive Board her goals, most importantly recommitting NWRO to its grassroots base. "There was a mandate put on the National Office by the delegates at the Convention for us to reorient our priorities and begin redeveloping our field operation, so that we can provide continuing build-up and support to local organizing groups."[8] She wanted to help "folks out there that are steadily organizing and sending in their memberships ... They need to be assured that we have on-going programs and something worthwhile for them to give to."[9] In July 1974, delegates voted to replace Beulah Sanders as national chairperson with Frankie Jeter as part of their effort to reorganize and change "its heavy emphasis on lobbying in Washington."[10] In response to the long-standing criticisms of staff domination, Tillmon promised to eliminate conflict between the staff and the Executive Board by respecting and following the policies outlined by the Board. The next year, at the 1973 convention, delegates decentralized the functions of the national office by creating regional representatives who would have more input into the programs of NWRO and be better able to communicate with the local and state offices. These reforms sought to redirect NWRO to its grassroots base.

The other important shift associated with the change in leadership was its feminist orientation. With black women more firmly in control of NWRO, the elements of radical black feminism that had taken root several years earlier cohered more visibly into an analysis that saw NWRO as part of the larger women's movement. Because of NWRO's internal conflict, recipients' experiences with the welfare system, and the greater salience of discussion of women's liberation in the larger political discourse, women in the welfare rights movement more overtly and with greater frequency spoke of themselves as a part of the women's movement.

Upon assuming control of the organization, recipient leaders immediately issued a "Women's Agenda," defining poverty and welfare as women's issues. A press release in July 1973 stated that "since the departure of founding Executive Director George Wiley, the women's leadership of NWRO has been considering radical revisions of the organization; prime among these consideration [sic] was a closer association with the women's movement." In the same press release, Tillmon asserted: "NWRO is primarily a women's organization in membership."[11] Reflecting the official shift in focus, recipient leaders began to refer to the convention chair as chairwoman rather than chairman.[12] Women in the welfare rights movement also endorsed the Equal Rights Amendment and, at one point, the Executive Committee considered changing the name of the organization to the National Women's Rights Organization.[13]

Black Feminism and Reproductive Rights

Welfare rights activists had advocated the elements of a feminist agenda for several years. This included defense of their status as single mothers, opposition to work requirements, financial support for mothering, and recipient control of NWRO. In the early 1970s, they also began to assert their reproductive rights. The introduction of the birth control pill, advancements in other forms of contraception, and more liberal attitudes about sexuality promoted greater sexual freedom, especially for women, in the 1960s. Many middle-class white feminists cast motherhood and the home as the cornerstone of their oppression and saw birth control as their ticket to freedom. Strategies limiting childbearing, such as contraception and abortion, dominated the agenda of the mainstream women's movement. Many women of color, on the other hand, had struggled for the right to raise their own children. Under slavery, slave masters often forcibly separated black children from their parents. At the turn of the century, social reformers launched campaigns to limit the fertility of the so-called "lower races."[14] As a result, many African American men and women had historically identified birth control with the eugenics movement. Because of this history, some male-dominated black nationalist organizations discouraged black women from participating in family-planning programs or using birth control. Some even argued that it was black women's revolutionary duty to have children.

Welfare recipients were as concerned with the right to bear children as the availability of contraception and framed reproductive rights as an issue of personal choice rather than simply access to birth control. They wanted to choose for themselves, whether or not and under what circumstances to have a child or have sex. Tillmon argued in 1971: "Nobody realizes more than poor women that all women should have the right to control their own reproduction."[15] Some handbooks and manuals created by local welfare organizations to educate recipients about their rights informed them of birth control. While providing information on birth control, they stressed that "this is your choice."[16] Olive Franklin, chair of the St. Louis City-Wide WRO, supported family planning if it gave poor women greater autonomy:

> Planned Parenthood should firstly be planned by the parent. No one from outside should be able to tell a parent when they may or may not, should or should not have a child. Just because a person happens to be poor and black and unmarried, uneducated, etc., does not in my opinion give some capitalistic pig the authority to set up genocidal clinics with some false façade that this is one of the answers to the many welfare related crises in this country.[17]

She, like Tillmon, wanted poor women to control their own reproduction.

Welfare rights activists also opposed coerced sterilization, practiced on poor, nonwhite, and so-called "feeble-minded" women since the Progressive Era.[18] Welfare recipients, in particular, were sometimes sterilized under the threat of losing their welfare payments.[19] In the early 1970s, in a notorious case, doctors sterilized two black teenagers in Alabama without their consent or knowledge. A lawsuit was brought on their behalf and a federal district court found

> uncontroverted evidence in the record that minors and other incompetents have been sterilized with federal funds and that an indefinite number of

poor people have been improperly coerced into accepting a sterilization operation under the threat that various federally supported welfare benefits would be withdrawn unless they submitted to irreversible sterilization.[20]

In the mid–1970s, women on public assistance with three children had a sterilization rate 67 percent higher than women with the same number of children but not on public assistance.[21]

Coerced sterilization of poor women and women on welfare was sometimes a blatant violation of an individual's civil rights, as in the case above, but at other times, it was less overt but more insidious. For some federal officials, sterilization represented a deliberate strategy to keep poor women from having children. According to one scholar: "The editors of *Family Planning Digest*, the official HEW family planning publication, prophetically hoped in 1972 to 'see sterilization become as important in family planning in the fifty states as it already is in Puerto Rico'"[22] Some policy analysts, such as Phillips Cutright and Frederick Jaffe, argued for the cost-effectiveness of family planning and estimated how much money is saved on welfare, social services, and medical care when social workers rely on family planning or sterilization.[23] Thus, it seems that for some policymakers, sterilization was used as a budgetary measure to reduce costs associated with the childbearing of poor women and women on welfare.

This history and political reality encouraged welfare recipients, both locally and nationally, to define sexual freedom not only as access to birth control, but complete control over one's reproduction, including the right to oppose sterilization and bear children.[24] Formed in the early 1960s, the Black Women's Liberation Group in Mount Vernon, New York, supported access to the birth control pill by 1968.[25] Members wrote in an essay in the landmark 1970 anthology *Sisterhood is Powerful*: "Poor black sisters decide for themselves whether to have a baby or not to have a baby ... Black women are able to decide for themselves, like poor people all over the world, whether they will submit to genocide. For us, birth control is the freedom to *fight* genocide of black women and children" (original italics).[26] Johnnie Tillmon explained NWRO's position on the issue. "We know how easily the lobby for birth control can be perverted into a weapon against poor women. The word is choice. Birth control is a right, not an obligation. A personal decision, not a condition of a welfare check."[27] In February 1974 NWRO's newsletter, the *Welfare Fighter*, outlined problems of forced sterilizations of "minority groups" and welfare recipients. It stated: "human reproduction should be entirely voluntary and the government has no right to force men or women to be sterilized ... It is NWRO's contention that all methods of birth control, including sterilization, be available for poor people as they are for all others."[28]

Although NWRO expanded the meaning of reproductive rights beyond birth control and insisted on women's right to bear children, the language of choice was a double-edged sword for welfare recipients. Arguing that women should and do have control over their reproduction could also hold them accountable for any children they chose to bear. The framework of choice reinforced the notion that poor women should simply use birth control, have abortions, or abstain from sex if they could not afford to raise their children.[29] Personal responsibility might easily replace public support. In this way, the politics of choice both provided an important opening for the welfare rights movement and may have worked against its long-term goals. Nevertheless, NWRO's approach to reproductive rights provided meaningful choices for poor women who wanted to control their own fertility.

NWRO's position on reproductive rights resonated with that of many black women at the time, including the National Black Feminist Organization, but it preceded mass movements of white and black women around this issue. As early as 1969, the Citywide Welfare Alliance in Washington, D.C. challenged restrictive eligibility procedures for free abortions at the city's only public hospital. They argued that a rigorous policy for deciding eligibility disadvantaged low-income women, since these women would most likely resort to an illegal abortion or attempt to self-induce, putting themselves in grave danger. After welfare activists picketed and filed a lawsuit, administrators appointed them to a committee to review the hospital's abortion policy.[30] For these activists, access to abortion meant not just demanding its legality, but assuring public funding for poor women who otherwise would not be able to afford these services. The concerns of welfare recipients with reproductive rights soon developed into a more widespread political movement. In the mid- and late 1970s feminists formed several local organizations to end sterilization abuse and protect women's right to abortion, including the Committee for Abortion Rights and Against Sterilization Abuse (CARASA), an interracial group in New York City. In 1981 a group of mostly white socialist-feminists formed the Reproductive Rights National Network, embodying NWRO's goals for both abortion rights and prevention of sterilization abuse.

Over the course of the welfare rights movement, women welfare activists slowly and haltingly developed a black feminist politics. Their politics was rooted in their day-to-day experiences as women of color on welfare, but was also influenced by the larger political climate. What started off as mothers' rights became women's rights. What began as a right to date became a demand for reproductive control. In the early 1970s these ideas became the basis of their philosophy of radical black feminism.

Radical Black Feminism

Women in the welfare rights movement articulated a black feminist politics that advocated autonomy for poor black women. Their notion of autonomy integrated an analysis of race, class, gender, and sexuality and included government financial support that would enable them to properly raise their children.

They saw economic independence for poor black women as crucial for their self-determination. They also advocated independence in the form of personal autonomy, whether this was in the arena of intimate relations, welfare administration, or political organizing. Women in the welfare rights movement pushed for reproductive rights, an easing of caseworker control over the lives of AFDC recipients, and welfare recipient control of the decision-making within NWRO. And they set an important precedent for how poor women can participate in policymaking. Through their articulation of a radical black feminist politics, they sought to empower poor women—especially poor black women—and provide them with economic security and personal autonomy.[31]

The welfare rights movement's call for autonomy and self-determination coupled with economic security set it apart from other Black Power and women's organizations. Its assertion of black empowerment centered poor black women and made support for motherhood a priority. And their call for women's rights took the racial identity and class position of welfare recipients seriously. Rather than an abstract demand for "power" or "choice" they insisted on material support to enable black women on welfare to live their lives without interference from government officials. Their grassroots campaign offers us a different way to re-conceptualize black radicalism and women's liberation. It shows black women not only as actors and practitioners, but as theoreticians as well. They articulated a philosophy that combined racial power, economic justice, and women's liberation.

The black feminist philosophy of the women activists was perhaps best summed up in an article written by Johnnie Tillmon in 1972 in *Ms. Magazine*, the preeminent feminist magazine of the time. Tillmon's widely circulated article symbolized the culmination of a long struggle within the welfare rights movement to define welfare as a women's issue and the welfare rights movement as a part of the larger women's movement. She wrote that women in the welfare rights movement were "the front line troops of women's freedom" and their primary aim to ensure the right to a living wage for women's work concerned all women.[32] In her 1972 article, Johnnie Tillmon articulated most clearly the movement's position of welfare as a women's issue:

> The truth is that AFDC is like a super-sexist marriage. You trade in *a* man for *the* man. But you can't divorce him if he treats you bad. He can divorce you, of course, cut you off anytime he wants. *The* man runs everything. In ordinary marriage sex is supposed to be for your husband. On AFDC you're not supposed to have any sex at all. You give up control of your own body. It's a condition of aid. You may even have to agree to get your tubes tied so you can never have more children just to avoid being cut off welfare. *The* man, the welfare system, controls your money. He tells you what to buy, what not to buy, where to buy it, and how much things cost. If things— rent, for instance—really cost more than he says they do, it's just too bad for you. He's always right. Everything is budgeted down to the last penny

and you've go to make your money stretch. *The* man can break into your house anytime he wants to and poke into your things. You've got no right to protest. You've got no right to privacy when you go on welfare. Like I said. Welfare's a super-sexist marriage.[33]

For Tillmon, "the man" was a metaphor for both the welfare system and institutionalized white racism. In her analysis, welfare combined racial, class, and gender oppressions, laying the basis for an argument that it should be defined as a feminist issue. She put forth an insightful critique of the welfare system and the ways in which it controlled and regulated the sexuality and lives of black women.

Although not founded specifically as a black women's organization, by the early 1970s, NWRO had been transformed into an organization controlled by poor black women speaking in a distinctly feminist voice. Their experiences with poverty and racism shaped both their understanding of gender and their platform for addressing gender oppression. In the process of building a movement, women activists challenged prescribed gender roles, attempted to legitimate their status as single mothers, and sought to ensure that women on welfare had greater control over their lives. In the struggle for welfare rights, motherhood and reproduction became a site of contestation for poor black women. Welfare rights activists initially demanded that society recognize and respect their work as mothers, but this soon evolved into a position of women's rights.

Some members believed adamantly that theirs was a women's organization at the forefront of the struggle for women's liberation. Some women in NWRO adopted a strategy of appealing broadly to women. Jennette Washington, a prominent welfare rights leader in New York City wrote:

> We women must stay together on this issue and not let anyone divide us. We can do this first by challenging the male power-holding groups of this nation. We must make them remember that we, as mothers and as women, are concerned about the survival of our children, of all human life. We women have to organize, agitate, pressure and demand; not beg. You see, in the past, women have always been told that they should stay behind their men and be nice and cool and don't rock the boat. Well, I just don't want to rock one boat, I want to rock all boats—the big boats. And I want all women to help me.[34]

Others may have been more reluctant than Washington to identify as women liberationists or feminists. Nevertheless, through the struggle to improve their economic situation, they articulated a program of economic demands that increasingly asserted a critique of gender roles, patriarchy, and proscribed sexuality. Although members may not have explicitly pushed for gender equality, in essence they advocated women's liberation: liberation from poverty and reproductive control. They tied their campaigns for economic security to their desire for autonomy as women. Even women who did not explicitly characterize their organization as part of the women's movement clearly identified as women and attempted to ally with other women's organizations. Rather than eclipsing their struggles for racial and economic justice, their identity as a women's group was firmly rooted in their struggle to mitigate the effects of poverty and racism. Far from being contradictory, the various goals of the movement lent strength and support to their agenda. Their struggle represented a strand of radical black feminism emerging in the 1960s, one that contributed to and expanded the boundaries of the existing women's movement as well as the black freedom movement.

NWRO Closes its Doors

When women activists gained control of NWRO in 1972 and began to implement a black feminist agenda, the movement had already begun its decline. Membership rolls shrank, the political climate became more hostile as the public and policymakers clamored for greater cutbacks in AFDC, and many staff members with fundraising skills left because of the internal conflict.

Even prior to the change in leadership, NWRO's financial situation was precarious. Although the organization's income, in the form of membership dues, grants and donations, had increased dramatically by 1969, its operating expenses grew even faster. NWRO's annual budget increased from $200,000 in 1968 to $500,000 in 1969 to $900,000 in 1970. But in 1969, expenses exceeded income by more than $50,000. Two-thirds of the 1969 budget was allotted to staff salaries.[35] By 1972, NWRO's financial situation was acute. Wiley estimated the organizational debt at about $150,000. At the same time, important funding sources began to dry up. Support from Protestant churches, the largest private source of funding for NWRO contributing close to half of its 1968 budget, had nearly vanished by 1973 because of a general decline in funding for social protest.[36] In a letter to supporters, Wiley wrote:

> Most of you are probably aware that NWRO has been going through one of the most serious financial crises [sic] in our history. We had invested every last nickel we could beg or borrow into the Children's March for Survival, the Democratic Convention platform fight and fight against FAP.[37]

At the NCC meeting in October 1972, Wiley warned that the lack of funds may force him to close the national office.[38] Questions about bookkeeping procedures and the handling of finances also plagued NWRO. The organization's accountant wrote to Wiley in September 1971, that they were "dissatisfied [sic] with the reliability of the internal control ... lack of written procedures in the fiscal department and the high turn-over of fiscal personnel."[39]

But some recipients had a different vision of fundraising for the organization. Catering to financial supporters, they believed, led to misguided priorities and concentrated power in those people in the national office with the skills and contacts to raise money. Relying on foundation money and grant writing, in effect, excluded poor women from control of the organization. A member of Mothers for Adequate Welfare (MAW) commented in 1969 about George Wiley's "relationship to the power structure. If he was an uneducated type of guy, how much would he really do? How many friends could he really get?" She believed that the work of MAW was far more important "because it was done on the local level with a handful of mothers, with the median education being the eighth grade…NWRO had money, people with doctorates."[40]

The departure of Wiley and much of the middle-class staff, the primary fund-raisers for NWRO, exacerbated financial constraints. When they left, 80 percent of the donations and pledges "went out the door," according to one observer.[41] This, in combination with the changing political climate crippled NWRO.[42] Contributions from white churches and liberal groups stopped coming in and, at Wiley's resignation, NWRO was $100,000 in debt.[43] Moreover, the unexpected and tragic death of George Wiley in August 1973 shook up the members and staff of NWRO, making organizing more difficult. Efforts to raise money, even among former supporters, were unsuccessful and the organization never funded its 1973 budget. In 1974 Johnnie Tillmon organized what she called the "Half-A-Chance" campaign. With a goal of making NWRO self-supporting, rather than relying on outside funding, the campaign appealed to all poor people in the country to give 50 cents each to the National Welfare Rights Organization. According to Tillmon:

> Organizations like ours could not continue to depend on grants and other resources from foundations at a time when everyone is caught us [sic] in the economic squeeze and governmental repression that exists in this nation today. Organizing the action campaigns that NWRO continues to wage against the nation's oppressive institutions almost requires us to be self-sufficient because too many of those foundations and funding groups are running scared—too scared to deal with us.[44]

Little came of the campaign, however.[45] At the moment when African American women were firmly in control, there was little left to control and the future of the organization looked bleak.

In July 1973 the Internal Revenue Service (IRS), after an audit, threatened to close down NWRO unless it paid back taxes of $20,000.[46] Along with other debts, this catapulted the organization into a period of severe financial difficulty, consuming time, energy, and resources to stay solvent. Through fundraising events, appeals to middle-class liberals, and support from members, Tillmon and other staff in the national office eventually paid off the IRS and brought down NWRO's debt from $100,000 in 1972 to $20,000 in 1975.[47] Despite this achievement, NWRO found it difficult to function effectively without operating funds.

In August 1973, the national staff shrank to eight, including four recipients working without pay. They published the newsletter and sent out mailings only intermittently.[48] Raising money to reduce the debt, rather than planning new campaigns, consumed the staff and, consequently, the organization's base of support continued to dwindle. In March 1975, NWRO declared bankruptcy and closed its doors.

New Community Activism

The closing of the NWRO national office did not signal the end of welfare rights activity. Most local groups were invested in national campaigns and relied on resources and information from the national office. They were empowered by the national network. But for nearly all of them, their organizing focus was the local welfare department in their community. When the NWRO officed close, the local groups that remained active tended to devote their energies to immediate and local issues. They organized around welfare, nutrition, education, and housing.[49]

In the late 1970s, the Baltimore Welfare Rights Organization (BWRO) maintained an exclusively local focus. Although formally headed by a man, Bobby Cheeks, women like Annie Chambers, chair of the Board of Directors, ran the organization. In 1978 the BWRO launched a rent strike in the O'Donnell Heights housing project to protest plumbing problems, dangerous electrical wiring, rodent infestation, and generally poor maintenance of the building. While a large number of residents wanted improvements in the housing complex, only a minority withheld their rent. A series of repairs by the housing authority to placate protesters and fear on the part of residents hindered full-fledged participation in the strike. BWRO found limited support for its more militant strategies. Its politics centered on quality-of-life issues, shying away from the more broadly based theme of economic justice that informed the welfare rights movement at its height.[50]

In many cases, welfare rights groups became less confrontational and more interested in social services and legal tactics. For example, the Clark County WRO in Las Vegas, in 1974, just two years after the struggle to roll back the state welfare reductions, adopted a helping-hand approach to poverty. With the aid of Legal Services and the League of Women Voters, the WRO, headed by Ruby Duncan and Mary Wesley, formed a nonprofit organization called Operation Life. The group leased a dilapidated hotel in a neglected neighborhood, renovated it, and turned it into a community center. Operation Life provided the black community an opportunity for "full participation in the economy—in the ownership and savings and the self-sufficiency which the more fortunate in our Nation already take for granted." The community center provided services for the needy, including a home for the elderly, a food commodity program, drug counseling and tutoring programs, vocational training for youth, aid to black-owned businesses, a public swimming pool, a child-care center, a community-run press, and a youth-run restaurant which also served as a training ground for food handling and preparation and restaurant management.[51] At the end of 1973, it opened a health center, the first medical facility on the Westside of Las Vegas. In 1974, Operation Life won a federal grant to operate a Women, Infant and Child nutrition program. Its slogan was "We can do it and do it better." Despite continual harassment by local officials, in 1978 Operation Life became a Community Development Corporation, running several low-income housing units, and by 1981 was the largest property owner in the community. In the late 1980s, the federal government pulled funding from Operation Life and subsequently many of its programs and services were either forced to shut down or handed over to another, more conservative community group. This undercut the many years of organizing by welfare mothers in Nevada. Renee Diamond, who worked with Operation Life, believed that federal agencies deliberately took "funding out of the hands of militant community groups, particularly black organizations, and [gave] what little federal money there was in the eighties to more conservative groups."[52]

Similarly, welfare recipients in Mud Creek, Kentucky formed the East Kentucky WRO (EKWRO). Organizing since 1969, the EKWRO never affiliated with NWRO, but worked to make government services available and more responsive to the needs of the poor. In 1973, members of EKWRO formed a free, community-run health-care clinic, the Mud Creek Citizens Health Project. While providing a much-needed service for residents of East Kentucky, they were consumed with the bureaucratic details of running a clinic: hiring a doctor, staff salaries, Medicaid reimbursement, state-licensing procedures, and purchasing medical supplies.[53]

A northern California group evolved in a parallel direction in the mid-1970s. Ethel Dotson, head of the Richmond, CA WRO, had served on the NCC and continued her involvement well after the national office closed its doors. In 1974 the group distributed food stamps and received a federal contract to run the Women, Infant and Children (WIC) program, to provide adequate nutrition for pregnant women and children. Dotson didn't see a distinction between social services and political organizing. She believed servicing the community created avenues to become educated and engaged in political activity. The organization was on the verge of becoming a holistic health clinic, when the federal government, after an audit, revoked its grant in 1980.[54] Ethel Dotson maintains they were "clean as a whistle," but that politicians, threatened by welfare rights, audited them to pave the way for "welfare reform." She explains:

> We was telling people, those mothers that need to stay at home should raise their kids. Stay at home and raise your children properly. Those that want to work, you know, develop your own self, jobs, etc ... [These politicians thought] the only way that welfare rights can exist is through food

stamp outreach and the WIC program. If we take [these] away, they will cease to exist.

While these examples demonstrate the fortitude and vigilance of welfare recipients in the face of enormous obstacles, they also mark a new phase in the welfare rights movement. The community activism of the 1970s tended to be atomized reforms, rooted in the politics of representation or social service. The tactics usually revolved around self-help or participation in formulating social policy, defined as civic action or community organizing, rather than the broad-based social changes that challenged the basic assumptions guiding the welfare system. Welfare rights activists turned to social service in the 1970s because of the retreat of state responsibility. Many of the community campaigns revolved around basic survival—health care, food programs, and education. On the one hand, the response of activists represented grassroots resistance to neglect of their communities. At the same time, they often became embroiled in the day-to-day requirements of running and maintaining a complex social service agency. Welfare recipients found community work empowering and an avenue to personal success, some gaining full-time, meaningful employment. Moiece Palladino, for example, landed a job with legal services as a "professional welfare mother" and worked her way through college and law school.[55] Many women for the first time sent their children to college. Others engaged in local and state politics. Former welfare recipients elected to public office or influential in public policy arenas often became advocates for the poor, consulting with nonprofit groups, foundations, or state and local agencies. They continued in the tradition of earlier welfare rights struggles, providing an alternative voice in policy discussions and working to achieve a more just public assistance program.

The protracted activity of welfare recipients suggests that welfare politics were not transitory, even if they did diminish in the early 1970s. These local movements demonstrate the tenacity of welfare recipients and chart the changing nature of political organizing in the 1970s.[56] These successes should not be underestimated, given the history and marginalization of women on welfare. But equally revealing was the circumscribed nature of their struggle. Gone was the language of a right to a basic standard of living. Gone was the language of entitlement. Moreover, because these service strategies often relied on government grants, federal authorities had the power to audit or revoke contracts, sometimes crippling welfare rights activism.

Like many other welfare rights activists, after NWRO folded, Johnnie Tillmon continued her political work. In 1975, she returned to California and, with her husband Harvey Blackston, bought a house just a few blocks from Nickerson Gardens where she first began organizing welfare recipients. She joined the local welfare rights chapter and got a job as a legislative aide on welfare issues for City Councilman Robert Farrell. She later served on a welfare advisory committee under Governor Jerry Brown and subsequently under the administration of Republican Governor George Deukmejian.

In many ways, Tillmon's life spans this important period of welfare reform and welfare activism. Like many other African American women who joined the welfare rolls in the 1950s and 1960s, she was part of a great migration that left the impoverished South in search of better work opportunities. As a single mother, she juggled her many responsibilities of working, mothering, and caring for a home. A combination of health problems and concern for her children prompted her to apply for welfare at the very moment when the debate about AFDC was reaching a fever pitch and federal officials were moving in a direction of requiring women on welfare to take paid employment. These experiences laid the basis for Tillmon's political analysis that combined race, class, gender, sexuality, and political and economic autonomy. As a leader of the welfare rights movement, Tillmon was an important oppositional voice to the dominant discourse about welfare, articulating the needs and concerns of poor women on welfare and placing them at the center.

Johnnie Tillmon was unable to parcel out her struggle for women's rights, Black Power, and economic justice because these goals were interlocking and mutually reinforcing. She adopted a rhetoric of autonomy and self-determination like many other Black Power activists, but developed its meaning through her own lens as a poor black woman struggling for economic justice and personal dignity. Tillmon's childhood and early adulthood in a rural black community in Arkansas instilled in her a deep sense of independence, autonomy, and self-pride. Her politics encompassed not only racial pride and self-determination, but the economic needs of women on welfare. She placed female independence and power at the center. For Tillmon, gender—in particular female autonomy—was central to her philosophy of black radicalism and thus she embraced a politics of radical black feminism. She was an unapologetic feminist who articulated a powerful gendered critique of the welfare system. Tillmon's radical black feminism advocated poor women's right to make decisions about childbearing, childraising, and their intimate lives. For this reason she rejected calls to restore the two-parent heterosexual black family and for black men to reassert their masculinity. Instead, she waged campaigns to enable poor women to live their lives with dignity, respect, and economic security. And she worked tirelessly to debunk the stereotypes that had become associated with receipt of welfare. Her black feminist politics grew out of her welfare activism and through it she modeled a positive black female identity that integrated class, race, gender, and sexuality.[57]

Even after the decline of welfare rights activity, as possibilities for radical protest diminished, Johnnie Tillmon continued her engagement with the politics of welfare, giving input wherever possible, whether a Republican or Democratic administration. This tactical flexibility is indicative of her political common sense that guided her through her career in the welfare rights movement.

Tillmon reached out to allies and supporters, embraced interracial activism; she was militant in the streets, yet poised in front of legislators. And through it all she remained committed to her core constituency of poor women on AFDC and fought relentlessly to defend their rights. Tillmon died of diabetes in 1995 at the age of sixty-nine, just one year before AFDC was permanently dismantled.[58]

CONCLUSION

The welfare rights movement left a permanent mark on the history and politics of the 1960s. It represented one of the most disenfranchised sectors of American society—and articulated a politics of black liberation, feminism, and economic justice. In doing so, the welfare rights movement reshaped the political landscape.

Its most obvious impact was on welfare policy, both locally and nationally. Welfare policy is frequently written from the point of view of policymakers, social workers, and politicians. The views of welfare recipients are more often than not brushed aside. The history of the welfare rights movement illustrates that the formation of social welfare policy is a negotiated process in which recipients of public welfare play an active part.[1] There is a rich history of poor people's movements, but the spectacle of single mothers militantly demanding state assistance to raise their children was rare prior to the emergence of the welfare rights movement in the 1960s. It provides an opportunity to examine the collective voice and political vision of this particular group of welfare recipients.

Welfare rights activists in the 1960s won concrete reforms such as higher monthly benefits and special grants for items they did not have. They lobbied for legislation, including the right to a fair hearing to appeal welfare department decisions, an end to residency laws denying assistance to recent migrants, and constitutional protection for recipients' right to due process. They challenged the basic tenets of the welfare system, which placed discretionary power in the hands of caseworkers and discouraged poor women from seeking assistance. Welfare recipients were accorded stature within policymaking circles that had, until then, not been granted to poor single mothers. They also attempted to influence public opinion by recasting their identities in ways that might make their status as welfare recipients more palatable. Their goal of a guaranteed annual income redefined the relationship of the state to poor black women (as well as other poor people) and claimed social reproduction as work. It made welfare a right regardless of personal morality or behavior. Moreover, although it would not have eliminated economic disparities, a guaranteed annual income, to some degree, would have narrowed the racial and gender gaps by aiding poor African American women. NWRO's proposal of $5,500 a year for a family of four, although never passed by Congress, became one measure by which policymakers judged other legislative proposals. The welfare rights movement, thus, influenced the discourse about poverty and helped shape the debate about welfare in the 1960s.

Rethinking the Black Freedom Movement

The welfare rights movement was an integral part of the black freedom movement. It teaches us, however, that the "typical" story of the emergence of black radicalism—in which activists turned their attention to poverty in the North only after their disillusionment with the Civil Rights Act of 1964 and Voting Rights Act of 1965—is a distortion of the historical record.[2] A transition from civil rights to economic justice, as the traditional narrative suggests, undoubtedly occurred in this period. But we need to be wary of the argument that the mid-1960s marks a clear break between the nonviolent struggle against legal segregation in the South and the more militant efforts to attack racism and poverty in the North. In reality the black freedom movement in the South, even prior to 1965, had many different strands.[3] Most of those participating in and affected by the southern movement were poor. And for some activists the struggle was always about both racism and economics.[4] There were also countless campaigns in the North in the 1950s and early 1960s that targeted black poverty and economic inequality.

The welfare rights movement disrupts the conventional periodization of the black freedom movement and the false North–South dichotomy. It was not a northern movement but a national one, with chapters all across the country. Moreover, the welfare rights movement did not have its roots in the transition of 1964.[5] It did not emerge simply as a frustrated response to the black activists' loss of direction after the passage of the Civil Rights Act and a desire to focus more attention on economic issues. Nor did it result primarily from the organizing efforts of middle-class activists on behalf of the poor. Women on welfare had organized around economic issues such as urban renewal, fair housing, and adequate income as early as the 1950s. Although support from middle-class activists aided tremendously in the formation of a national movement, the impetus for organizing came from the women themselves and was rooted in their day-to-day experiences with AFDC.

Welfare rights activists also pushed mainstream civil rights leaders to deal more seriously with issues of poverty and forced them to engage in social policy. Perhaps the best example of this was when Martin Luther King Jr. met with welfare rights activists in Chicago to garner support for his Poor People's Campaign in 1968.

As he sat on a panel with Johnnie Tillmon and other welfare rights leaders, they queried him about welfare legislation about which he clearly knew very little. Tillmon told him, "You know, Dr. King, if you don't know about these questions, you should say you don't know, and then we could go on with the meeting." King replied, "You're right, Mrs. Tillmon. We don't know anything about welfare. We are here to learn." Welfare rights activists were a significant component of the antipoverty movement and other African American leaders, such as Dr. King, had to cooperate with and sometimes earn the respect of these poor black women.

Although the welfare rights movement is often not considered part of the Black Power movement, in many ways its campaigns and political views were fundamentally about empowering poor black women. Activists articulated a version of Black Power that was not premised on recreating two-parent families or reasserting black patriarchy but rather about maintaining their dignity, ensuring adequate state assistance, and supporting their children. Welfare rights activists' political positions posed an alternative to the masculinity that had permeated many black nationalist groups. Their defense of black womanhood and their demands for social support carved out a political space that spoke to the specific needs of women on welfare. They nurtured a pride in who they were as black welfare recipients and sought to reclaim their womanhood. Their political vision offers a fresh angle to look beyond the banners and headlines, and explore how Black Power was understood, adopted, and theorized by poor black women. In sum, the history of the welfare rights movement forces us to expand our understanding and definition of Black Power politics to include grassroots welfare rights campaigns. It also encourages us to recognize how the boundaries between women's liberation and Black Power activism were fluid, overlapping, and permeable.

Redefining Liberalism

Apart from its role in the black freedom movement, how did the welfare rights movement engage with the broader political discourses of liberalism and conservatism? What does it tell us about radicalism in the 1960s? Many scholars argue that by 1965 the political consensus characterizing the early 1960s had frayed, the political center was undermined, and support for both the left and right increased. It was, they suggest, a period of polarization fueled by protests such as those for welfare rights. Such protests may have contributed to the weakening of the Democratic Party by pushing many working-class white Americans into Republican hands.[6] "Ordinary" white Americans, the silent majority, these scholars argue, had to choose between the increasingly militant voices of students, the poor, and people of color, on the one hand, and the appeals on the right for law and order, on the other. They ultimately chose stability and the status quo, as was symbolized most clearly in the election of Richard Nixon in 1968.[7]

But the history of the welfare rights movement shows us that reform in the 1960s is more complicated than the ultimate victory of conservatism. Many of the radical protest movements both incorporated mainstream values and challenged them. They self-consciously placed themselves outside the mainstream of American politics and proudly adopted an image of rebelliousness. The welfare rights movement drew upon a radical tradition that, for example, demanded material assistance apart from market employment. It put forth alternatives to and patriarchal norms and challenged the ideal of the two-parent family. It questioned the belief that employment outside the home was the only valuable work of women of color, and asserted that welfare and a basic subsistence income were rights, rather than privileges. While in these respects the movement departed from popularly accepted wisdom, in other ways, it did not.

The movement also espoused ostensibly core American beliefs and reflected mainstream values. The welfare rights movement's focus on civil rights, legal protections, and electoral politics did little to challenge the underlying assumptions of liberal economic and political policy.[8] The welfare rights movement was entangled with the dominant discourse of the period, but came to their own sense of radicalism, blurring the boundaries among radical, liberal, and even conservative ideas.

The welfare rights movement incorporated into its policy platforms some key ideas that had come to define liberalism in the 1960s. Welfare rights activists fought for representation both in welfare departments and within the electoral and policymaking arenas. They waged a political and legal struggle to ensure protection of their civil rights. They did not demand a different kind of economic system, but wanted to share in the prosperity that had come to define postwar America. The movement, therefore, borrowed rhetoric and concepts most closely associated with "western" liberal values and made them its own. In doing so, activists defined radicalism on their own terms and expanded and revised the liberal discourse of the day. Most of the "liberal" reforms the welfare rights movement struggled for—more formalized welfare procedures, protection of their civil rights, the right to stay home and care for their children, and representation in policymaking bodies—challenged the status quo for poor black women on welfare. Their status quo included arbitrary and demeaning treatment by caseworkers, requirements to work outside their home and find day care for their children, routine violations of their civil rights, and silencing and marginalization. By insisting that they had the same rights and privileges as other people, women on welfare questioned the boundaries that had come to circumscribe and control their lives. They formulated a politics that drew upon radical, conservative, and liberal discourses as it suited their needs. The welfare rights movement challenged and, at the same time, worked within the framework of liberal American democracy. In this way, the ideology of the movement, at least on the surface, seemed to converge with many liberal and some conservative thinkers of the time.

On some topics, there was more consensus than conflict. Not only Democrats, but many Republicans and some radicals subscribed to dominant New Deal liberal ideas such as an activist federal government, commitment to a minimum standard of living, the politics of representation, and protection of civil rights. Both Richard Nixon and the National Welfare Rights Organization, for example, agreed on the need for an income floor, although they differed on where that floor should be set. Activists on the right and the left supported government action to alleviate poverty. This consensus demonstrates that, on some issues, we see not the unraveling of liberalism, as historian Allen Matusow suggested, but its triumph.

Suggesting that a certain level of consensus characterized welfare politics in the late 1960s does not mean glossing over the many differences among these ideologies. This was a period of profound conflict and hostility, when people from competing political factions rarely felt common cause with one another. However, precisely because of the intensity of disagreement it is important to recognize how the larger political dialogue and economic and political context influenced people across the political spectrum. This is not to say that either radicals or conservatives mindlessly absorbed the messages penetrating their society. Clearly their activism, their initiative, their willingness to tackle difficult problems is a testament that they did not. But the level of consensus many activists did reach—albeit strategic rather than "real" agreement—is instructive for political struggles today. The conciliatory approach of politicians to political protest can also teach us much, for it differed from earlier and later approaches to similar problems. This might lead us to conclude that the militant movements of the late 1960s and early 1970s cannot be assessed in terms of failure or success of their particular programs. Instead, we should look at their impact and influence on American culture.

Competing Visions

The welfare rights movement was also politically and intellectually sophisticated. Welfare rights activists voiced a world view that grew from their experiences as poor black women. They articulated a philosophy that combined racial power, economic justice, sexual autonomy and women's liberation. Many in the welfare rights movement had observed or participated in consciousness raising, examined patterns of institutional racism had come to view government action with a critical eye, recognized the ways in which individuals wielded racial power, and learned to speak the language of women's rights. The tactics, strategies, and array of protest options available to them were impressive, as were the discourses and dialogues in which they engaged.

Welfare recipients constructed alternative narratives about the politics of welfare. In making claims upon the state for higher monthly benefits and a guaranteed annual income, activists asserted their right to food, shelter, and basic subsistence. They justified welfare assistance as mothers caring for and rearing their children, and as citizens entitled to the same benefits and opportunities as all other Americans. The language of citizenship and rights is laced throughout the campaigns waged by the welfare rights movement. Recipients suggested that citizenship ought to guarantee them a basic standard of living and a right to stay home and care for their children. In making these claims, they built upon the work of economists and policymakers, who in an era of abundance had moved beyond a discussion of basic human survival to broach topics such as quality of life and emotional and psychological well-being. But welfare recipients went further than that and attempted to expand the definition of "rights" as it was used in the 1960s to demand economic resources independent of the market or their status as workers.[9]

The various narratives articulated by welfare rights activists was never as influential, didn't have access to the same channels of information as those of social workers or politicians, and had less legitimacy than competing discourses. Even within the welfare rights movement, conflicting interpretations between staff and recipients and among recipients were characterized by differences in resources and political clout. There is no question that the movement, both staff and recipients, articulated liberal ideals—but it also challenged certain core values. In sum, resistance and accommodation coexisted.[10]

As the movement evolved, the central internal conflict was between the predominantly male, middle-class staff in the national office and the black women on welfare, most of whom worked on the grassroots level. The middle-class staff countered the stereotypes about black women's dishonesty and laziness by asserting that black women did, in fact, want to work, but that the lack of jobs and adequate day care prevented them from seeking paid employment. When public hostility did not subside, and seemed to intensify, the staff considered ways to divert attention from black women and shift the movement's political focus by organizing poor working men, who they believed would be more sympathetic advocates of public assistance.

The black women on welfare in the organization had a different approach. Since the movement's inception, they articulated their concerns as mothers and had put forth a critique of the way in which the AFDC program controlled the lives of poor women. They justified welfare assistance by arguing that as mothers, they *were* working and, therefore, contributing to society. Few black women had the "luxury" of being full-time mothers. Wage work for poor women and most black women was more often a source of oppression than a means for empowerment and had most often meant long hours, drudgery, and meager rewards, not a fulfilling career. Family often provided some of the few comforts poor and working-class black families could enjoy.[11] For poor or low-income black women, their struggle to preserve the right to be mothers was a long-standing one and, historically, has been viewed as a challenge to the subordination of African Americans.[12]

Through the process of organizing, a core group of women in the welfare rights movement began to see themselves not just as mothers working to improve their children's lives, but as women struggling for autonomy and self-determination. Their political struggles with welfare officials as well as internal conflicts between the staff and the recipients over organizational platforms, fundraising, and leadership pushed the women leaders toward advocating independence. These internal tensions led women welfare rights activists to become more aware of sexism in the organization, which in turn influenced their political development and thinking about feminism. Many welfare recipients were not self-avowed feminists and most cannot be called intellectuals, in the traditional sense of the word.[13] Nevertheless, they forged an analysis and voiced a world view on their own terms. The material reality of their lives and the culture surrounding them shaped their notions of racial and gender politics and their identity as black women. Through their struggle for economic security and welfare rights, they expressed many of the basic tenets of a distinctive feminist ideology. By the time the welfare rights movement began to wane, they had formulated a full-fledged black feminist agenda, one reflecting their own priorities and sensibilities.

Fighting Sexism and Racism

The radical black feminist analysis offered by welfare rights activists integrated aspects of class empowerment, racial liberation, and a gender analysis. While they understood the importance of gender in shaping their lives and attempted to connect with other women, they also realized that all women were not treated equally. Thus, their conceptualization of womanhood was dialectical rather than one-dimensional. They did not see their oppression through the additive components of race, class, and gender, separate identities that they could turn to as it suited them. Their analysis was more accurately one of "multiple jeopardy, multiple consciousness": where race and class transformed the way they experienced gender; and class and gender transformed the way they experienced race.[14] They believed that their treatment was determined not just by their status as black people or women, but as poor black women. Racism and poverty influenced their opportunities and day-to-day experiences as women. In this way, their feminism differed from that of other women's liberationists who prioritized gender.

The welfare rights movement's distinctive feminist analysis had a perceptible impact on the mainstream women's movement. The publication of Johnnie Tillmon's 1972 article in *Ms.* signaled the women's movement's willingness, however limited, to address issues of concern to poor women and women of color.[15] In 1970, the National Organization of Women (NOW) passed a resolution supporting NWRO and recognizing poverty as a woman's issue. It called for an "immediate and continuing liaison with the National Welfare Rights Organization ... in support of our sisters in poverty."[16] Both NOW and the National Women's Political Caucus endorsed NWRO's guaranteed income proposal. These alliances, however, were both temporary and superficial. Although NWRO and mainstream women's organizations never developed a successful

long-term relationship, the attempts at cooperation reveal the possibilities for alliances across race and class among women. A common interest in empowering
women brought NWRO and NOW together in the late 1960s and early 1970s.
The resolutions and symbolic actions by other feminist organizations demonstrate
the impact of the welfare rights movement on the priorities of more mainstream
feminist groups.[17] By the early seventies welfare had become clearly identified as
a woman's issue.

Understanding the welfare rights movement as simultaneously a part of the
antipoverty, black, and women's liberation struggles of the 1960s enables us to
redraw the map of social reform in the 1960s. The welfare rights movement
expanded the notion of black liberation and feminism by defining welfare and
poverty as black women's issues. Activists explored in sophisticated ways the
relationship among race, class, and gender. They did not separate their oppression
as women from their oppression as poor black people. As Patricia Hill Collins
says, black feminists often reject the oppositional, dichotomized model.[18] They
organized for their own benefit, while also improving their community. They
attempted to make the system work for them as well as to challenge it. And in
the process, they created a movement that was as much a feminist movement as
a movement for racial equality and economic justice.

Welfare Reform after Welfare Rights

Despite the victories, the pervasiveness of stereotyping and its policy implications
were difficult to disrupt. In the long run, these successes had little impact on the
demonized public status of welfare recipients or the uncertain fate of the welfare
system. Welfare recipients wielded some power to reform AFDC, but had little
power to define their own lives. The characterization of welfare recipients as
undeserving, lazy, freeloading, promiscuous, and morally bankrupt remained and
may even have intensified in the years after NWRO folded. Welfare recipients
were still on the margins.

In the 1970s and 1980s, Democrats and Republicans found common ground
in the racialized and gendered stereotypes of recipients. Liberal and conservative
reformers portrayed black women as unworthy of assistance. Politicians suggested
that recipients' economic independence from men and the labor market, via the
welfare system, was detrimental and threatened the stability of the black family
and the viability of urban centers, where African Americans were concentrated.
As Bill Moyers depicted so vividly in his 1980s documentary *The Vanishing
Family*, an entire generation of poor African Americans was ostensibly at risk
because welfare bred teenage pregnancy, male irresponsibility, crime, drug use,
and the unraveling of the fabric of home and community life.

But as many ordinary Americans not on welfare feared—and as conservative
Charles Murray explained—the black community was not the only one in jeopardy. Welfare, they argued, endangered core American values of the work ethic and

family values. If working people subsidized the promiscuity, laziness, debauchery, and irresponsibility of some people, critics asked, then what will become of American society and its economic vitality? In the 1970s and 1980s, AFDC became a touchstone for a general anti-social welfare program position, a mantra for people calling for fewer taxes, smaller government, and an end to handouts for the poor. Historians sometimes explain this hostility as a response to the expansion of social welfare programs in the 1960s: that the white working class became angered and disaffected by Great Society programs funded by their tax dollars to benefit the poor and people of color.[19] While the sentiment may have been real, the analysis was misdirected. Poor people of color were not the largest beneficiaries of the Great Society programs, if spending on education, social security, food stamps and medical assistance is considered. According to historian Michael Katz, 75 percent of federal social welfare dollars between 1965 and 1971 went to the non poor. In addition, the hostility towards AFDC predated the social spending of the 1960s and is rooted in social and political changes in the immediate postwar period. Widespread disdain for women on AFDC can be traced back to the late 1950s and preceded civil rights legislation, Great Society programs, and dramatic increases in the welfare rolls which only occurred in the mid-1960s. It was rooted in the changing racial composition of the welfare rolls, black migration into predominantly white northern communities, and stereotypes about black women's sexual mores and work habits.[20]

Clearly, the welfare backlash cannot be divorced from the issue of race. Continuing a trend begun in the 1950s, welfare in the 1980s became even more closely associated with nonwhites, especially African Americans, and its failures were erroneously tied to the gains of the civil rights movement and Great Society programs. Conservatives framed welfare as representative of all that had gone wrong with 1960s liberalism (despite the fact that most Republicans and Democrats concurred on many issues). In the 1980s, few Republicans or Democrats found it politically palatable to publicly support welfare programs for fear of being labeled beholden to special interests. Kenneth Neubeck and Noel Cazenave, in their important book *Welfare Racism*, argue that the backlash of the 1960s brought welfare into the national spotlight.[21] In response to broader social and political changes in the postwar era, they suggest, welfare politics became a way to reestablish racial control in order to maintain white racial supremacy.

Welfare rights activists were ultimately unable to overcome these long-standing stereotypes and misconceptions. This failure points to the enduring presence of racism and sexism in American political ideology and culture. As long as black women were not legitimately considered mothers; as long as the work of mothering was devalued; as long as independent women raising children apart from men seemed to threaten the patriarchal norm; as long as black women were characterized by a racial/class/gender stereotype that not only stigmatized welfare, but placed them at the bottom of the social and economic hierarchy, then the forces that made the welfare system politically unpopular would remain.

In this way this history of the welfare rights movement reveals the place of welfare in the larger American political system. Welfare was an integral component of American capitalism, political ideology, and culture in the postwar era. The ideology and rhetoric surrounding AFDC and the structure of the program helped to define appropriate and inappropriate behavior, shaped notions of government responsibility, and contributed to the restructuring of social hierarchies. AFDC cast a dark shadow on many public welfare programs, bolstered the individualist ethos and the work ethic, and was used as a metaphor for race to discredit much of the liberal agenda of the postwar period. Welfare was essential to the dominant political discourse and served as a launching pad for a whole host of other issues. In the ensuing decades, the lives of the poor in this country, especially poor women, have only worsened.[22] By the 1980s, the rhetoric and discourse around welfare were more virulent and less tolerant than they had been in the early 1960s. Stereotypes emanated from the press, politicians, popular culture, and ordinary working-class Americans—black and white. They targeted welfare recipients as the root of many evils: from the tax burden, to the decline of family values, to the rise in drug use.[23] This discourse laid the basis for passage of the Personal Responsibility and Work Opportunity Act in 1996, which dismantled AFDC, our only guaranteed system of support for poor women.[24] Consequently, the trajectory of the welfare rights movement is also about the persistence and deep-seated nature of racism and sexism experienced by poor black women on AFDC. Welfare is not an isolated issue, but is a product of larger economic, political, social, and cultural systems. As many welfare recipients so clearly understood in the 1960s, overcoming the problems inherent in our system of public assistance requires that we address the broader problems of racism, sexism, and class bias.

The Organizing Tradition/Activist Legacy

African American women in the welfare rights movement waged an admirable battle to better their own and their children's lives, despite encountering problems of minimal resources, personal shame, and public hostility. Their momentary victories of engaging the public dialogue and reforming the welfare system are important, particularly in light of the powerful forces arrayed against them. Their personal journeys from silence and marginalized welfare recipient to political and/or community leader testify to the strength of who they are and what they achieved. Their sustained commitment to a more just society, to helping those less fortunate than them, and to dismantling the racial/gender structures that continue to silence many poor women, are important examples for anyone committed to social justice. They offer hope and inspire others through their work. The life of Roxanne Jones appropriately illustrates the enormous accomplishments the movement achieved as well as the obstacles it encountered. Jones led the Philadelphia WRO since its inception in 1968. She was a fierce critic of punitive welfare policies and a relentless proponent of recipient leadership.

After the movement declined, Jones served as a member of the Pennsylvania state senate from 1984 until 1996, the first black woman elected to that position. She became a role model and advocate for poor African Americans in North Philadelphia. In a period of renewed welfare rights activism in the mid-1990s, Jones extended practical support to welfare rights groups in Philadelphia.[25] She worked with the Kensington Welfare Rights Union and other welfare rights groups in Pennsylvania, providing assistance to individuals, speaking at rallies, attending demonstrations, and lobbying on their behalf in the state senate. Her status as a former welfare recipient and activist proved important to these modern-day welfare activists.

Women like Jones don't provide a blueprint for the political struggles of the poor, but they are part of an organizing tradition that has profoundly shaped and attempted to redefine what our society stands for, particularly the role of poor people in political debate. The most powerful component of the welfare rights movement was the way in which poor women of color, battling social and economic exclusion, stood up and articulated their needs and desires. Their struggles with the welfare department and their political allies suggest that social movements and political reform cannot filter down from the top. Instead the poor and disenfranchised need to be empowered to act on their own behalf, to think and speak for themselves. This process of empowerment is an essential part of restructuring and envisioning a different kind of society. Black women on welfare in the 1960s created a political space to challenge their marginalization and modeled an alternative black female identity, one predicated on autonomy and self-determination. They formulated a theoretical position that addressed both economic oppression and dehumanization. In the face of daunting odds, they spoke on behalf of a different set of economic values and worked to establish new racial and gendered images of poor women of color. The welfare rights movement provides a window into the organizing tradition of a group of people from whom there is much to learn. We can learn from the obstacles it encountered as well as the victories it achieved; from its contradictions and its moments of consensus. Their campaigns were a critical part of the push and pull of history: to reframe political debates, to think about what we value as a society, to demand more equitable and just social programs. There is never an end to political struggle, when we can say we have reached our goal. As the welfare rights movement demonstrates, "winning" and "losing" are never absolutes, because the only certainty of history is change. What is won in one moment can be lost in the next.

Over the past twenty-five years, welfare recipients have been speaking out and acting out to halt the deliberate and dramatic moves that have shredded the safety net for poor women. Groups like the National Welfare Rights Union (NWRU), Welfare Warriors, Kensington Welfare Rights Union in Philadelphia, the New York–based Community Voices Heard, the Contact Center in Cincinnati, and People Organized to Win Employment Rights (POWER) in San Francisco, as well as countless other groups of women in local settings, have staged massive protests and have resisted in minor ways to express their dismay at these develop-ments. Although the agenda of the renewed movement is different from its pred-ecessor and the political landscape is drastically different, it is nevertheless a part of a continuity of activism that has its peaks and troughs. People like Marion Kramer, chair of NWRU, and Roxanne Jones of Philadelphia bridge the two periods of struggle. But, in addition, many contemporary activists know about the earlier struggles for welfare and draw inspiration and strength from the women who came before them.

The recent activism reminds us, that, in a period when there seems to be a consensus and only a few lone voices in the public discourse defend the welfare state, welfare recipients have helped to destabilize assumptions about poverty, welfare, and welfare recipients. The dismantling of AFDC and implementation of draconian work requirements have forged a tenuous, but symbolically impor-tant, alliance between labor and welfare constituencies. Workfare programs throughout the country often require welfare recipients to work in unsafe and unhealthy environments for nothing more than their welfare check (which falls well below minimum wage). The mutual interests of unions representing work-ers in these occupations and welfare advocates have converged to demand that municipalities extend labor standards and union membership to workfare work-ers. Living-wage campaigns also draw from the ranks of labor and welfare. These campaigns seek not just wages that correlate to the cost of living, but also push for child care and health insurance. The rationale is that if the state requires work, then the state must ensure that jobs are available and well paid and that supports are in place to enable recipients to work. Other activists have invoked the 1948 United Nations Universal Declaration of Human Rights to insist on a basic min-imum standard of living. Some activists have pushed for direct cash assistance, addressed problems of racial discrimination and attempted to place value on the work of parenting. But others have not gone far enough to challenge the assump-tions of work or to address the particular problems of women, especially women of color. Nevertheless, taken together, these campaigns are an important and effective mobilizing strategy that has the potential to turn the work requirement on its head. It can also broaden the labor movement, recognize the diverse needs of workers, and begin to reconceptualize working-class activism.

Whatever particular path organizers choose, they have much to learn from the courage of welfare rights activists, who can teach us to question, speak out, challenge, contest, and be angry. The lessons of the welfare rights movement should warn against apathy and complacency in the face of dramatic assaults on our collective well-being. Future activists might find in this history the seeds to germinate new movements in different political contexts. They will be part of an ongoing negotiation and dialogue as we struggle to define our country's economic and political priorities as we enter a new historical moment.

NOTES

Introduction

1 Colleen Agnew. Eyewitness Walk Report. n.d., Whitaker Papers, box 1, folder 22.
2 This was called the standard of need. The 1935 Social Security Act allowed each state to set its own standard of need, but did not require it to actually pay recipients this amount.
3 OSCAW leaflet, 1966. Rally for Decent Welfare. June 30, Whitaker Papers, box 1, folder 22. NASW leaflet, 1966. Ohio Walk for Decent Welfare. June 30, Whitaker Papers, box 1, folder 22.
4 After 1962, the program was extended in some states to two-parent families in which both parents were unemployed.
5 Jennifer Ann Frost, "Participatory Politics: Community Organizing, Gender, and the New Left in the 1960s," Ph.D. diss., University of Wisconsin, 1996. p. 507.
6 *New York Times*, July 1, 1966.
7 Michael Harrington, *The Other America: Poverty in the United States* (New York: Macmillan, 1962), p. 1.
8 U.S. Bureau of the Census, *Historical Statistics of the United States: Colonial Times to 1970.* (Washington, D.C: GPO, 1975): Series G 16–30. Family and Individual Income, p. 291.
9 For more on the welfare rights movement, see for example Premilla Nadasen, *Welfare Warriors: The Welfare Rights Movement in the United States* (New York: Routledge, 2004), Rhonda Williams, *The Politics of Public Housing: Black Women's Struggles against Urban Inequality* (Cambridge: Oxford University Press, 2005), Annelise Orleck, *Storming Caesar's Palace: How Black Mothers Fought Their Own War on Poverty* (Boston: Beacon Press, 2005), Felicia Kornbluh, *The Battle for Welfare Rights: Politics and Poverty in Modern America* (University of Pennsylvania Press, 2007), Nick Kotz and Mary Lynn Kotz, *A Passion for Equality: George A. Wiley and the Movement* (New York: W.W. Norton, 1977), Frances Fox Piven and Richard Cloward, "The Welfare Rights Movement" in *Poor People's Movements: Why they Fail and How they Succeed* (New York: Vintage, 1977), Guida West, *The National Welfare Rights Movement: The Social Protest of Poor Women* (New York: Praeger, 1981), Lawrence Neil Bailis, *Bread or Justice: Grassroots Organizing in the Welfare Rights Movement* (Lexington, Mass.: D.C.

Heath., 1972), Deborah Gray White, *Too Heavy a Load: Black Women in Defense of Themselves, 1894–1994* (New York: W. W. Norton, 1999), Rose Ernst, *The Price of Progressive Politics: The Welfare Rights Movement in an Era of Color Blind Racism* (New York: New York University Press, 2010).

10 I distinguish between the NWRO, a national organization comprising local groups, and the welfare rights movement more broadly, which included organizations not affiliated with NWRO.

1 The Origins of the Welfare Rights Movement

1 Jill Quadagno, *Transformation of Old Age Security: Class and Politics in the American Welfare State* (Chicago: University of Chicago Press, 1988), Mimi Abramovitz, *Regulating the Lives of Women: Social Welfare Policy from the Colonial Times to the Present* (Boston: South End Press, 1989), Barbara Nelson, "Origins of the Two-Channel Welfare State: Workmen's Compensation and Mothers' Aid" in *Women, the State, and Welfare*, ed. Linda Gordon (Madison: University of Wisconsin Press, 1990), Gwendolyn Mink, *The Wages of Motherhood: Inequality in the Welfare State, 1917–1942* (Ithaca: Cornell University Press, 1995), Theda Skocpol, *Protecting Soldiers and Mothers: The Origins of Social Policy in the United States* (Cambridge: Harvard University Press, 1992), Michael Katz, *The Price of Citizenship: Redefining the American Welfare State* (Philadelphia: University Press, 2001).

2 Robert Lieberman, *Shifting the Color Line: Race and the American Welfare State* (Cambridge: Harvard University Press: 1998), Yvonne Zylan, "The Divided Female State: Gender, Citizenship and US Social Policy Development, 1945–90," Ph.D. diss., New York University, 1994.

3 Linda Gordon, *Pitied but not Entitled: Single Mothers and the History of Welfare* (New York: The Free Press, 1994), Alice Kessler-Harris, *In Pursuit of Equity: Women, Men, and the Quest for Economic Citizenship in Twentieth-Century America* (New York: Oxford University Press, 2001).

4 For a discussion of wage-earning and welfare see Joanne Goodwin, *Gender and the Politics of Welfare Reform: Mothers' Pensions in Chicago, 1911–1929* (Chicago: University of Chicago Press, 1997), Joanne Goodwin, "'Employable Mothers' and 'Suitable Work': A Re-Evaluation of Welfare and Wage Earning for Women in the Twentieth-Century United States," *Journal of Social History* 29 (1995): 253–274, Gordon, *Pitied but not Entitled*, Gordon, *Women, the State and Welfare*, Nelson, "The Two-Channel Welfare State," Gwendolyn Mink, *The Wages of Motherhood: Inequality in the Welfare State, 1917–1942* (Ithaca: Cornell University Press, 1995), Abramovitz, *Regulating the Lives of Women*.

5 See Goodwin, "'Employable Mothers,'" Ellen Reese, *Backlash against Welfare Mothers Past and Present* (Berkeley: University of California Press, 2005) and Jennifer Mittelstadt, *From Welfare to Workfare: The Unintended Consequences of Liberal Reform, 1945–1965* (Chapel Hill: University of North Carolina Press, 2005). For more on patterns of discrimination in the early years of ADC see Kenneth Neubeck and Noel A. Cazenave, *Welfare Racism: Playing the Race Card Against America's Poor* (New York: Routledge, 2001), Chap. 3.

6 Frances Fox Piven and Richard Cloward, *Regulating the Poor: The Functions of Public Welfare* (New York: Pantheon Books, 1971), Winifred Bell, *Aid to Dependent Children* (New York: Columbia University Press, 1965), Zylan, "The Divided Female State," Abramovitz, *Regulating the Lives of Women*.

7 Abramovitz, *Regulating the Lives of Women*, Gordon, *Pitied but not Entitled*.

8 Winifred Bell suggests that between 1937 and 1940 African Americans made up 14 to 17 percent of the ADC caseload. Bell, *Aid to Dependent Children*, p. 34.

9 Bell, *Aid to Dependent Children*, Chap. 3.

10 Mary S. Larabee, "Unmarried Parenthood Under the Social Security Act," *Proceedings of the National Conference of Social Work, 1939* (New York: Columbia University Press, 1939), p. 449. Quoted in Bell, *Aid to Dependent Children*, pp. 34–35.

11 Piven and Cloward, *Regulating the Poor,* and Zylan, "The Divided Female State," p. 104.

12 See, for example, Jacqueline Jones, *Labor of Love, Labor of Sorrow: Black Women, Work, and the Family from Slavery to the Present* (New York: Vintage Books, 1985) and Eileen Boris, "The Power of Motherhood: Black and White Activist Women Redefine the Political" in *Mothers of a New World: Maternalist Politics and the Origins of the Welfare States,* eds. Seth Koven and Sonya Michel (New York: Routledge, 1993), pp. 214–245.

13 U.S. Bureau of the Census, *Statistical Abstracts of the United States* (Washington, D.C.: GPO, 1970): Table no. 428. Public Assistance—Recipients and Payments by Program: 1950–65.

14 U.S. Advisory Council on Social Security, 1938 Final Report, pp. 17–19, in Robert Bremner, *From the Depths: The Discovery of Poverty in the U.S.* (New York: New York University Press, 1956), p. 535, cited in Abramovitz, *Regulating the Lives of Women*, p. 321.

15 U.S. Congress, *House Ways and Means Committee, Background Material and Data on Programs Within the Jurisdiction of the Committee on Ways and Means, 1986 Edition* (Washington, D.C. Government Printing Office, 1986), p. 392. Quoted in Abramovitz, *Regulating the Lives of Women.*

16 U. S. Bureau of the Census, *Historical Statistics of the United States: Colonial Times to 1970* (Washington, D.C.: GPO, 1975): Series D 87–101. Unemployment Rates for Selected Groups in the Labor Force: 1947–70, p. 135.

17 Robert Grove and Alice Hetzel, *Vital Statistics Rates in the United States, 1940–1960* (Washington D.C.: U.S. Department of Health, Education and Welfare, 1968): Table no. 29. Ratios of Illegitimate Live Births by Color, p. 185.

18 See Rickie Solinger, *Wake Up Little Susie: Single Pregnancy and Race Before Roe v. Wade* (New York: Routledge, 1994) and Regina Kunzel, "White Neurosis, Black Pathology: Constructing Out-of-Wedlock Pregnancy in the Wartime and Post-War US" in *Not June Cleaver: Women and Gender in Postwar America*, ed. Joanne Meyerowitz (Philadelphia: Temple University Press, 1994).

19 According to a HEW report, 4.5 percent of the nation's children in 1961 were illegitimate, but only 0.5 percent were illegitimate and on ADC. U.S. Department of Health, Education and Welfare, *Public Assistance 1961, reprinted from the Annual Report 1961* (Washington), p. 31. Cited in Gilbert Steiner, *Social Insecurity: The Politics of Welfare* (Chicago: Rand McNally & Co, 1966), p. 125.

20 Bell, *Aid to Dependent Children*, p. 62.

21 "Cheating on Relief: Investigation Shows This," *US News and World Report*, July 16, 1962.

22 Lois Chevalier, "The Welfare Mess," *Saturday Evening Post*, May 11, 1963.

23 "The Mystery of Rising Relief Costs," *US News and World Report*, March 8, 1965.

24 "After 30 Years—Relief a Failure," *US News and World Report,* 17 July 1967.

25 This conclusion is based upon an extensive review of the popular press from 1945 to 1967. The review includes coverage about welfare in *Time, US News and World Report, New York Times Magazine, Saturday Evening Post, Nation's Business, Atlantic Monthly*, and *Business Week.* See, for example, *New York Times Magazine*, December 17, 1961, *US News and World Report*, July 24, 1961, *Saturday Evening Post*, May 11, 1963, *Business Week*, July 22, 1961.

26 "The Mystery of Rising Relief Costs," *US News and World Report*, March 8, 1965.

27 For more on the history of race and social welfare, see Gunja Sengupta, *From Slavery to Poverty: The Racial Origins of Welfare in New York, 1840–1918* (New York: New York University Press, 2009).

28 Zylan, "The Divided Female State," James Patterson, *America's Struggle Against Poverty, 1900–1980* (Cambridge: Harvard University Press.1981), pp. 107–109.

29 Bell, *Aid to Dependent Children*, p. 87.

30 For more on the history of AFDC, see Piven and Cloward, *Regulating the Poor*, Abramovitz, *Regulating the Lives of Women*, Reese, *Backlash against Welfare*, Mittelstadt, *From Welfare to Workfare*, Mink, *The Wages of Motherhood*, Lisa Levenstein, "From Innocent Children to Unwanted Migrants and Unwed Moms: Two Chapters in the Public Discourse on Welfare in the United States, 1960–61," *Journal of Women's History* 11 (Winter 2000): 10–33, Gordon, *Pitied but not Entitled*, Neubeck and Cazenave, *Welfare Racism*, Lieberman, *Shifting the Color Line*.

31 U.S. Bureau of the Census, *County and City Data Book, 1962: A Statistical Abstract Supplement* (Washington, D.C.: GPO, 1967).

32 U.S. Commission on Civil Rights. *Children in Need: A Study of a Federally Assisted Program of Aid to Needy Families with Children in Cleveland and Cuyahoga County, Ohio* (Washington, D.C.: GPO, 1966).

33 See Kenneth Wayne Rose, "The Politics of Social Reform in Cleveland, 1945–1967: Civil Rights, Welfare Rights, and the Response of Civic Leaders," Ph.D. diss., Case Western Reserve University, 1988.

34 U.S. Bureau of the Census, *Statistical Abstracts of the United States*, Table no. 404. Public Assistance: Payments to Recipients, by Program, by States and Other Areas (Washington, D.C.: GPO, 1962), p. 299.

35 For an extended discussion see Bell, *Aid to Dependent Children*.

36 Welfare Recipients in Action's Organization History. Undated, Wiley Papers. *New York Amsterdam News*, July 23, 1966.

37 See Premilla Nadasen, *Welfare Warriors: The Welfare Rights Movement in the United States* (New York: Routledge, 2004), Rhonda Williams, *The Politics of Public Housing: Black Women's Struggles against Urban Inequality* (Cambridge: Oxford University Press, 2005), Annelise Orleck, *Storming Caesar's Palace: How Black Mothers Fought Their Own War on Poverty* (Boston: Beacon Press, 2005), Felicia Kornbluh, *The Battle for Welfare Rights: Politics and Poverty in Modern America* (Philadelphia: University of Pennsylvania Press, 2007), Nick Kotz and Mary Lynn Kotz, *A Passion for Equality: George A. Wiley and the Movement* (New York: W.W. Norton, 1977), Frances Fox Piven and Richard Cloward, "The Welfare Rights Movement" in *Poor People's Movements: Why They Fail and How They Succeed* (New York: Vintage, 1977), Guida West, *The National Welfare Rights Movement: The Social Protest of Poor Women* (New York: Praeger, 1981), Lawrence Neil Bailis, *Bread or Justice: Grassroots Organizing in the Welfare Rights Movement* (Lexington, Mass.: D.C. Heath., 1972).

38 H. Lawrence Lack, "People on Welfare Form Union," *Los Angeles Free Press,* April 28, 1967, Whitaker Papers, box 1, folder 19.

39 Dorothy Moore, quoted in Ibid.

40 Hobart A. Burch, "Insights of a Welfare Mother: A Conversation with Johnnie Tillmon," *The Journal* (Jan.–Feb. 1971): 13–23, Wiley Papers [27].

41 Lawrence Witmer and Gibson Winter, "The Problem of Power in Community Organization" (paper presented at Conference on Community Organization, University of Chicago, April 12, 1968), p. 11, MFY (Mobilization For Youth) Papers, box 27.

42 Ibid.

43 Guaranteed Annual Income Newsletter, August 1966, pp. 3–5, MFY Papers, box 14.

44 MAW Member, Speech to VISTA Training Conference, Boston, May 31, 1969, Whitaker Papers, box 3, folder 4.

45 Ibid.

46 Gordon Brumm, "Mothers for Adequate Welfare—AFDC from the Underside," in *Dialogues Boston*, January 1968 [1–12], Whitaker Papers, box 3, folder 3.

47 Anne Whitaker, "Contacting People—Notes," May 31, 1968, Whitaker Papers, box 3, folder 8.

48 Ibid.
49 Jennifer Ann Frost, "Participatory Politics: Community Organizing, Gender, and the New Left in the 1960s," Ph.D. diss., University of Wisconsin, 1996, p. 203.
50 Milwaukee County Welfare Rights Organization, *Welfare Mothers Speak Out: We Ain't Gonna Shuffle Anymore*, (New York: Norton, 1972), pp. 25–26.
51 George Wiley. Round-Up of June 30th Welfare Demonstrations. June 28, 1966, Whitaker Papers, box 1, folder 22.
52 MAW, Press Release, May 13, 1968, Whitaker Papers, box 3, folder 8.
53 Guida West interview with Beulah Sanders, July 7, 1983, New York, NY.
54 Guida West interview with Jennette Washington, September 25, 1981, New York, NY. Profile of a Welfare Fighter. March 1971, MSRC, Washington (1981). Citywide Executive Board to Commissioner Jack Goldberg, December 3, 1968, and Minutes of the Executive Board Meeting, November 21, 1971, George Wiley Papers. She was on the Board during these years, but she may also have been involved during an earlier and later period.
55 Author interview with Frank Espada, 9 October 2003.
56 Author interview with Frank Espada, 9 October 2003.
57 Lawrence Witmer and Gibson Winter, "The Problem of Power in Community Organization," Paper presented at Conference Community Organization, Univ. of Chicago, p. 12, 12 April 1968, MFY Papers, Box 27.
58 Guaranteed Annual Income Newsletter, June 1966, MFY Papers, Box 14.
59 Pat Wagner, "Bread and Justice," *Voice of the West End Community Council*, June 14, 1967, Wiley Papers, box 14, folder 9.
60 David Street, George T. Martin, Jr., and Laura Kramer Gordon, *The Welfare Industry: Functionaries and Recipients of Public Aid* (Beverly Hills, CA: Sage, 1979), p. 124. Cited in West, *The National Welfare Rights Movement*, p. 45.
61 Brumm, "Mothers for Adequate Welfare," p. 9.
62 Milwaukee County WRO (1972: 68).
63 Lack, "People on Welfare Form Union."
64 Gluck interview #2 with Tillmon, 1991.
65 Gluck interview #3 with Tillmon, 1991.
66 Gluck interview #3 with Tillmon, 1991.
67 Burch, "Insights of a Welfare Mother," p. 14.
68 *New York Times*, November 21, 1995.
69 Gluck interview #3 with Tillmon, 1991.

2 Forming a National Organization

1 John Kenneth Galbraith, *The Affluent Society* (Boston: Houghton Mifflin, 1958).
2 Michael Harrington, *The Other America: Poverty in the United States* (New York: Macmillan, 1962).
3 Lyndon B. Johnson, "Annual Message to the Congress on the State of the Union," 8 January 1964. *Public Papers of the Presidents of the United States: Lyndon B. Johnson, 1963–1964*. Volume i, pp. 112–118. Washington, D. C.: Government Printing Office, 1965.
4 Hobart A. Burch, "Insights of a Welfare Mother: A Conversation with Johnnie Tillmon," *The Journal* (Jan.–Feb. 1971): 13–23, Wiley Papers [27], p. 18. Tillmon's understanding of how this phrase could be used by the poor points to the divergence between those who inserted the phrase in the Economic Opportunity Act and those who sought to put it into practice. See, for example, Daniel Patrick Moynihan, *Maximum Feasible Misunderstanding* (New York: Free Press, 1970).
5 Hurbert James. Statement to VISTA Training Institute, Boston, 1 June 1969, Whitake Papers, Box 3, Folder 4.

6 Jennifer Ann Frost, "Participatory Politics: Community Organizing, Gender, and the New Left in the 1960s," Ph.D. diss., University of Wisconsin, 1996.

7 For more on early organizing in Cleveland, see Kenneth Wayne Rose, "The Politics of Social Reform in Cleveland, 1945–1967: Civil Rights, Welfare Rights, and the Response of Civic Leaders," Ph.D. diss., Case Western Reserve University, 1988.

8 OSCAW. Ohio Adequate Welfare News. Newsletter, June 30, 1970, Whitaker Papers, box 1, folder 17. Also see Rose, "The Politics of Social Reform in Cleveland, 1945–1967."

9 Lillian Craig, with Marge Gravett, *Just a Woman: Memoirs of Lillian Craig* (Cleveland, OH: Orange Blossom Press, 1981), p. 17.

10 Guida West, *The National Welfare Rights Organization: The Social Protest of Poor Women* (New York: Praeger, 1981), Chaps. 2 and 4.

11 John H. Ehrenreich, *The Altruistic Imagination: A History of Social Work and Social Policy in the United States* (Ithaca: Cornell University Press, 1985), Chap. 7.

12 Author interview with Cloward, June 19, 1997.

13 Linda Cherrey Reeserand Irwin Epstein, *Professionalization and Activism in Social Work: The Sixties, Eighties, and the Future* (New York: Columbia University Press, 1990).

14 Milwaukee County Welfare Rights Organization, *Welfare Mothers Speak Out: We Ain't Gonna Shuffle Anymore.* (New York: Norton, 1972): p. 41.

15 Myles Horton, "Efforts to Bring About Radical Change in Education," *Cutting Edge* 4: 10 (1973), Highlander Collection, box 24.

16 Harold H. Weissman, ed., *Community Development in the Mobilization for Youth Experience* (New York: Association Press, 1969), p. 106. *New York Amsterdam News*, April 2, 1966.

17 James Farmer, *Lay Bare the Heart: An Autobiography of the Civil Rights Movement* (New York: Plume, 1986), pp. 302–303.

18 For more details on Wiley's life see Nick Kotz and Mary Lynn Kotz, *A Passion for Equality: George A. Wiley and the Movement* (New York: W. W. Norton & Co., 1977).

19 Author interview with Cloward, June 19, 1997.

20 Richard Cloward and Frances Fox Piven, "A Strategy to End Poverty," *The Nation,* May (1966): 510–517.

21 Barbara Schmoll, "Center Set up for War on Guaranteed Poverty," *The Milwaukee Journal*, March 3, 1967, Wiley Papers, box 27, folder 7.

22 For more on the disagreement between Wiley and Piven and Cloward, see Frances Fox Piven and Richard Cloward, *Poor People's Movements: How They Succeed, Why They Fail* (New York: Pantheon, 1977).

23 Ibid.

24 Author interview with Tim Sampson, April 21, 1997.

25 Robert E. Huldschiner, "Fighting Catherine Gets Welfare Mothers Together," *Lutheran Women*, October (1968), Wiley Papers, box 27, folder 7. Barbara Schmoll, *The Milwaukee Journal*, March 3, 1967, Wiley Papers, box 27, folder 7.

26 The conference, on May 21, 1966, was also attended by Richard Cloward and seventy welfare recipients and welfare rights organizers.

27 P/RAC. Summary Report of Welfare Action Meeting May 21, 1966. May 27, 1966, MSRC Author interview with Frank Espada, 9 October 2003.

28 P/RAC. Summary Report of Welfare Action Meeting May 21, 1966. May 27, 1966, MSRC.

29 Alex Efthim to Val Coleman. May 23, 1966. The Chicago Conference. MFY Papers, box 14.

30 Kotz and Kotz, *A Passion for Equality*, p. 188.

31 P/RAC. Notes of Fund Raising Meeting. June 8, 1966, MSRC.

32 Seymour M. Hersh, "Seek Welfare Power Bloc," *National Catholic Reporter,* June 29, 1966. Wiley Papers, box 27, folder 7.

33 Guida West interview with Hulbert James, February 6, 1981, New York, NY.

34 Hobart A. Burch, "A Conversation with George Wiley," *The Journal* (Nov.–Dec. 1970): 2–12, Wiley Papers [27], p. 8.
35 Guida West interview with Beulah Sanders, July 7, 1983, New York, NY. Citywide Prospectus, 1968, Wiley Papers.
36 Author interview with Catherine Jermany, October 11, 2003.
37 Author interview with Frances Fox Piven, June 19, 1997.
38 NWRO. Meeting Minutes for Poverty Line Discussion. February 1967. MSRC. They defined poverty according to the Bureau of Labor Statistics figures rather than the official poverty line set by the Department of Agriculture.
39 West, *The National Welfare Rights Organization*, pp. 54–55.
40 At the founding of NWRO, the women adopted the title chairman. In the early 1970s, when they articulated feminist goals, they changed the title to chairwoman.

3 Motherhood and the Making of Welfare Policy

1 For more on racial stereotypes and welfare policy see Sue K. Jewell, *From Mammy to Miss American and Beyond: Cultural Images and the Shaping of US Social Policy* (New York: Routledge, 1993), Martin Gilens, *Why Americans Hate Welfare: Race, Media and the Politics of Antipoverty Policy* (Chicago: University of Chicago Press, 1999), and Kenneth Neubeck and Noel A. Cazenave, *Welfare Racism:Playing the Race Card Against America's Poor* (New York: Routledge, 2001).
2 Lisa Levenstein, *A Movement Without Marches: African American Women and the Politics of Poverty in Postwar Philadelphia* (Chapel Hill: University of North Carolina Press, 2009), Chap. 1, pp. 31–62.
3 Ange-Marie Hancock, *The Politics of Disgust: The Public Identity of the Welfare Queen*, (New York: New York University Press, 2004).
4 Hobart A. Burch, "Insights of a Welfare Mother: A Conversation with Johnnie Tillmon," *The Journal* (Jan.–Feb. 1971): 13–23, Wiley Papers [27].
5 Beulah Sanders. Statement Before the Presidential Commission on Income Maintenance. June 5, 1969, Wiley Papers, box 22, folder 4.
6 Joe McDermott. Congressional Record. April 3, 1969, Wiley Papers, box 21, folder 2.
7 Lloyd Ohlin and Richard Cloward, *Delinquency and Opportunity: A Theory of Delinquent Gangs* (Glencoe, IL: Free Press, 1960) argued that institutions serving the poor would best be reformed by the poor.
8 Author interview with Jon Van Til, October 6, 2003.
9 A similar policy about decision making guided the United Auto Workers in the 1960s. See Kevin Boyle, *The UAW and the Heyday of American Liberalism 1945–1968* (Ithaca: Cornell University Press, 1995), Chap. 8.
10 See bell hooks, *Talking Back: Thinking Feminist, Thinking Black* (Boston: South End Press, 1989).
11 See Nancy Fraser, *Unruly Practices: Power, Discourse, and Gender in Contemporary Social Theory* (Minneapolis: University of Minnesota Press, 1989) and Gayatri Spivak, "Can the Subaltern Speak?" in *Marxism and the Interpretation of Culture*, eds. Cary Nelson and Lawrence Grossberg, (Chicago: University of Illinois Press, 1988), pp. 271–313.
12 Mary Davidson, "Interviews," October 1968, Whitaker Papers, box 3, folder 6.
13 *New York Times*, July 1, 1966, July 16, 1966. Ezra Birnbaum and Mary Rabagliati, "Organizations of Welfare Clients," in *Community Development in the MFY Experience*, ed. Harold H. Weissman (New York: Association Press), pp. 69–105.
14 Neil Gilbert, *Capitalism and the Welfare State: Dilemmas of Social Benevolence* (New Haven: Yale University Press, 1983).
15 Stanley Kravitz quoted in *Administrative History of the Office of Economic Opportunity*, Vol. 1, p. 681, Office of Economic Opportunity Collection Box 1, Lyndon B. Johnson Library.

16 Fraser, *Unruly Practices*, p. 161 suggests that the negotiation takes place in the "social" which she defines as a sphere of public discourse that cuts across economic, political, and domestic arenas.

17 Cynthia Edmonds-Cady, "Mobilizing Motherhood: Race, Class, and the Uses of Maternalism in the Welfare Rights Movement," *Women's Studies Quarterly* 37, 3–4 (2009): 206–222.

18 Joseph E. Paull, "Recipients Aroused: The New Welfare Rights Movement," *Social Work*, Vol. 12, April 1967, pp. 101–106, Wiley Papers, box 27, folder 7. Also see no author, 1965. Northern Colorado: AFDC Mothers Clubs. News from the Chapters, NASW News. 10: 11.

19 Minnie Bradford, President of North Branch AFDC League. Letter to George Wiley. January 7, 1967, MSRC.

20 OSCAW. Ohio Adequate Welfare News. Newsletter, June 13, 1966, Whitaker Papers, box 1, folder 17.

21 Ezra Birnbaum and Mary Rabagliati, "Organizations of Welfare Clients," in *Community Development in the MFY Experience* ed. Harold H. Weissman (NY: Association Press): 117.

22 Lois Walker. Virginia Welfare Rights Organization Proposal. December 1970, Wiley Papers, box 27, folder 3.

23 Author interview with Ethel Dotson, April 27, 1997.

24 For a discussion of race and social science theory see Daryl Michael Scott, *Contempt and Pity: Social Policy and the Image of the Damaged Black Psyche, 1880–1996* (Chapel Hill: University of North Carolina Press, 1997), Chaps. 5 and 6, and Alice O'Connor, "From Lower Class to Underclass: The Poor in American Social Science, 1930–1970," Ph.D. diss., Johns Hopkins University, 1991, Chap. 4.

25 Daniel Patrick Moynihan, *The Negro Family: A Case for National Action* (Washington, D.C.: Office of Policy Planning and Research, U.S. Dept. of Labor, 1965).

26 See for example, Oscar Lewis, La Vida: A Puerto Rican Family in the Culture of Poverty San Juan and New York (New York: Random House, 1966).

27 Scott J. Spitzer, "The Liberal Dilemma: Welfare and Race, 1960–1975," Ph.D. diss., Columbia University, 2000, makes a similar argument that race and welfare became inseparable in the mid-1960s. He ties this development, however, more to the passage of the 1967 Social Security Amendments.

28 George Wiley to Daniel P. Moynihan, no date, Wiley papers, box 29.

29 Richard Cloward, "The War on Poverty: Are the Poor Left Out?," *The Nation*, August 2, 1965 [55].

30 Guida West, *The National Welfare Rights Organization: The Social Protest of Poor Women* (New York: Praeger, 1981), p. 86.

31 Marisa Chappell, "From Welfare Rights to Welfare Reform: The Politics of AFDC, 1964–1984," Ph.D. diss., Northwestern University, 2002, Chap. 1, makes a similar argument about the political consensus on the family-wage system.

32 See, for example, Ula Taylor, "Elijah Muhammad's Nation of Islam: Separatism, Regendering, and a Secular Approach to Black Power after Malcolm X (1965–1975)," in *Freedom North: Black Freedom Struggles Outside the South, 1940–1980*, eds. Jeanne Theoharis and Komozi Woodard (New York: Palgrave, 2003, pp. 177–198), and Komozi Woodard, *A Nation Within a Nation: Amiri Baraka (LeRoi Jones) and Black Power Politics* (Chapel Hill: University of North Carolina Press, 1999).

33 In 1972, Daphne Busby formed the Sisterhood of Black Single Mothers. This organization, much like welfare rights organizing, navigated the path between feminism and nationalism and defended black single motherhood. See Barbara Omolade, *It's a Family Affair: The Real Lives of Black Single Mothers* (Albany, NY: Kitchen Table Press, 1986), Chap. 11.

34 Welfare Rights Committee, Mohongalia County, West Virginia, "Your Welfare Rights" Handbook, no date, Whitaker Papers, box 3.
35 Allan Becker, Robert Daniels, and Susan Wender, "Proposed Action: Public Assistance" (paper submitted to Metropolitan Detroit Branch, ACLU), November 17, 1968, ACLU Archives, boxes 1134–36.
36 Gordon Brumm, "Mothers for Adequate Welfare—AFDC from the Underside," in *Dialogues Boston*, January 1968 [1–12], Whitaker Papers, box 3, folder 3.
37 Ibid.
38 Welfare Rights Committee, Mohongalia County, West Virginia, "Your Welfare Rights" Handbook, no date, Whitaker Papers, box 3.
39 Brumm, "Mothers for Adequate Welfare."
40 Nancy Naples coined the phrase "activist mothering" to refer to women whose activism grew out of struggles on behalf of their children. See Nancy A. Naples, "Activist Mothering: Cross-Generational Continuity in the Community Work of Women From Low-Income Urban Neighborhoods," *Gender and Society* (1992) 6: 441–463. See also Alexis Jetter, Annelise Orleck, and Diana Taylor, eds., *The Politics of Motherhood: Activist Voices from Left to Right* (Hanover: University Press of New England, 1997).
41 Jennifer Mittelstadt, *From Welfare to Workfare: The Unintended Consequences of Liberal Reform, 1945–1965* (Chapel Hill: University of North Carolina Press, 2005), Nancy Rose, *Workfare or Fair Work: Women, Welfare, and Government Work Programs* (New Brunswick: Rutgers University Press, 1995).
42 Congressional Quarterly Almanac, 1967, pp. 902–903. Quoted in Spitzer, "The Liberal Dilemma," p. 126.
43 For a discussion of civil rights organizations' positions see Dona Cooper Hamilton and Charles Hamilton, *The Dual Agenda: Race and Social Welfare Policies of Civil Rights Organizations* (New York: Columbia University Press, 1997).
44 *Washington Post*, August 29, 1967.
45 Ibid.
46 "Six Myths About Welfare," NWRO pamphlet, 1971, Welfare Rights Collection, Lehman Library.
47 *Washington Daily News*, September 20, 1967.
48 Ibid.
49 Interview with Tim Sampson, April 21, 1997.
50 *Washington Post*, 20 September, 1967 and *Washington Daily News*, September 20, 1967.
51 Mittelstadt, *From Welfare to Workfare*.
52 U.S. Dept of Labor, Contract with the National Welfare Rights Organization, December 24, 1968, Wiley Papers, box 30, folder 3.
53 Martha Davis, *Brutal Need, Lawyers and the Welfare Rights Movement, 1960–1973* (New Haven: Yale University Press, 1993), p. 121.
54 NWRO, NOW!, Newsletter, July 1969, Wiley Papers, box 17, folder 3.
55 Interview with Tim Sampson, April 21, 1997.
56 George Wiley, quoted in *Washington Post*, August 29, 1967.
57 NashCo, "Contract Proposal for a Technical Assistance and Citizen Participation project to the Bureau of Work Training Programs, U.S. Department of Labor," October 1969, Wiley Papers, box 30, folder 3.
58 The professional staff of MFY who worked with the Committee of Welfare Families took a similar position. In 1966 they wrote a proposal to OEO for a summer training program to help women get jobs and get off the welfare rolls. They were granted $19,000, which was used to hire four professionals to train thirty recipients "to interview,…fill out questionnaires…do elementary filing, and…deal with unexpected situations during work with other people." Birnbaum and Rabagliati, "Organizations of Welfare Clients," p. 119.
59 Interview with Marjorie Caesar, March 4, 1996.

60 Interview with Catherine Jermany, October 11, 2003.
61 Philadelphia Welfare Rights Organization, "To: All Persons Attending the National Conference of Social Welfare," May 1969, MSRC. *New York Times,* May 29, 1969.
62 Virginia Snead, NCC Representative, "Report from NCC Meeting in New York, May 23–28," May 1969, MSRC and NCC Meeting, May 28, 1969, MSRC.
63 Jon Van Til, "Becoming Participants: Dynamics of Access Among the Welfare Poor," Ph.D. diss., University of California, Berkeley, 1970, pp. 211–213.
64 Massachusetts Welfare Information Center Newsletter, April 7, 1969, Whitaker Papers, box 2, folder 38.
65 Brumm, "Mothers for Adequate Welfare," p. 11.
66 Massachusetts Welfare Information Center Newsletter, April 7, 1969, Whitaker Papers, box 2, folder 38.
67 Andrea Jule Sachs, "The Politics of Poverty: Race, Class, Motherhood, and the National Welfare Rights Organization, 1965–75," Ph.D. diss., University of Minnesota, 2001, Chap. 3, also deals with the differences between staff and recipients on this point.
68 Skocpol, Theda, *Protecting Soldiers and Mothers: The Origins of Social Policy in the United States* (Cambridge: Harvard University Press, 1992), Linda Gordon, *Pitied but not Entitled: Single Mothers and the History of Welfare* (New York: Free Press, 1994).
69 Gordon, *Pitied but not Entitled,* Gwendolyn Mink, *The Wages of Motherhood: Inequality in the Welfare State, 1917–1942* (Ithaca: Cornell University Press, 1995).
70 Boris, Eileen, "The Power of Motherhood: Black and White Activist Women Redefine the Political,"in *Mothers of a New World: Maternalist Politics and the Origins of the Welfare States,* eds. Seth Koven and Sonya Michel (New York: Routledge, 1993 pp. 214–245), Looks at strategies used by women during the progressive era and similarly concludes that black defense of motherhood challenged subordination of African Americans.
71 Nancy Fraser and Linda Gordon, "A Genealogy of Dependency: Tracing a Keyword of the U.S. Welfare State," *Signs* 19 (1994): 303–336.
72 O'Connor, "From Lower Class to Underclass."
73 For more on child care and working women see Sonya Michel, *Children's Interests, Mother's Rights: The Shaping of America's Child Care Policy* (New Haven: Yale University Press, 1999).
74 Quoted in Daniel Patrick Moynihan, *Politics of Guaranteed Income: The Nixon Administration and the Family Assistance Plan* (New York: Random House, 1973), pp. 89–91.
75 "Ohio Adequate Welfare News," April 18, 1968, Whitaker Papers, box 1.
76 For more on ideological differences between black and white activists in the 1960s see M. Rivka Polatnick, "Diversity in Women's Liberation Ideology: How a Black and a White Group of the 1960s Viewed Motherhood," *Signs* 21 (1996): 679–706.
77 West, *The National Welfare Rights Organization,* p. 253.
78 Tera Hunter, *To 'Joy My Freedom: Southern Black Women's Lives and Labors after the Civil War* (Cambridge: Harvard University Press, 1997), Elizabeth Clark-Lewis, *Living In, Living Out: African American Domestics in Washington, D.C., 1910–1940* (Washington: Smithsonian Institution Press, 1994).

4 We Demand a Right to Welfare

1 Minutes of the Committee on Individual, Group, and Family Services. February 2, 1966, MFY Papers, box 8, and Ezra Birnbaum and Mary Rabagliati. "Organizations of Welfare Clients," in *Community Development in the MFY Experience,* ed. Harold H. Weissman (New York: Association Press, 1969), p. 112.
2 The Welfare Marches. *Trans-Action* 4, 2 (December 1966), Wiley Papers, box 27, folder 7. Brooklyn Welfare Action Council. A Description of the Birth and Growth of

the Brooklyn Welfare Action Council, Wiley Papers. *New York Times*, January 19, 1968. *New York Times*, November 20, 1966. *New York Times*, November 5, 1966.

3 Welfare Grievance Committee, Newsletter, June 28, 1966, Whitaker Papers, box 1, folder 18.

4 OSCAW, Telegram to Governor Rhodes, October 26, 1966, Whitaker Papers, box 1, folder 1.

5 Judy Rensberger, *Detroit's Daily Express*, December 9, 1967, Wiley Papers.

6 *New York Times*, May 30, 1968, May 31, 1968, June 1, 1968.

7 *New York Times*, July 16, 1968, August 31, 1968.

8 Citywide Coordinating Committee of Welfare Rights Groups, "Tell it Like it is," Newsletter, May 22, 1968, Wiley Papers. *New York Times*, May 30, 1968.

9 "Citywide Demands", June 28, 1968, Wiley Papers, box 26, folder 1.

10 "Tell it Like it is," Citywide Newsletter, July 19, 1968, Wiley Papers. *New York Times*, July 4, 1968, July 17, 1968, July 15, 1968, August 14, 1968. Beulah Sanders, Press Statement, July 3, 1968, Wiley Papers. and "Citywide Demands," June 28, 1968, Wiley Papers.

11 Rhonda Williams, "Nonviolence and Long Hot Summers: Black Women and Welfare Rights Struggles in the 1960s," *Borderlands E Journal* 4, 3 (2005): 2–4.

12 *New York Times*, August 31, 1968.

13 Johnnie Tillmon, Speech, United Presbyterian Woman National Meeting, 1970.

14 See Timothy Tyson, *Radio Free Dixie: Robert F. Williams and the Roots of Black Power* (Chapel Hill: University of North Carolina Press, 1999); Barbara Bansby, *Ella Baker and the Black Freedom Movement: A Radical Democratic Vision*, (Chapel Hill: University of North Carolina Press, 2003); Chana Kai Lee, *For Freedom's Sake: The Life of Fannie Lon Hamer*. (Urbana: University of Illinois Press, 1999); Simon Hall, "The NAACP, Black Power, and the African American Freedom Struggle, 1966–69," *The Historian* 69: 49–82.

15 Author interview with Tim Sampson, April 21, 1997.

16 "Ohio Adequate Welfare News," OSCAW Newsletter, January 23, 1969, Whitaker Papers, box 1, folder 17.

17 Gloria Brown, Report to NWRO, before January 2, 1969, Wiley Papers, box 25, folder 4. Westside Mothers ADC, Report to NWRO, December 30, 1968, Wiley Papers, box 25, folder 4.

18 "NWRO in Action" Booklet, Welfare Rights Collection, Lehman Library.

19 John Lewis, "Black Voices." *Washington Afro-American*, 14 September, 1968, Wiley Papers, box 27.

20 Columbus WRO, flier, no date, Whitaker Papers, box 1, folder 12.

21 *Evening Gazette*, August 14, 1968, Welfare Rights Handbook, Whitaker Papers, box 3, folder 5.

22 OSCAW, "Ohio Adequate Welfare News" Newsletter, January 9, 1967, Whitaker Papers, box 1, folder 17.

23 See, for example, Evelyn Brooks Higginbotham, *Righteous Discontent: The Women's Movement in the Black Baptist Church 1880–1920* (Cambridge: Howard Press, 1993).

24 Author interview with Tim Sampson, April 21, 1997.

25 NWRO, NWRO Winter Action Campaign Ideas, fall 1968, MSRC.

26 West, Guida, *The National Welfare Rights Organization: The Social Protest of Poor Women* (New York: Praeger, 1980), p. 50.

27 Philadelphia WRO, "A Study Document on Welfare Rights Goals," no date, Wiley Papers, box 27, folder 1.

28 Mary Wallace, "Welfare Mothers Seek Clothing Funds," *Ann Arbor News*, September 4, 1968, Wiley Papers.

29 Mary Wallace, "Mothers Reject Offer," *Ann Arbor News*, September 6, 1968, Wiley Papers.

30 Mary Wallace, "$60 ADC Grants to be Ready Monday," *Ann Arbor News*, September 7, 1968, Wiley Papers.
31 Birnbaum and Rabagliati, "Organizations of Welfare Clients," p. 110.
32 Rhode Island Fair Welfare, Flier, "Experimental Title I Clothing Proposal," July 30, 1970, Wiley Papers, box 27, folder 2.
33 Philadelphia WRO, "A Study Document on Welfare Rights Goals," no date, Wiley Papers, box 27, folder 1.
34 See, for example, Daniel Bell, *Work and Its Discontents* (Boston: Beacon Press, 1956) and Betty Friedan, *The Feminine Mystique* (New York: Norton, 1963).
35 The Clarks found similar results for black children in the North. In addition, their research did not address the specific issue of school segregation, rather segregation, or racism, generally. See Richard Kluger, *Simple Justice: The History of Brown v. Board of Education and Black America's Struggle for Equality* (New York: Knopf, 1976) and Gerald Markowitz and David Rosner, *Children, Race, and Power: Kenneth and Mamie Clark's Northside Center* (Charlottesville, VA: University Press of Virginia, 1996).
36 For a discussion of the evolution of social science and liberal racial ideology see Daryl Michael Scott, *Contempt and Pity: Social Policy and the Image of the Damaged Black Psyche, 1880–1996* (University of North Carolina Press: Chapel Hill, 1997). For more on the Brown decision see Kluger, *Simple Justice*.
37 Author interview with Moiece Palladino, April 27, 1997.
38 *New York Times*, July 17, 1968, July 15, 1968. *New York Daily News*, July 4, 1968.
39 *New York Times*, June 26, 1968, August 27, 1968.
40 *Boston Globe*, April 20, 1969, Welfare Rights Handbook, Whitaker Papers, box 3, folder 5.
41 Citizens Committee to Change Welfare, Newsletter, June 21, 1970, Whitaker Papers, box 3, folder 5. Date of proposed change was August 15, 1970.
42 "Tell It Like it is," Citywide Newsletter, August 16, 1968, Wiley Papers, box 26.
43 Guida West interview with Beulah Sanders, July 7, 1983, New York, NY. *New York Times*, August 28, 1968, August 29, 1968. *New York Amsterdam News*, September 7, 1968.
44 *New York Times*, August 30, 1968, August 31, 1968, September 4, 1968, September 5, 1968, September 6, 1968. *New York Amsterdam News*, September 7, 1968.
45 In addition to the cases discussed here, the U.S. Supreme Court struck down substitute-father laws in *King v. Smith* (1968) and declared residency laws unconstitutional in *Shapiro v. Thompson* (1969).
46 Minneapolis Community Union Project Welfare Committee. Status Report. Late Summer 1968, Wiley Papers, box 25, folder 6.
47 Collection of WRO Handbooks, Whitaker Papers, box 3, folder 17.
48 Charles Sutton. Newspaper Article. *Independent Press Telegram*. May 26, 1968, Wiley Papers, box 24, folder 13.
49 Gordon Brumm, "Mothers for Adequate Welfare—AFDC from the Underside," in *Dialogues Boston*, January 1968 [1–12], Whitaker Papers, box 3, folder 3.
50 Hinds County Welfare Rights Movement. Your Welfare Rights. Handbooks. July 1967 and March 1968. ACLU Archives, boxes 1134–1136.
51 Ibid.
52 *Beckley Post Herald*, February 25, 1971, Wiley Papers, box 27, folder 3.
53 LA County WRO. Newsletter, November 1, 1968, Wiley Papers, box 24, folder 13.
54 D.C. Citywide WRO. We Rap. Newsletter, June 10, 1969, Wiley Papers, box 24, folder 11.
55 Robert Maier. Field Notes. April 8, 1968, Whitaker Papers, box 3, folder 3.
56 Naomi Gottlieb Shreshinsky, "Welfare Rights Organizations and the Public Welfare System: An Interaction Study," Ph.D. diss., University of California, 1970, p. 103.
57 Ibid., p. 115.

58 No author (probably NWRO staff). Project in Lay Advocacy. 1967, Wiley Papers. *New York Times*, July 15, 1968. Ann Fagan Ginger, ed, *Civil Liberties Docket* (Meiklejohn Civil Liberties Libraries: Oakland, CA, 1970), no. 673, p. 111.

59 OSCAW. Press Release. November 22, 1967, Whitaker Papers, box 1, folder 16.

60 MAW member. Speech to VISTA Training Conference, Boston. May 31, 1969, Whitaker Papers, box 3, folder 4.

61 Brumm, "Mothers for Adequate Welfare." Massachusetts WRO. The Adequate Income Times. Newsletter, January 7, 1969, Whitaker Papers, box 3, folder 5.

62 Englewood WRO. Report. August 16, 1968, Wiley Papers, box 25, folder 6.

63 NWRO. Report on Welfare Rights Organization Conference on Minimum Standards Campaigns. January 12, 13, 1968, MSRC.

64 Citywide Coordinating Committee of Welfare Rights Groups. "Tell it Like it is." Newsletter, May 22, 1968, Wiley Papers. Ginger, *Civil Liberties Docket*, pp. 110–111, 115–116, *New York Times*, January 30, 1968, November 27, 1968. Martha Davis, *Brutal Need, Lawyers and the Welfare Rights Movement, 1960–1973* (New Haven, CT: Yale University Press, 1993).

65 See Charles Reich, "Individual Rights and Social Welfare: The Emerging Legal Issues," *Yale Law Journal* 74 (1965): 1245–1257; Charles Reich, "New Property," *Yale Law Journal* 73 (1964): 733–787.

66 NWRO, "402(a) (23): A New Weapon to Fight for More Money Now," April 18, 1969, Wiley Papers, box 23, folder 3. National Organization for Women, Newsletter, August 7, 1969, Wiley Papers, box 23, folder 3.

67 For more details, see Davis, *Brutal Need*, Chap. 9.

68 Milton Berliner, "Welfare Voice: We are Living Like Dogs," *Daily News*, April 27, 1966, Whitaker Papers, box 3, folder 14.

69 Brumm, "Mothers for Adequate Welfare."

70 Welfare Grievance Committee (Cleveland), Leaflet, "Something is Wrong," August 1966, Whitaker Papers, box 1, folder 35.

71 James T. Patterson, *America's Struggle Against Poverty, 1900–1980* (Cambridge: Harvard University Press, 1981).

72 Joseph McCarthy, *Sun-Telegram*, no date, Wiley Papers, box 14, folder 9.

73 Laurens Silver (Deputy Director, Law Reform and Education), Letter to Wylie [sic], 9 October 1968, Wiley Papers, box 24, folder 11.

74 Diana Karter Appelbaum, "The Level of the Poverty Line: A Historical Survey," *Social Service Review* 5 (1977): 514–523, Greg Duncan, *Years of Poverty, Years of Plenty: The Changing Economic Fortunes of American Workers and Families* (Ann Arbor: Institute for Social Research, University of Michigan, 1984), Patterson, *America's Struggle Against Poverty, 1900–1980.*

75 This is very similar to a development in the labor movement in the 1930s when unions shattered management's arbitrary power over labor. David Brody, "Workplace Contractualism in Comparative Perspective," in *Industrial Democracy in America: The Ambiguous Promise*, eds. Nelson Lichtenstein and Howell Harris (Boston: Cambridge University Press, 1993), pp. 176–205, calls the new system of procedures "workplace contractualism."

5 The Fight for a Guaranteed Annual Income

1 Guida West, *The National Welfare Rights Organization: The Social Protest of Poor Women* (New York: Praeger, 1981), p. 50. Bailis writes that NWRO claimed a membership of between 75,000 and 125,000. Lawrence Bailis, *Bread or Justice: Grassroots Organizing in the Welfare Rights Movement.* Lexington, MA: Lexington Books, 1972.

2 Ibid., p. 55.

3 West, *The National Welfare Rights Organization*, p. 51.
4 Ibid., p. 52.
5 Ibid., p. 51.
6 Jennette Washington, "I Challenge," published article, source unknown, date unknown, Wiley Papers, box 28.
7 Richard Cloward and Frances Fox Piven, "A Strategy to End Poverty," *The Nation* (May 1966): 510–517.
8 Grier Horner, "PAPAW: How It Started, What It's Hoping To Do," *Berkshire Eagle*, June 30, 1967.
9 Loretta Domencich, quoted in Milwaukee County Welfare Rights Organization; *Welfare Mothers Speak Out: We Ain't Gonna Shuffle Anymore* (New York: Norton, 1972): 51.
10 Robert E. Huldschiner, "Fighting Catherine Gets Welfare Mothers Together," *Lutheran Women*, October 1968, Wiley Papers, box 27, folder 7.
11 Philadelphia WRO, "A Study Document on Welfare Rights Goals," no date, Wiley Papers, box 27, folder 1.
12 OSCAW, "Ohio's Continuing Welfare Disgrace," flyer, 1969, Whitaker Papers, box 1, folder 1.
13 MAW member, Speech to VISTA Training Conference, Boston, May 31, 1969, Whitaker Papers, box 3, folder 4.
14 Joy Stanley, President LA County WRO, Speech before the Public Forum, Citizens Committee for a Decent Welfare System, September 5, 1966, MSRC. LA County WRO, Press Release, June 30, 1969, MSRC.
15 Hobart A. Burch, "A Conversation with George Wiley," *The Journal* (Nov.–Dec. 1970): 2–12, Wiley Papers [27], p. 10.
16 "Welfare Reform Called Repression of the Poor," *Greensboro Daily News*, November 15, 1970.
17 Johnnie Tillmon, "Welfare is a Woman's Issue," *Ms. Magazine* 1 (1972): 115.
18 OSCAW, "Ohio Adequate Welfare News," Newsletter, April 18, 1968, Whitaker Papers, box 1.
19 Cassie B. Downer, quoted in Milwaukee County WRO (1972: 135–136).
20 Philadelphia WRO, "A Federal Family Investment Program: The Basic Goal of the Philadelphia WRO," no date, Wiley Papers, box 27, folder 1.
21 Ibid.
22 MWRO Chair, Speech at MWRO Rally, Boston, June 30, 1969, Whitaker Papers, box 3, folder 6.
23 NWRO, "Adequate Income Plan: $5500 or Fight," pamphlet, April 1970, Welfare Rights Collection, Lehman Library.
24 NWRO, Adequate Income Plan, June 25, 1971, Lehman Library.
25 U.S. Department of Labor, "Three Standards of Living for an Urban Family of Four Persons," Bulletin No. 1570–1575, quoted in ibid.
26 NWRO, Adequate Income Plan, June 25, 1971, Lehman Library.
27 Vincent J.,Burke and Vee Burke, *Nixon's Good Deed: Welfare Reform* (New York: Columbia University Press, 1974), pp. 49–50.
28 National Council of Churches, "Proposed Policy Statement on Guaranteed Income," June 10, 1967, ACLU Archives, boxes 1134–1136.
29 *Providence Evening Bulletin*, August 17, 1966, Wiley Papers, box 27, folder 7.
30 Daniel Patrick Moynihan, *Politics of Guaranteed Income: The Nixon Administration and the Family Assistance Plan* (New York: Random House, 1973), p. 126.
31 National Association of Social Workers, Press Release, June 11, 1968, ACLU Archives, boxes 1134–1136.
32 T. H. Marshall, *Class, Citizenship and Social Development: Essays by T. H. Marshall* (Garden City: NY, Doubleday & Co, 1964), p. 72.
33 Milton Friedman, *Capitalism and Freedom* (Chicago: University of Chicago Press, 1962), p. 191.

34 Ibid., p. 192.
35 John Kenneth Galbraith, *The Affluent Society* (Boston: Houghton Mifflin, 1958), p. 266.
36 Ibid., p. 292.
37 Robert Theobald, for example, argued that scientific and technological advancements would give a productive potential in western nations that would enable breaking the link between jobs and income and ensuring everyone a decent standard of living. Robert Theobald, *The Guaranteed Income: The Next Step in Economic Evolution?* (New York: Doubleday, 1966), p. 83. See also Robert Theobald, *Free Men and Free Markets* (Garden City, NY: Doubleday & Co, 1965).
38 Galbraith, *The Affluent Society*, p. 292.
39 For more on the liberal orientation of Nixon, see Joan Hoff, *Nixon Reconsidered* (New York: Basic Books, 1994). Scott J. Spitzer, "The Liberal Dilemma: Welfare and Race, 1960–1975." Ph.D. diss., Columbia University, 2000, Chap. 5, similarly argues that, despite his conservative rhetoric, Nixon was liberal on welfare policy.
40 Statistical Abstracts, Table no. 431 "Public Assistance—Expenditures, by Source of Funds, and Monthly Payments to Recipients, by Program, States and Other Areas: 1965."
41 Richard Nixon, "Welfare Reform Message to the Congress of the United States, 8/11/69," in *Nixon: The First Year of His Presidency* (Washington, D.C.: Congressional Quarterly, 1970).
42 Ibid.
43 For more on what motivated Nixon see Spitzer, "The Liberal Dilemma," Chap. 7 and Burke and Burke, *Nixon's Good Deed*, p. 39.
44 Gareth Davies, *From Opportunity to Entitlement: The Transformation and Decline of Great Society Liberalism* (Lawrence: University Press of Kansas, 1996).
45 "Text of President's Welfare—Workfare Speech, 8/8/69,"in Nixon, *Nixon: The First Year.*
46 Ibid.
47 Burke and Burke, *Nixon's Good Deed*, p. 5.
48 "Text of President's Welfare—Workfare Speech, 8/8/69," in Nixon, *Nixon: The First Year.*
49 David G. Gil, "Mothers' Wages or Social Security for Mothers: An Alternative Approach to Attack Poverty" (paper presented at Brandeis University, July 23, 1968), ACLU Archives, boxes 1134–1136.
50 *Historical Statistics* (1975: 346–367).
51 U.S. Bureau of the census, *Statistical Abstracts of the United States*, Table no. 431 "Public Assistance—Expenditures, by Source of Funds, and Monthly Payments to Recipients, by Program, States and Other Areas: 1965."
52 Nick Kotz and Mary Lynn Kotz, *A Passion for Equality: George A. Wiley and the Movement* (New York: W. W. Norton & Co., 1977), p. 260.
53 For more on the impact of political protest on pushing politics to the left see Davies, *From Opportunity to Entitlement*, Chap. 6.
54 U.S. Riot Commission, *Report of the National Advisory Commission on Civil Disorders* (New York: Bantam Books, 1968), pp. 34–35, 37–38.
55 Robert Finch, "Memo to the President: Response to Arthur Burns Welfare Proposal," April 30, 1969, quoted in Burke and Burke, *Nixon's Good Deed*, p. 75.
56 Burke and Burke, *Nixon's Good Deed*, p. 77.
57 Richard Nixon, quoted in Ibid., p. 106.
58 Burke and Burke, *Nixon's Good Deed*, p. 78.
59 For more on internal discussion about the guaranteed income, see Burke and Burke, *Nixon's Good Deed*, and Moynihan, *Politics of Guaranteed Income.*
60 Burke and Burke, *Nixon's Good Deed*, p. 126 and Moynihan, *Politics of Guaranteed Income*, p. 251.

61 Gilbert Steiner, *The State of Welfare* (Washington, D.C.: Brookings Institution, 1971), p. 77.
62 Burke and Burke, *Nixon's Good Deed*, p. 127.
63 Robert Finch, "Statement Before the Senate Finance Committee on Family Assistance Act of 1970, HR16311," Hearings Before the Committee on Finance, United States Senate, 91st Congress, 2nd session, *Congressional Record*, April 29, 1970.
64 NWRO, fliers and position papers, 1969–72, Wiley Papers, boxes 17 and 18.
65 NWRO, "NWRO Position on the Nixon Welfare Plan," July 25, 1970, Wiley Papers, box 17, folder 4.
66 Marisa Chappell, "Rethinking Women's Politics in the 1970s: The League of Women's Voters and the National Organization for Women Confront Poverty," *Journal of Women's History* 13 (2002), and Mansa Chappell, The War on Welfare: Gender, Family and the Politics of AFDC in Modern America (Philadelphia: University of Pennsylvania Press, 2009).
67 Beulah Sanders, George Wiley, and Carl Rachlin, "Statement to the House Ways and Means Committee," October 27, 1969, Wiley Papers, box 17, folder 3.
68 Ibid.
69 Nixon, "Welfare Reform Message to Congress of the United States 8/11/69," in *Nixon: The First Year*.
70 Statement by George A. Wiley at the Institute for Black Elected Officials, September 13, 1969, NOW!, NWRO Newsletter, Wiley Papers, box 17, folder 3. George Wiley, Untitled Speech, 1973, Wiley Papers, box 17, folder 3.
71 NWRO, "Fact Sheet on the New Nixon Welfare Plan," no date (fall 1969?), Lehman Library.
72 Statement by George A. Wiley at the Institute for Black Elected Officials, September 13, 1969, NOW!, NWRO Newsletter, Wiley Papers, box 17, folder 3. See also Beulah Sanders, George Wiley and Carl Rachlin, "Statement to the House Ways and Means Committee," October 27, 1969, Wiley Papers, box 17, folder 3.
73 Jon Kaufman, "Memo to NWRO Research Staff," March 18, 1970, Wiley Papers, box 22, folder 4.
74 Congressman George McGovern introduced this as a bill into Congress in July 1971.
75 NWRO, fliers and position papers, 1969–72, Wiley Papers, boxes 17 and 18.
76 George Wiley, untitled document, March 16, 1971, Wiley Papers, box 17, folder 5.
77 George Wiley, Packet for Welfare Rights Leaders and Friends, September 1970 and September 1971, Wiley Papers, box 17, folder 4.
78 "Welfare Reform Called Repression of the Poor," *Greensboro Daily News*, November 15, 1970.
79 "Welfare Unit Blasts Nixon Reform Plan," *The Pittsburgh Press*, July 23, 1970, Wiley Papers, box 26, folder 2.
80 George Wiley, Packet for Welfare Rights Leaders and Friends, September 1970 and September 1971, Wiley Papers, box 17, folder 4.
81 NWRO, "The Gaps in Fap: Ways and Means Welfare Bill, HR1," November 18, 1971. MSRC.
82 NWRO, "What Your Group Can Do," May 21, 1971, MSRC.
83 Burke and Burke, *Nixon's Good Deed*, p. 173.
84 The vote was 234–187 in the House and 52–34 in the Senate.
85 His 1974 state of the union address did not even mention a basic minimum income. "Special Message to Congress on Welfare Reform," March 27, 1972 and "State of the Union Address," January 1, 1974, Richard Nixon, *Public Papers of the President, 1969–1974* (Washington D.C.: Government Printing Office, 1970–75).
86 H.R. Haldeman, *The Haldeman Diaries: Inside the Nixon White House* (New York: GP Putnam's Sons, 1994), Entry 187.

87 Johnnie Tillmon and George Wiley to Richard Nixon, August 5, 1969, Wiley Papers, box 17, folder 4.

88 Brian Jeffrey and Tom Glynn, "Notes from Meeting with John Price, Assistant to Moynihan," July 28, 1969, Wiley Papers, box 18, folder 1.

89 NWRO, Press Release, February 20, 1969, Wiley Papers, folder 7, box 11.

90 Johnnie Tillmon and George Wiley to Richard Nixon, August 5, 1969, Wiley Papers, box 17, folder 4.

91 John Montgomery (Department of HEW), "Evaluation of NWRO Demands," September 25, 1970, Wiley Papers, box 17, folder 11.

92 Elliot Richardson, "Telegram to George Wiley," November 19, 1970, Wiley Papers, box 19, folder 11.

93 Davies, *From Opportunity to Entitlement*, recounts some liberals who were influenced by NWRO.

94 National Federation of Social Service Employees, "Resolutions Adopted at the 1970 Annual Convention," Wiley Papers, box 20, folder 7. National Association of Laymen, "Convention Resolution," July 11, 1970, Wiley Papers, box 20, folder 4. Bella Abzug, "Speech to NWRO Convention in Miami Beach," July 9, 1972, Wiley Papers, box 19, folder 1.

95 Burke and Burke, *Nixon's Good Deed*, pp. 136–137, 173.

96 Henry J. Pratt, *The Gray Lobby* (Chicago: University of Chicago Press, 1976), Chap. 11.

97 Roger Sanjek, *Gray Panthers* (Philadelphia: University of Pennsylvania Press, 2009).

98 Ibid. pp. 88–89. The American Association of Retired Persons, chartered in 1958, had a membership of nine million in 1975. But the AARP was more of a service and business association than a lobbyist.

99 Ibid. pp.167–68.

100 Martin Gilens, *Why Americans Hate Welfare: Race, Media and the Politics of Antipoverty Policy* (Chicago: University of Chicago Press, 1999) makes a similar argument. He suggests that Americans are generally not opposed to government programs aiding the poor, except when recipients are considered undeserving, a perception colored by race.

101 See Richard Iton, *Solidarity Blues: Race, Culture, and the American Left* (Chapel Hill: University of North Carolina Press, 2000), Chap. 5, for influence of race on public policy.

102 For more on the relationship between liberal policy and race, see Spitzer, "The Liberal Dilemma."

103 See Joseph Pechman and Michael Timpane, eds. *Work Incentives and Income Guarantees: The New Jersey Experiment* (Washington D.C.: The Brookings Institution, 1975), Peter H. Ross and Katherine C. Lyall, *Reforming Public Welfare: A Critique of the Negative Income Tax Experiment* (New York: Russel Sage, 1976).

104 For more on the racial politics of Nixon's FAP strategy see Spitzer, "The Liberal Dilemma."

105 *Congressional Record*, April 15, 1970.

106 James Welsh, "Welfare Reform: Born Aug. 8, 1969; Died, Oct. 4, 1972: A Sad Case Study of the American Political Process," *New York Times Magazine*, January 7, 1973. Jill Quadagno, "Race, Class, and Gender in the U.S. Welfare State: Nixon's Failed Family Assistance Plan," *American Sociological Review* 55 (1990): 11–28, suggests that the work requirement in FAP was directed primarily at men. On this point I would disagree with her.

107 Russell Long, Hearings Before the Committee on Finance, United States Senate, 91st Congress, 2nd Session, *Congressional Record*, April 29, 1970.

108 Welsh, "Welfare Reform."

109 "Work and Welfare," *New Republic*, January 15, 1972.

110 *New York Times*, October 25, 1971.

6 Reckoning with Internal Tensions

1 Guida West, *The National Welfare Rights Organization: The Social Protest of Poor Women* (New York: Praeger, 1981), p. 84.
2 Minutes of NWRO Executive Committee Meeting, January 24–27, 1969, MSRC, NWRO Executive Committee with Betty Younger and Helen Williams, May 2, 1969, MSRC, Executive Committee Meeting, October 30, 1969, MSRC, "Executive Committee," December 5, 1970, MSRC.
3 George Martin, "Emergence and Development of a Social Movement Organization among the Underclass: A Case Study of the National Welfare Rights Organization," Ph.D. diss., University of Chicago, 1972, p. 94.
4 Dora Bonfanti, Letter to George Wiley, May 15, 1969, MSRC.
5 Sally Ylitalo, Letter to George Wiley, May 14, 1969, MSRC.
6 Dora Bonfanti and other recipients, Letter to Johnny Tillman, May 26, 1969, MSRC.
7 *Washington Post*, August 27, 1967.
8 George Wiley, "The Challenge of the Powerless," Speech at Consultation of Economic Power and Responsibility Meeting, March 29, 1968, Wiley Papers, box 36, folder 5.
9 *Evening Star*, August 29, 1967.
10 Hulbert James, Speech to VISTA Training Institute, Boston, 1 June 1969, Whitaker Papers, box 3, folder 4.
11 Bill Pastreich to Tim Sampson, July 26, 1969, Wiley Papers, box 25. Bill Pastreich, Speech to the Student Health Organization, June 1969, Whitaker Papers, box 3.
12 Bill Pastreich to Tim Sampson, July 26, 1969, Wiley Papers, box 25. Bill Pastreich, Speech to the Student Health Organization, June 1969, Whitaker Papers, box 3.
13 See Sara Evans, *Personal Politics: The Roots of Women's Liberation in the Civil Rights Movement and the New Left* (New York: Vintage, 1979).
14 "Log of Columbus WRO Activities," December 8, 1968, Whitaker Papers, box 2, folder 1.
15 Anonymous Welfare Recipient from Chicago, August 1969, quoted in Martin, "Emergence and Development of a Social Movement Organization Among the Underclass," p. 148.
16 The Chicago Friends of Welfare Rights Organization, "To the 'Concerned': An Invitation to Help Welfare Clients Help Themselves," May 25, 1968, MSRC.
17 Anonymous (probably Dovie Coleman), "Resignation Letter to Executive Committee," possibly February 1969, Wiley Papers, box 25, folder 1. Author unknown, "Some Facts on Chicago Welfare Unions," 1967? MSRC.
18 The Chicago Friends of Welfare Rights Organization, "To the 'Concerned': An Invitation to Help Welfare Clients Help Themselves," May 25, 1968, MSRC.
19 Anonymous (probably Dovie Coleman), "Resignation Letter to Executive Committee," possibly February 1969, Wiley Papers, box 25, folder 1.
20 Virginia WRO, "Newsheet: What's Been Happening Around the State," Early 1970, MSRC.
21 Loretta Johnson, quoted in "Proposal: Virginia WRO," December 1970, Wiley Papers, box 27, folder 3.
22 Author interview with Rhoda Linton, October 4, 2003.
23 MAW member, Speech to VISTA Training Conference, Boston, May 31, 1969, Whitaker Papers, box 3, folder 4.
24 Mary Davidson, "Interviews," October 1968, Whitaker Papers, box 3, folder 6, 4.
25 John Lewis, "Black Voices," *Washington Afro-American*, 19 August 1969, Wiley Papers, box 27.
26 Ibid.

27 Martin, "Emergence and Development of a Social Movement Organization among the Underclass," p. 99.

28 Ibid., p. 100.

29 *Record American*, August 27, 1968, in Welfare Rights Handbook, Whitaker Papers, box 3, folder 5.

30 Mary Davidson, "Interviews," October 1968, Whitaker Papers, box 3, folder 6, 3.

31 Ibid.

32 George Wiley to Michigan WRO, June 4, 1969, MSRC.

33 Members of MWRO to George Wiley, July 17, 1969, MSRC.

34 Martin, "Emergence and Development of a Social Movement Organization among the Underclass."

35 Pamela Blair, "Memo to The Executive Committee of Michigan WRO," November 11, 1969, Wiley Papers, box 25, folder 5.

36 NWRO Executive Committee Meeting, October 30, 1969, MSRC.

37 Gary Delgado, *Organizing the Movement: The Roots and Growth of the Association of Community Organizations for Reform Now (ACORN)* (Philadelphia: Temple University Press, 1986).

38 Marie Ratagick to George Wiley, possibly November 1970, Wiley Papers, box 8, folder 8.

39 Author interview with Catherine Jermany, October 11, 2003.

40 Author unknown, "Evaluation of NWRO and Affiliates" 22 December 1970, MSRC.

41 Evelyn Brooks Higginbotham, "African American Women and the Metalanguge of Race," *Signs* (Winter 1992): 251–274.

42 Robert E. Huldschiner, "Fighting Catherine Gets Welfare Mothers Together," *Lutheran Women*, October 1968, Wiley Papers, box 27, folder 7.

43 Author interview with Catherine Jermany, October 11, 2003. For more on US, see Scot Brown, "The Politics of Culture: The US Organization and the Quest for Black 'Unity,'" in *Freedom North: Black Freedom Struggles Outside the South, 1940–1980*, eds. Jeanne Theoharis and Komozi Woodard (New York: Palgrave, 2003), pp. 223–253.

44 Huldschiner, "Fighting Catherine Gets Welfare Mothers Together."

45 Ibid.

46 Los Angeles County WRO, Newsletter, November 1, 1968, Wiley Papers, box 24, folder 13.

47 Meeting Minutes of the Ohio Training Steering Committee, April 3, 1968, Whitaker Papers, box 2, folder 17.

48 Loretta Domencich, quoted in Milwaukee County Welfare Rights Organization, *Welfare Mothers Speak Out: We Ain't Gonna Shuffle Anymore*, (New York: Norton, 1972), p. 59.

49 Jennifer Ann Frost "Participatory Politics: Community Organizing, Gender, and the New Left in the 1960s," Ph.D. diss., University of Wisconsin, p. 62.

50 Ibid, p. 76.

51 Lillian Craig, with Marge Gravett, *Just a Woman: Memoirs of Lillian Craig* (Cleveland, OH: Orange Blosson Press, 1981), p. 54.

52 Ibid., p. 19.

53 Studs Terkel, *Race: How Black and Whites Think and Feel About the American Obsession* (New York: New Press, 1992), p. 55. Many of the studies of "whiteness" focus on poor white people in the South. For some examples of whites in the North, see Matt Wray and Annalee Newitz, eds., *White Trash: Race and Class in America* (New York: Routledge, 1996) and Jacqueline Jones, *The Dispossessed: America's Underclass from the Civil War to the Present* (New York: Basic Books, 1992).

54 Terkel, *Race*, p. 54.

55 For more on interracial organizing, see Rose Ernst, *The Price of Progressive Politics: The Welfare Rights Movement in an Era of Color Blind Racism* (New York: New York

University Press, 2010). In her study of the contemporary welfare rights movement she argues that women of color employ an intersectional analysis, while white women avoid discussions of race, making it hard to address the racism inherent in welfare politics. Premilla Nadasen, "'Welfare's Green Problem': Cross-Race Coalitions in Welfare Rights Organizing" in *Feminist Coalition: Historical Perspectives on Second-Wave Feminism in the United States*, ed. Stephanie Gilmore (Urbana: University of Illinois Press, 2008): 178–195.

56 Martin, "Emergence and Development of a Social Movement Organization among the Underclass," p. 98.

57 Rosie Hudson, quoted in Milwaukee Country WRO (1972: 81).

58 Author interview with Moiece Palladino, April 27, 1997.

59 Author interview with Catherine Jermany, October 11, 2003.

60 Hobart A. Burch, "Insights of a Welfare Mother: A Conversation with Johnnie Tillmon," *The Journal* (Jan.–Feb. 1971): 13–23, Wiley Papers [27].Tillmon actively recruited white recipients and wanted to dispel the myth that most recipients were black. When some members dressed up in African garb for a press conference, she urged them to change. *New York Times*, July 9, 1995. For more on Tillmon and her particular philosophy of Black Power and interracialism, see Premilla Nadasen, "We Do Whatever Becomes Necessary: Johnnie Tillmon, Welfare Rights. and Black Power" in *Want to Start a Revolution?: Women in the Black Revolt,* eds. Jeanne Theoharis, Dayo Gore, and Komozi Woodard (New York University Press, 2009), pp. 317–338.

61 Johnnie Tillmon Speech, United Presbyterian Women National Meeting, 1970.

62 Roxanne Jones, PWRO, "Report of the Chairman" in Straight Talk Newsletter, June 11, 1969, MSRC.

63 Kansas WRO, "A Proposal to Help Ghetto Families Help Themselves," January 12, 1970, MSRC.

64 Rudell Martin quoted in Rhonda Y. Williams, "Living Just Enough in the City: Change and Activism in Baltimore's Public Housing, 1940–1980," Ph.D. diss., University of Pennsylvania, 1998. p. 283.

65 Terkel, *Race*, p. 55.

66 Catherine Jermany, "Testimony Presented by Catherine Jermany Before the Annual Conference of State Welfare Finance Officers," September 24, 1969, MSRC.

67 For more on racial stereotypes and welfare policy see Sue K. Jewell, *From Mammy to Miss American and Beyond: Cultural Images and the Shaping of US Social Policy* (New York: Routledge, 1993), Martin Gilens, *Why Americans Hate Welfare: Race, Media and the Politics of Antipoverty Policy* (Chicago: University of Chicago Press, 1999) and Kenneth Neubeck and Noel A. Cazenave, *Welfare Racism: Playing the Race Card Against America's Poor* (New York: Routledge, 2001).

68 Emilye J. Crosby, "'This nonviolent stuff ain't no Good. It'll get ya killed': Teaching About Self-Defense in the African American Freedom Struggle," in *Teaching the American Civil Rights Movement: Freedom's Bittersweet Song*, eds. Julie B. Armstrong, Susan H. Edwards, Houstan B. Roberson, and Rhonda Y. Williams (New York: Routledge, 2002): 159–169.

7 Resisting External Backlash

1 Guida West, *The National Welfare Rights Organization: The Social Protest of Poor Women* (New York: Praeger, 1981), p. 50.

2 www.allcountry.ed/Songbook/Texte_W/Welfare_Cadillac/body_welfare_cadillac. html.

3 Rickie Solinger, *Beggars and Choosers: How the Politics of Choice Shapes Adoption, Abortion, and Welfare in the United States* (New York: Hill and Wang, 2001).

4 Doris Lurie, Letter to the Editor, *New York Times*, April 1, 1971.

5 As a result of special-grant protests in Massachusetts, the furniture guidelines, explaining recipients' entitlements, were publicized and caused some anger. See *Boston Globe*, September 9, 1968, in Welfare Rights Booklet, Whitaker Papers, box 3, folder 5.

6 Table no. 571. "Unemployed and Unemployment Insurance—Summary: 1960–75," US Bureau of the Census, *Statistical Abstracts of the United States* (1975).

7 Table no. 679. "Percent Change Per Year in Selected Price Indexes: 1961–74," US Bureau of the Census, *Statistical Abstracts of the United States* (1975).

8 Bruce Schulman, *The Seventies: The Great Shift in American Culture, Society and Politics* (Cambridge: Da Capo Press, 2001).

9 Mrs. Anna Marie Mullen to Phillip E. George (Director, Blair County WRO), June 28, 1972, Wiley Papers, box 27, folder 1.

10 www.ntu.org.

11 Roger A. Freeman, "Wayward Ambitions of the Welfare State," *New York Times*, December 4, 1971, 31. Quoted in Marisa Chappell, "Rethinking Women's Politics in the 1970s: The League of Women's Voters and the National Organization for Women Confront Poverty," *Journal of Women's History* 13 (2002): 180.

12 Public Aid includes AFDC, Medicaid, Old Age Assistance, Aid to the Disabled and Supplemental Security Income. Social Insurance includes Social Security, Medicare, Unemployment Insurance, Workers' Compensation, Disability Insurance. Table no. 446. "Social Welfare Expenditures Under Public Programs: 1950–74," US Bureau of the Census, *Statistical Abstracts of the United States* (1975: 280).

13 George Gallup, *The Gallup Poll, 1959–1971* (Wilmington, DE: Scholarly Resources, 1972).

14 John Williamson, "Beliefs about the Welfare Poor," *Sociology and Social Research* 58 (1973): 163–175.

15 Martin Gilens, *Why Americans Hate Welfare: Race, Media and the Politics of Antipoverty Policy* (Chicago: University of Chicago Press, 1999), pp. 122–123. For extended discussion, see Chap. 5 of Gilens. Gerald C. Wright, "Racism and Welfare Policy in America," *Social Science Quarterly* 57 (1976): 718–730.

16 Kenneth Neubeck and Noel A. Cazenave, *Welfare Racism: Playing the Race Card against America's Poor* (New York: Routledge, 2001), Chap. 5.

17 "Welfare Fraud: The Backlash," *Newsweek*, January 31, 1972.

18 Susan Sheehan, "A Welfare Mother," *The New Yorker*, 29 September 1975: 42–99.

19 *Review Journal*, March 15, 1971, Wiley Papers, box 32, folder 1. Also see Annelise Orleck, "If it Wasn't For You I'd Have Shoes for My Children": The Political Education of Las Vegas Welfare Mothers," in *The Politics of Motherhood: Activist Voices from Left to Right*, eds. Alexis Jetter, Annelise Orleck, and Diana Taylor (Hanover: Dartmouth College, 1997), p. 109.

20 Annelise Orleck, *Storming Caesar's Palace: How Black Mothers Fought Their Own War on Poverty* (Boston: Beacon Press, 2005).

21 Ruby Duncan, "'I Got to Dreamin': An Interview with Ruby Duncan, conducted by Annelise Orleck. in *The Politics of Motherhood*, eds. Jetter et al., pp. 119–126.

22 Ibid.

23 "Staff Retreat," NWRO report, January 29–31, 1971, Wiley Papers, box 8, folder 1.

24 James Evans to George Wiley, March 24, 1971, Wiley Papers, box 8, folder 8.

25 "Staff Retreat," NWRO report, January 29–31, 1971, Wiley Papers, box 8, folder 1.

26 NCC Meeting, Las Vegas, Nevada, February 1971, MSRC.

27 Author interview with Moiece Palladino, April 27, 1997.

28 *The Las Vegas Voice*, February 11, 1971, v. 8 (22) Wiley Papers, box 32, folder 1.

29 NWRO, News Release, February 21, 1971, Wiley Papers, box 32, folder 1.
30 *Washington Post*, March 7, 1971, Wiley Papers, box 32, folder 1. Also see Orleck, "If it Wasn't For You," p. 109.
31 *Los Angeles Times*, March 14, 1971, Wiley Papers, box 32, folder 1. *Las Vegas Sun*, March 14, 1971, Wiley Papers, box 32, folder 1. *Las Vegas Sun*, March 13, 1971, Wiley Papers, box 32, folder 1.
32 *Las Vegas Sun*, March 20, 1971, Wiley Papers, box 31, folder 1. *New York Times*, March 21, 1971, Wiley Papers, box 32, folder 1.
33 Frances Fox Piven and Richard Cloward, *Regulating the Poor: The Functions of Public Welfare* (New York: Pantheon Books, 1971), pp. 373–381.
34 *Las Vegas Sun*, March 16, 1971 and *Las Vegas Sun*, March 18, 1971, Wiley Papers, box 32, folder 1.
35 "Romney," Summary of Staff Retreat, 1970, Wiley Papers, box 8, folder 1.
36 George Martin, "Emergence and Development of a Social Movement Organization among the Underclass: A Case Study of the National Welfare Rights Organization," Ph.D. diss., University of Chicago, 1972, p. 128.
37 Brooklyn Welfare Action Committee, flier, no date, Wiley Papers, box 26, folder 4. Citywide Coordinating Committee of Welfare Rights Groups, flier, no date, Wiley Papers, box 26, folder 4. Unemployed Workers Union, flier, possibly early 1971, Wiley Papers, box 27, folder 2.
38 Hulbert James, Speech to VISTA Training Institute, Boston, June 1, 1969, Whitaker Papers, box 3, folder 4.
39 Bill Pastreich to Tim Sampson, July 26, 1969, Wiley Papers, box 25, folder 3.
40 Frances Fox Piven and Richard Cloward, quoted in Michael C. C. Macdonald, "Organizing for Welfare: Knock on any Door," *The Village Voice*, 4 September 1969 [18–35], Wiley Papers, box 25, folder 3.
41 Macdonald, "Organizing for Welfare."
42 Ibid.
43 Massachusetts Wage Supplement Organization, flier, after August 6, 1969, Wiley Papers, box 25, folder 3.
44 Hulbert James, Speech to VISTA Training Institute, Boston, June 1, 1969, Whitaker Papers, box 3, folder 4.
45 Macdonald, "Organizing for Welfare."
46 For more on black popular culture see William Van Deburg, *New Day in Babylon: The Black Power Movement and American Culture, 1965–1975* (Chicago: University of Chicago Press, 1992).
47 Martin, "Emergence and Development of a Social Movement Organization among the Underclass," p. 132.
48 Milwaukee County Welfare Rights Organization, *Welfare Mothers Speak Out: We Ain't Gonna Shuffle Anymore*, (New York: Norton, 1972), p. 77.
49 Martin, "Emergence and Development of a Social Movement Organization among the Underclass," p. 132.
50 George Wiley, "Memorandum to WRO Leaders, Staff, and Friends Re: Children's March for Survival," April 12, 1972, Wiley Papers, box 15, folder 5.
51 Bert DeLeeuw, "Memo to NWRO Department Heads, Re: Draft for Internal Use Only of Proposed NWRO Spring Campaign," January 22, 1972, Wiley Papers, box 15, folder 5.
52 George Wiley, "Memorandum to WRO Leaders, Staff, and Friends Re: Children's March for Survival," April 12, 1972, Wiley Papers, box 15, folder 5.
53 Bert DeLeeuw, "Memo to NWRO Department Heads, Re: Draft for Internal Use Only of Proposed NWRO Spring Campaign," January 22, 1972, Wiley Papers, box 15, folder 5.
54 *New York Times*, March 26, 1972, p. 20.
55 Ibid., p. 42.

56 See William J. Wilson, *The Truly Disadvantaged: The Inner City, The Underclass, and Public Policy* (Chicago: University of Chicago Press, 1987), Jill Quadagno, *The Color of Welfare: How Racism Undermined the War on Poverty* (New York: Oxford University Press, 1994).

57 Miriam Cohen and Michael Hanagan, "The Politics of Gender and the Making of the Welfare State, 1900–1940: A Comparative Perspective," *Journal of Social History* 24 (1991): 469–484, argue that programs relying on women's role as childbearer were appealing.

58 Andrea Jule Sachs, "The Politics of Poverty: Race, Class, Motherhood, and the National Welfare Rights Organization, 1965–75." Ph.D. diss., University of Minnesota, 2001, Chap. 6.

8 A Radical Black Feminist Movement

1 Tracye Matthews, "'No One Ever Asks What a Man's Place in the Revolution Is': Gender and the Politics of the Black Panther Party, 1966–1971," in *The Black Panther Party Reconsidered*, ed. Charles P. Jones (Baltimore, MD: Black Classic Press, 1998). Robyn Ceanne Spencer, "Engendering the Black Freedom Struggle: Revolutionary Black Womanhood and the Black Panther Party in the Bay Area, California," *Journal of Women's History* 20, 1 (Spring 2008): 90–113.

2 Author interview with Tim Sampson, April 21, 1997.

3 "Report of Program Services Task Force," August 22, 1972, Wiley Papers, box 14. "Romney: Staff Meeting and Training Conference," probably 1970, Wiley Papers. "Staff Retreat," January 1971, Wiley Papers.

4 Johnnie Tillmon, Interview with Guida West, quoted in Guida West, *The National Welfare Rights Organization: The Social Protest of Poor Women* (New York: Praeger, 1981), p. 101.

5 Marisa Chappell, "From Welfare Rights to Welfare Reform: The Politics of AFDC, 1964–1984," Ph.D. diss., Northwestern University, 2002, Chap. 3, explains this development to address broader issues of economic justice as one that characterized the left more generally in the 1970s.

6 Gary Delgado, *Organizing the Movement: The Roots and Growth of the Association of Community Organizations for Reform Now (ACORN)* (Philadelphia: Temple University Press, 1986), pp. 112–13.

7 Johnnie Tillmon, "Memorandum to the Executive Board," December 8, 1972, Wiley Papers, box 36, folder 6.

8 "NWRO 1973 Convention Report," July 1973, Welfare Rights Collection, Lehman Library.

9 Johnnie Tillmon, "Memorandum to the Executive Board," December 8, 1972, Wiley Papers, box 36, folder 6.

10 NWRO Press Release 18 July 1974 MSRC.

11 NWRO Press Release, "Women's Rights To Be a Major Topic at NWRO Convention," July 9, 1973, MSRC.

12 "Strategies for Survival," NWRO pamphlet, 1973, Wiley Papers, box 7.

13 West, *The National Welfare Rights Organization*, p. 49.

14 Linda Gordon, *Woman's Body, Woman's Right: Birth Control in America* (New York: Penguin, 1974).

15 Johnnie Tillmon, "Welfare is a Woman's Issue," *Ms. Magazine* 1 (1972): 111–116.

16 Chicago Welfare Rights Organization, Handbook, June 1968, Whitaker Papers, box 3. Mothers for Adequate Welfare, "Your Welfare Rights Manual," undated, Whitaker Papers, box 3.

17 Olive Franklin, Chair of the St. Louis City-Wide WRO, "Letter to Johnnie Tillmon," September 13, 1972, MSRC.

18 Dorothy Roberts, *Killing the Black Body: Race, Reproduction, and the Meaning of Liberty* (New York: Pantheon Books, 1997), Chap. 2 and Gordon, *Woman's Body, Woman's Right*, Chap. 14.

19 Betsy Hartmann, *Reproductive Rights and Wrongs: The Global Politics of Population Control and Contraceptive Choice* (New York: Harper & Row, 1995), p. 255.

20 This was known as the Relf case. Rosalind Petchesky, "Reproductive Ethics and Public Policy" (Hastings Center Report, October 1979), quoted in Hartmann, *Reproductive Rights and Wrongs*, p. 255.

21 Thomas Shapiro, *Population Control Politics: Women, Sterilization and Reproductive Choice* (Philadelphia: Temple University Press, 1985), pp. 103–104.

22 *Family Planning Digest* (1972), quoted in Ibid. p. 124.

23 Phillips Cutright and Fredrick Jaffe, *The Impact of Family Planning Programs on Fertility: The U.S. Experience* (New York: Praeger, 1976).

24 Toni Cade, "The Pill: Genocide or Liberation," in *The Black Woman: An Anthology*, ed. Toni Cade Bambara (New York: New American Library, 1970), pp. 162–169.

25 M. Rivka Polatnick, "Diversity in Women's Liberation Ideology: How a Black and a White Group of the 1960s Viewed Motherhood," *Signs* 21(1996): 679–706.

26 Black Women's Liberation Group, Mount Vernon, New York, "Statement on Birth Control," in *Sisterhood is Powerful: An Anthology of Writings from the Women's Liberation Movement*, ed. Robin Morgan (New York: Random House. 1970), 360–361.

27 Tillmon, "Welfare is a Woman's Issue."

28 NWRO, "Forced Sterilization: Threat to Poor," *The Welfare Fighter*, 4 (February 1974), MSRC.

29 Rickie Solinger, *Beggars and Choosers: How the Politics of Choice Shapes Adoption, Abortion, and Welfare in the United States* (New York: Hill and Wang, 2001), Chap. 5.

30 Anne Valk, "Mother Power: The Movement for Welfare Rights in Washington, D.C., 1966–1972," *Journal of Women's History* 11 (2000): 41–42.

31 For more on women and Black Power politics in this period, see, for example, Rhonda Williams, "We're tired of being treated like dogs': Poor Women and Power Politics in Black Baltimore," *Black Scholar* 31(3–4) (2001): 31–41, Matthews, "No One Ever Asks What a Man's Place in the Revolution is", Spencer, "Engendering the Black Freedom Struggle," Rhonda Y. Williams, "Black Women, Urban Politics and Engendering Black Power" in *The Black Power Movement: Rethinking the Civil Rights-Black Power Era*, ed. Paniel Joseph (New York: Routledge, 2006), pp. 79–103, Kimberley Springer, "Black Feminists Respond to Black Power Masculinism," in *The Black Power Movement*, ed. Joseph, pp. 105–118, Stephan Ward, "The Third World Women's Alliance," in *The Black Power Movement*, ed. Joseph, pp. 119–144, Dayo F. Gore, Jeanne Theoharis, and Komozi Woodard, eds., *Want to Start a Revolution: Radical Women in the Black Freedom Struggle* (New York: New York University Press, 2009), Bettye Collier-Thomas and V.P. Franklin, eds., *Sisters in the Struggle: African American Women in the Civil Rights-Black Power Movement* (New York: New York University Press, 2001).

32 Tillmon, "Welfare is a Woman's Issue."

33 Ibid.

34 Jennette Washington, "I Challenge," published article, source unknown, date unknown, Wiley Papers, box 28.

35 West, *The National Welfare Rights Organization*, pp. 28–30.

36 Ibid.

37 George Wiley, "Letter to Welfare Rights Leaders, Members, Friends, and Supporters, Re: Resignation," December 15, 1972, Wiley Papers, box 36, folder 6.

38 NCC, "General Session," October 1972, MSRC.

39 Bert N. Mitchell to George Wiley, September 2, 1971, Wiley Papers, box 9, folder 4.

40 MAW Member, Speech to VISTA Training Conference, Boston, May 31, 1969, Whitaker Papers, box 3, folder 4.

41 Taped interview 151. Quoted in West, *The National Welfare Rights Organization*, p. 35.

42 Personnel Committee, "Recommendations to the N.W.R.O. Executive Board," no date, Wiley Papers. "Executive Directors Report," May 17, 1972, Wiley Papers.

43 West, *The National Welfare Rights Organization*, p. 36.

44 NWRO Press Release, July 18, 1974, MSRC.

45 NWRO, Welfare Fighter, 4 (February 1974) MSRC, NWRO Press Release, July 18, 1974, MSRC.

46 Washington, D.C. Government, "Letter to NWRO," Wiley Papers, box 9, folder 10. Johnnie Tillmon and Faith Evans, "Letter to all WRO's and Friends from Tillmon and Evans," July 1973, Wiley Papers, box 9, folder 10.

47 West, *The National Welfare Rights Organization*, p. 36.

48 Johnnie Tillmon and Faith Evans, "Memo to All WRO's and Friends," August 16, 1973, MSRC.

49 Author interview with Rhoda Linton, October 4, 2003.

50 Rhonda Y. Williams, "Living Just Enough in the City: Change and Activism in Baltimore's Public Housing, 1940–1980," Ph.D. diss., University of Pennsylvania, 1998, Chap. 7.

51 Bill Vincent, "Operation Life Has Brought Hope," *The Nevadan*, January 28, 1973, Wiley Papers, box 25, folder 6. See also Annalise Orleck, "'If it Wasn't for You I'd Have Shoes for My Children': The Political Education of Las Vegas Welfare Mothers," in *The Politics of Motherhood: Activist Voices From Left to Right*, eds. Alexis Jetter, Annelise Orleck, and Diana Taylor (Hanover: Dartmouth College, 1997), p. 109; Annelise Orleck, *Storming Caesar's Palace: How Black Mothers Fought Their Own War on Poverty* (Boston: Beacon Press, 2005).

52 Annelise Orleck interviews with Renee Diamond, September 5, 1992 and December 9, 1994, quoted in Orleck, "If it Wasn't for You," p. 114.

53 Richard Couto, "Mud Creek, Kentucky: Sick for Clinics," *Southern Exposure* 6(1978): 76–79.

54 Author interview with Ethel Dotson, April 27, 1997.

55 Author interview with Moiece Palladino, April 27, 1997.

56 Orleck, "If It Wasn't for You," p. 115 looks at the evolution in political consciousness of welfare rights activists.

57 Premilla Nadasen, "'We Do Whatever Becomes Necessary': Johnnie Tillmon, Welfare Rights, and Black Power," in *Want to Start a Revolution? Radical Women in the Black Freedom Struggle*, eds. Dayo F. Gore, Jeanne Theoharis, and Komozi Woodard (New York: New York University Press, 2009), pp. 317–338.

58 *New York Times*, July 9, 1995 and *New York Times*, November 21, 1995.

Conclusion

1   Mimi Abramovitz, *Regulating the Lives of Women: Social Welfare Policy From the Colonial Times to the Present* (Boston: South End Press, 1988), Frances Fox Piven and Richard Cloward, *Regulating the Poor: The Functions of Public Welfare* (New York: Pantheon Books, 1971), Seth Koven and Sonya Michel, eds. *Mothers of a New World: Maternalist Politics and the Origins of the Welfare States* (New York: Routledge, 1993), Linda Gordon, *Pitied but not Entitled: Single Mothers and the History of Welfare* (New York: Free Press, 1994), Michael Katz, *In the Shadow of the Poorhouse: A Social History of Welfare in America* (New York: Basic Books, 1986), James T. Patterson, *America's Struggle Against Poverty, 1900–1980* (Cambridge: Harvard University Press, 1981),

Theda Skocpol, *Protecting Soldiers and Mothers: The Origins of Social Policy in the United States* (Cambridge: Harvard University Press, 1992), Gwendolyn Mink, *The Wages of Motherhood: Inequality in the Welfare State, 1917–1942* (Ithaca: Cornell University Press, 1995), Mimi Abramovitz, *Under Attack, Fighting Back: Women and Welfare in the US* (New York: Monthly Review, 1995) details a history of organizing within the welfare system in Part 4 of her overview of the welfare system.

2   See, for example, Robert Weisbrot, *Freedom Bound: A History of the Civil Rights Movement* (New York: W.W. Norton, 1990), Juan Williams, *Eyes on the Prize: America's Civil Rights Years, 1954–1965* (New York: Penguin, 1987), Harvard Sitkoff, *Struggle for Black Equality, 1954–1980* (New York: Hill and Wang, 1981), John Dittmer, *Local People: The Struggle for Civil Rights in Mississippi* (Urbana: University of Illinois Press, 1994), Allan Matusow, *The Unraveling of America: A History of Liberalism in the 1960s* (New York: Harper & Row, 1984), Clay Carson, *In Struggle: SNCC and the Black Awakening of the 1960s* (Cambridge: Harvard University Press, 1981). There is much important scholarship that has already challenged this narrative. Jeanne Theoharis and Komozi Woodard, eds., *Freedom North: Black Freedom Struggles Outside the South, 1940–1980* (New York: Palgrave, 2003), Martha Biondi, *To Stand and Fight: The Struggle for African American Rights in Postwar New York City* (Cambridge: Harvard University Press, 2003), Robert Self, *American Babylon: Class, Race, and Power in Oakland and the East Bay, 1945–1978* (Princeton: Princeton University Press, 2003), Matthew J. Countryman, *Up South: Civil Rights and Black Power in Philadelphia* (Philadelphia: University of Pennsylvania Press, 2005), Thomas Sugrue, *Sweet Land of Liberty: The Forgotten Struggle for Civil Rights in the North* (New York: Random House, 2008).

3   See Timothy Tyson, *Radio Free Dixie: Robert F. Williams and the Roots of Black Power* (Chapel Hill: University of North Carolina Press, 1999), Charles Payne, *I've Got the Light of Freedom: The Organizing Tradition and the Mississippi Freedom Struggle* (Berkeley: University of California Press, 1995), Clay Carson, *In Struggle: SNCC and the Black Awakening of the 1960s* (Cambridge: Harvard University Press, 1981).

4   See Payne, *I've Got the Light of Freedom*, and Chana Kai Lee, *For Freedom's Sake: The Life of Fannie Lou Hamer* (Urbana: University of Illinois Press, 1999).

5   This is probably true of other radical movements of the late 1960s as well. Biondi, *To Stand and Fight*, in her study of the civil rights movement in New York City, and Self, *American Babylon*, in his work on Oakland, both look at the roots of northern movements and suggest these were not simply outgrowths of the southern struggle.

6   See Gareth Davies, *From Opportunity to Entitlement: The Transformation and Decline of Great Society Liberalism* (Lawrence: University Press of Kansas, 1996), Thomas Byrne Edsall and Mary Edsall, *Chain Reaction: The Impact of Race, Rights and Taxes on American Politics* (New York: W.W. Norton, 1992).

7   For the standard interpretation of the decline of liberalism see Allan Matusow, *The Unraveling of America: A History of Liberalism in the 1960s* (New York: Harper & Row, 1984). See also Edsall and Edsall, *Chain Reaction*, Weisbrot, *Freedom Bound*, and Jill Quadagno, *The Color of Welfare: How Racism Undermined the War on Poverty* (New York: Oxford University Press, 1994).

8   Rand E. Rosenblatt, "Social Duties and the Problem of Rights in the American Welfare State," in *The Politics of Law: A Progressive Critique*, ed. David Kairys (New York: Pantheon Books, 1982), pp. 90–114.

9   Felicia Kornbluh, "A Right to Welfare? Poor Women, Professionals, and Poverty Programs, 1935–1975," Ph.D. diss., Princeton University, 2000, makes a persuasive case for the way in which NWRO made a claim for credit as a right of American citizenship and how this emphasis on consumerism departed from traditional work-oriented strategies.

10 See Antonio Gramsci, *Selections from the Prison Notebooks* (New York: International Publishers, 1971), Gayatri Spivak, "Can the Subaltern Speak?" in *Marxism and the Interpretation of Culture*, eds. Cary Nelson and Lawrence Grossberg (Chicago: University of Illinois Press, 1988), pp. 271–313.

11 Tera Hunter, *To 'Joy My Freedom: Southern Black Women's Lives and Labors After the Civil War* (Cambridge: Harvard University Press, 1997), Patricia Hill Collins, *Black Feminist Thought: Knowledge, Consciousness, and the Politics of Empowerment* (New York: Routledge, 1990), Herbert Gutman, *The Black Family in Slavery and Freedom* (New York: Vintage Books, 1976), Jacqueline Jones, *Labor of Love, Labor of Sorrow: Black Women, Work, and the Family from Slavery to the Present* (New York: Vintage Books, 1985).

12 Jones, *Labor of Love, Labor of Sorrow*, Eileen Boris, "The Power of Motherhood: Black and White Activist Women Redefine the Political," in *Mothers of a New World: Maternalist Politics and the Origins of the Welfare States*, ed. Seth Koven and Sonya Michel (New York: Routledge, 1993), pp. 213–245.

13 See Edward Said, *Representations of the Intellectual: The Reith Lectures* (New York: Pantheon, 1994).

14 Deborah King, "Multiple Jeopardy, Multiple Consciousness: The Context of a Black Feminist Ideology," *Signs* 14 (1988): 42–72, Evelyn Brooks Higginbotham, "African-American Women's History and the Metalanguage of Race," *Signs* 17 (1992): 254.

15 See Marisa Chappell, *The War on Welfare: Gender, Family and the Politics of AFDC in Modern America* (Philadelphia: University of Pennsylvania Press, 2009), Martha Davis, "Welfare Rights and Women's Rights in the 1960s," *Journal of Policy History* 8 (1996): 144–165.

16 "Women in Poverty," Statement Adopted by the NOW Executive Committee, November 29, 1970, Wiley Papers, box 21.

17 See Johnnie Tillmon, Interview with Guida West, quoted in Guida West, *The National Welfare Rights Organization: The Social Protest of Poor Women* (New York: Praeger, 1981), Chap. 5.

18 Collins, *Black Feminist Thought*, 69–70.

19 See, for example, Quadagno, *The Color of Welfare*, Edsall and Edsall, *Chain Reaction*.

20 See Yvonne Zylan, "The Divided Female State: Gender, Citizenship and US Social Policy Development, 1945–1990," Ph.D. diss., New York University, 1994, Abramovitz, *Regulating the Lives of Women*, Richard Iton, *Solidarity Blues: Race, Culture, and the American Left* (Chapel Hill: University of North Carolina Press, 2000) also argues that the "white backlash" predated the CRM. For other roots of white hostility, see Thomas Sugrue, *The Origins of the Urban Crisis: Race and Inequality in Postwar Detroit* (Princeton, NJ: Princeton University Press, 1996).

21 Kenneth Neubeck and Noel A. Cazenave, *Welfare Racism: Playing the Race Card Against America's Poor* (New York: Routledge, 2001), Chap. 5.

22 For a discussion of domestic violence and welfare reform, see Dana-Ain Davis, *Battered Black Women and Welfare Reform: Between a Rock and a Hard Place* (Albany: State University of New York Press, 2006).

23 For a discussion of stereotypes associated with welfare, see Ange-Marie Hancock, *The Politics of Disgust: The Public Identity of the Welfare Queen* (New York: New York University Press, 2004), Neubeck and Cazenave, *Welfare Racism*, Martin Gilens, *Why Americans Hate Welfare: Race, Media and The Politics of Antipoverty Policy* (Chicago: University of Chicago Press, 1999), Sue K. Jewell, *From Mammy to Miss American and Beyond: Cultural Images and the Shaping of US Social Policy* (New York: Routledge, 1993), Vanessa Sheared, *Race, Gender, and Welfare Reform: The Elusive Quest for Self-Determination* (New York: Garland Publishing, 1998).

24 For impact of welfare reform see Alejandra Marchevsky and Jeanne Theoharis, *Not Working: Latina Immigrant, Low-Wage Jobs, and the Failure of Welfare Reform* (New York: New York University Press, 2006).

25 David Zucchino, *Myth of the Welfare Queen* (New York: Simon & Schuster, 1997).

REFERENCES

Primary Sources

Manuscript Collections

American Civil Liberties Union National Archives. Mudd Library, Princeton University.
Highlander Research and Education Center Collection. State Historical Society of Wisconsin.
Johnson, Lyndon Baines. Presidential Papers. Lyndon B. Johnson Library, Austin.
Mobilization for Youth. Papers. Rare Book and Manuscript Library. Columbia University.
National Welfare Rights Organization. Papers. Moorland-Spingarn Research Center. Howard University.
Welfare Rights Collection. Lehman Library, Columbia University.
Whitaker, William Howard. Papers. Ohio Historical Society, Columbus.
Wiley, George Alvin. Papers. State Historical Society of Wisconsin.

Periodicals and Newspapers

Atlantic Monthly
Berkshire Eagle
Business Week
Congressional Record
The Nation
Nation's Business
New Republic
New York Amsterdam News
New York Daily News
New York Times
New Yorker
Newsweek

NOW!
Time
Saturday Evening Post
U.S. New and World Report
Washington Daily News
Washington Post
Welfare Fighter

Publications

Ezra Birnbaum and Mary Rabagliati. 1969. Organizations of Welfare Clients. In *Community Development in the MFY Experience*, ed. Harold H. Weissman,102–136. New York: Association Press.

Brumm, Gordon. 1968. Mothers for Adequate Welfare—AFDC from the Underside. In *Dialogues Boston*, January, 1–12, Whitaker Papers, box 3, folder 3.

Burch, Hobart A. 1970. A Conversation with George Wiley. *The Journal* (Nov.–Dec.): 2–12, Wiley Papers 27.

Burch, Hobart A. 1971. Insights of a Welfare Mother: A Conversation with Johnnie Tillmon. *The Journal* (Jan.–Feb.): 13–23, Wiley Papers 27.

Craig, Lillian with Marge Gravett. 1981. *Just a Woman: Memoirs of Lillian Craig*. Cleveland, OH: Orange Blosson Press.

Gallup, George. 1972. *The Gallup Poll, 1959–1971*. Wilmington, DE: Scholarly Resources.

Grove, Robert and Alice Hetzel. 1968. *Vital Statistics Rates in the United States, 1940–1960*, Washington D.C.: U.S. Department of Health, Education and Welfare.

Haldeman, H.R. 1994. *The Haldeman Diaries: Inside the Nixon White House*. New York: G.P. Putnam's Sons.

Huldschiner, Robert E. 1968. Fighting Catherine Gets Welfare Mothers Together. *Lutheran Women*, October Wiley Papers, box 27, folder 7.

Johnson, Lyndon. 1968. *Public Papers of the Presidents of the United States*. Washington: GPO.

Lewis, John. 1968. Black Voices. *Washington Afro-American*, September 14. Wiley Papers, box 27.

Macdonald, Michael C.C. 1969. Organizing for Welfare: Knock on any Door. *The Village Voice*, September 4, 18–35, Wiley Papers, box 25, folder 3.

Milwaukee County Welfare Rights Organization. 1972. *Welfare Mothers Speak Out: We Ain't Gonna Shuffle Anymore*. New York: Norton.

Moynihan, Daniel Patrick. 1965. *The Negro Family: A Case for National Action*. Washington, D.C.: Office of Policy Planning and Research, U.S. Dept. of Labor.

Nixon, Richard. 1970. *Setting the Course, The First Year: Major Policy Statements by President Richard Nixon*. New York: Funk and Wagnalls.

Nixon, Richard. 1970 *Nixon: The First Year of His Presidency*. Washington, D.C.: Congressional Quarterly.

Nixon, Richard. 1970–1975. *Richard Nixon: Public Papers of the President, 1969–1974*. Washington D.C.: Government Printing Office.

Tillmon, Johnnie. 1972. Welfare is a Woman's Issue. *Ms. Magazine* 1: 111–116.

U.S. Bureau of the Census. 1967. *County and City Data Book, 1962: A Statistical Abstract Supplement*. Washington, D.C.: Government Printing Office.

U.S. Bureau of the Census. 1970. *Statistical Abstracts of the United States*. Washington, D.C.: Government Printing Office.

U.S. Bureau of the Census. 1975. *Historical Statistics of the United States: Colonial Times to 1970.* Washington, D.C.: Government Printing Press.

U.S. Commission on Civil Rights. 1966. *Children in Need: A Study of a Federally Assisted Program of Aid to Needy Families with Children in Cleveland and Cuyahoga County, Ohio.* Washington, D.C.: Government Printing Office.

U.S. Riot Commission. 1968. *Report of the National Advisory Commission on Civil Disorders.* New York: Bantam Books.

Weissman, Harold H., ed. 1969. *Community Development in the Mobilization for Youth Experience.* New York: Association Press.

Weissman, Harold H., ed. 1969. *Individual and Group Services in the Mobilization for Youth Experience.* New York: Association Press.

Oral Sources

Interviews by Author

Marjorie Caesar, March 4, 1996

Tim Sampson, April 21, 1997

Ethel Dotson, April 27, 1997

Moiece Palladino, April 27, 1997

Frances Fox Piven, June 19, 1997

Richard Cloward, June 19, 1997

Rhoda Linton, October 4, 2003

Jon Van Til, October 6, 2003

Frank Espada, October 9, 2003

Catherine Jermany, October 11, 2003

Interviews by Sherna Berger Gluck

Johnnie Tillmon, 1991, The Virtual Oral/Aural History Archive, University of Southern California.

Interviews by Guida West

Hulbert James, February 6, 1981, New York, NY

Jeanette Washington, September 25, 1981, New York, NY

Beulah Sanders, July 7, 1983, New York, NY

Secondary Sources

Books

Abramovitz, Mimi. 1989. *Regulating the Lives of Women: Social Welfare Policy from the Colonial Times to the Present.* Boston: South End Press.

Abramovitz, Mimi. 1995. *Under Attack, Fighting Back: Women and Welfare in the US.* New York: Monthly Review, Press.

Bailis, Lawrence. 1972. *Bread or Justice: Grassroots Organizing in the Welfare Rights Movement.* Lexington, MA: Lexington Books.

Bell, Daniel. 1956. *Work and Its Discontents*. Boston: Beacon Press.

Bell, Winifred. 1965. *Aid to Dependent Children*. New York: Columbia University Press.

Biondi, Martha. 2003. *To Stand and Fight: The Struggle for African American Rights in Postwar New York City*. Cambridge: Harvard University Press.

Boyle, Kevin. 1995. *The UAW and the Heyday of American Liberalism 1945–1968*. Ithaca: Cornell University Press.

Bremner, Robert. 1956. *From the Depths: The Discovery of Poverty in the U.S.* New York: New York University Press.

Burke, Vincent J. and Vee Burke. 1974. *Nixon's Good Deed: Welfare Reform*. New York: Columbia University Press.

Carson, Clay. 1981. *In Struggle: SNCC and the Black Awakening of the 1960s*. Cambridge: Harvard University Press.

Chappell, Marisa. 2009. *The War on Welfare: Gender, Family and the Politics of AFDC in Modern America*. Philadelphia: University of Pennsylvania Press.

Clark, Kenneth. 1965. *Dark Ghetto: Dilemmas of Social Power*. New York: Harper and Row.

Clark-Lewis, Elizabeth. 1994. *Living In, Living Out: African American Domestics in Washington, D.C., 1910–1940*. Washington: Smithsonian Institution Press.

Collier-Thomas, Bettye and V.P. Franklin, eds. 2001. *Sisters in the Struggle: African American Women in the Civil Rights-Black Power Movement*. New York: New York University Press.

Collins, Patricia Hill. 1991. *Black Feminist Thought: Knowledge, Consciousness, and the Politics of Empowerment*. New York: Routledge.

Countryman, Matthew J. 2005. *Up South: Civil Rights and Black Power in Philadelphia* Philadelphia: University of Pennsylvania Press.

Cutright, Phillips, and Fredrick Jaffe. 1976. *The Impact of Family Planning Programs on Fertility: The U.S. Experience*. New York: Praeger.

Davies, Gareth. 1996. *From Opportunity to Entitlement: The Transformation and Decline of Great Society Liberalism*. Lawrence: University Press of Kansas.

Davis, Dana-Ain. 2006. *Battered Black Women and Welfare Reform: Between a Rock and a Hard Place*. Albany: State University of New York Press.

Davis, Martha. 1993. *Brutal Need, Lawyers and the Welfare Rights Movement, 1960–1973*. New Haven: Yale University Press.

Delgado, Gary. 1986. *Organizing the Movement: The Roots and Growth of the Association of Community Organizations for Reform Now (ACORN)*. Philadelphia: Temple University Press.

Dittmer, John. 1994. *Local People: The Struggle for Civil Rights in Mississippi*. Urbana: University of Illinois Press.

Duncan, Greg. 1984. *Years of Poverty, Years of Plenty: The Changing Economic Fortunes of American Workers and Families*. Ann Arbor: Institute for Social Research, University of Michigan.

Edsall, Thomas Byrne, and Mary Edsall. 1992. *Chain Reaction: The Impact of Race, Rights and Taxes on American Politics*. New York: W.W. Norton.

Ehrenreich, John H. 1985. *The Altruistic Imagination: A History of Social Work and Social Policy in the United States*. Ithaca: Cornell University Press.

Ernst, Emily Rose. 2010. *The Price of Progressive Politics: The Welfare Rights Movement in an Era of Color Blind Racism*. New York: New York University Press.

Evans, Sara. 1979. *Personal Politics: The Roots of Women's Liberation in the Civil Rights Movement and the New Left*. New York: Vintage.

Farmer, James. 1986. *Lay Bare the Heart: An Autobiography of the Civil Rights Movement.* New York: Plume.

Fraser, Nancy. 1989. *Unruly Practices: Power, Discourse, and Gender in Contemporary Social Theory.* Minneapolis: University of Minnesota Press.

Friedan, Betty. 1963. *The Feminine Mystique.* New York: Norton.

Friedman, Milton. 1962. *Capitalism and Freedom.* Chicago: University of Chicago Press.

Galbraith, John Kenneth. 1958. *The Affluent Society.* Boston: Houghton Mifflin.

Gilbert, Neil. 1983. *Capitalism and the Welfare State: Dilemmas of Social Benevolence.* New Haven: Yale University Press.

Gilens, Martin. 1999. *Why Americans Hate Welfare: Race, Media and the Politics of Antipoverty Policy.* Chicago: University of Chicago Press.

Gilroy, Paul. 1987. *There Ain't No Black in the Union Jack: The Cultural Politics of Race and Nation.* Chicago: University of Chicago Press.

Ginger, Ann Fagan, ed. 1970. *Civil Liberties Docket.* no. 673: 110–111, 114–116. Meiklejohn Civil Liberties Libraries, Oakland, CA.

Goodwin, Joanne. 1997. *Gender and the Politics of Welfare Reform: Mothers' Pensions in Chicago, 1911–1929.* Chicago: University of Chicago Press.

Gore, Dayo F., Jeanne Theoharis, and Komozi Woodard, eds. 2009. *Want to Start a Revolution: Radical Women in the Black Freedom Struggle.* New York: New York University Press.

Gordon, Linda. 1994. *Pitied but not Entitled: Single Mothers and the History of Welfare.* New York: The Free Press.

Gordon, Linda. 1974. *Woman's Body, Woman's Right: Birth Control in America.* New York: Penguin.

Gordon, Linda, eds. 1990. *Women, the State and Welfare.* Madison: University of Wisconsin Press.

Gramsci, Antonio. 1971. *Selections from the Prison Notebooks.* New York: International Publishers.

Gutman, Herbert. 1976. *The Black Family in Slavery and Freedom.* New York: Vintage Books.

Hamilton, Dona Cooper, and Charles Hamilton. 1997. *The Dual Agenda: Race and Social Welfare Policies of Civil Rights Organizations.* New York: Columbia University Press.

Hancock, Ange-Marie. 2004. *The Politics of Disgust: The Public Identity of the Welfare Queen.* New York: New York University Press.

Harrington, Michael. 1962. *The Other America: Poverty in the United States.* New York: Macmillan.

Hartmann, Betsy. 1995. *Reproductive Rights and Wrongs: The Global Politics of Population Control and Contraceptive Choice.* New York: Harper & Row.

Higginbotham, Evelyn Brooks. 1993. *Righteous Discontent: The Women's Movement in the Black Baptist Church, 1880–1920.* Cambridge: Harvard University Press.

hooks, bell. 1989. *Talking Back: Thinking Feminist, Thinking Black.* Boston: South End Press.

Hoff, Joan. 1994. *Nixon Reconsidered.* New York: Basic Books.

Hunter, Tera. 1997. *To 'Joy My Freedom: Southern Black Women's Lives and Labors after the Civil War.* Cambridge: Harvard University Press.

Iton, Richard. 2000. *Solidarity Blues: Race, Culture, and the American Left.* Chapel Hill: University of North Carolina Press.

Jetter, Alexis, Annelise Orleck, and Diana Taylor, eds. 1997. *The Politics of Motherhood: Activist Voices from Left to Right.* Hanover: University Press of New England.

Jewell, K. Sue. 1993. *From Mammy to Miss American and Beyond: Cultural Images and the Shaping of US Social Policy*. New York: Routledge.

Jones, Jacqueline. 1985. *Labor of Love, Labor of Sorrow: Black Women, Work, and the Family from Slavery to the Present*. New York: Vintage Books.

Jones, Jacqueline. 1992. *The Dispossessed: America's Underclass from the Civil War to the Present*. New York: Basic Books.

Joseph, Paniel, ed. 2006. *Black Power Movement: Rethinking the Civil Rights-Black Power Era*. New York: Routledge.

Katz, Michael. 1986. *In the Shadow of the Poorhouse: A Social History of Welfare in America*. New York: Basic Books.

Katz, Michael. 2001. *The Price of Citizenship: Redefining the American Welfare State*. Philadelphia: University of Pennsylvania Press.

Kessler-Harris, Alice. 2001. *In Pursuit of Equity: Women, Men, and the Quest for Economic Citizenship in 20th Century America*. New York: Oxford University Press.

Kluger, Richard. 1976. *Simple Justice: The History of Brown v. Board of Education and Black America's Struggle for Equality*. New York: Knopf.

Kornbluh, Felicia. 2007. *The Battle for Welfare Rights: Politics and Poverty in Modern America*. Philadelphia: University of Pennsylvania Press,

Kotz, Nick, and Mary Lynn Kotz. 1977. *A Passion for Equality: George A. Wiley and the Movement*. New York: W.W. Norton & Co.

Koven, Seth, and Sonya Michel, eds. 1993. *Mothers of a New World: Maternalist Politics and the Origins of the Welfare States*. New York: Routledge.

Lee, Chana Kai. 1999. *For Freedom's Sake: The Life of Fannie Lou Hamer*. Urbana: University of Illinois Press.

Lewis, Oscar. 1966. *La Vida: A Puerto Rican Family in the Culture of Poverty—San Juan and New York*. New York: Random House.

Levenstein, Lisa. 2009. *A Movement Without Marches: African American Women and the Politics of Poverty in Postwar Philadelphia*. Chapel Hill: University of North Carolina Press.

Lieberman, Robert. 1998. *Shifting the Color Line: Race and the American Welfare State*. Cambridge: Harvard University Press.

Marchevsky, Alejandra and Jeanne Theoharis. 2006. *Not Working: Latina Immigrants, Low-Wage Jobs, and the Failure of Welfare Reform*. New York: New York University Press.

Markowitz, Gerald and David Rosner. 1996. *Children, Race, and Power: Kenneth and Mamie Clark's Northside Center*. Charlottesville: University Press of Virginia.

Marshall, T. H. 1964. *Class, Citizenship and Social Development: Essays by T. H. Marshall*. Garden City: Doubleday & Co.

Matusow, Allan. 1984. *The Unraveling of America: A History of Liberalism in the 1960s*. New York: Harper & Row.

Michel, Sonya. 1999. *Children's Interests, Mothers' Rights: The Shaping of America's Child Care Policy*. New Haven: Yale University Press.

Mink, Gwendolyn. 1995. *The Wages of Motherhood: Inequality in the Welfare State, 1917–1942*. Ithaca: Cornell University Press.

Mittelstadt, Jennifer. 2005. *From Welfare to Workfare: The Unintended Consequences of Liberal Reform, 1945–1965*. Chapel Hill: University of North Carolina Press.

Moynihan, Daniel Patrick. 1970. *Maximum Feasible Misunderstanding*. New York: Free Press.

Moynihan, Daniel Patrick. 1973. *Politics of Guaranteed Income: The Nixon Administration and the Family Assistance Plan*. New York: Random House.

Nadasen, Premilla. 2004. *Welfare Warriors: The Welfare Rights Movement in the United States.* New York: Routledge.

Neubeck, Kenneth, and Noel A. Cazenave. 2001. *Welfare Racism: Playing the Race Card Against America's Poor.* New York: Routledge.

Ohlin, Lloyd and Richard Cloward. 1960. *Delinquency and Opportunity: A Theory of Delinquent Gangs.* Glencoe: Free Press.

Omolade, Barbara. 1986. *It's a Family Affair: The Real Lives of Black Single Mothers.* Albany: Kitchen Table Press.

Orleck, Annelise. 2005. *Storming Caesar's Palace: How Black Mothers Fought Their Own War on Poverty.* Boston: Beacon Press.

Ovesey, Lionel and Abram Kardiner. 1951. *Mark of Oppression: A Psychological Study of the American Negro.* New York: Norton.

Patterson, James T. 1981. *America's Struggle Against Poverty, 1900–1980.* Cambridge: Harvard University Press.

Payne, Charles. 1995. *I've Got the Light of Freedom: The Organizing Tradition and the Mississippi Freedom Struggle.* Berkeley: University of California Press.

Pechman, Joseph, and Michael Timpane, eds. 1975. *Work Incentives and Income Guarantees: The New Jersey Experiment.* Washington, D.C.: The Brookings Institution.

Piven, Frances Fox and Richard Cloward. 1971. *Regulating the Poor: The Functions of Public Welfare.* New York: Pantheon Books.

Piven, Frances Fox and Richard Cloward. 1977. *Poor People's Movements: How They Succeed, Why They Fail.* New York: Pantheon.

Pratt, Henry J. 1976. *The Gray Lobby.* Chicago: University of Chicago Press.

Quadagno, Jill. 1988. *Transformation of Old Age Security: Class and Politics in the American Welfare State.* Chicago: University of Chicago Press.

Quadagno, Jill. 1994. *The Color of Welfare: How Racism Undermined the War on Poverty.* New York: Oxford University Press.

Rainwater, Lee. 1970. *Behind Ghetto Walls: Black Families in a Federal Slum* (Chicago: Aldine Publishing, 1970).

Ransby, Barbara. 2003. *Ella Baker and the Black Freedom Movement: A Radical Democratic Vision.* Chapel Hill: University of North Carolina Press.

Reese, Ellen. 2005. *Backlash Against Welfare Mothers Past and Present.* Berkeley: University of California Press.

Reeser, Linda Cherrey and Irwin Epstein. 1990. *Professionalization and Activism in Social Work: The Sixties, Eighties, and the Future.* New York: Columbia University Press.

Roberts, Dorothy. 1997. *Killing the Black Body: Race, Reproduction, and the Meaning of Liberty.* New York: Pantheon Books.

Rose, Nancy. 1995. *Workfare or Fair Work: Women, Welfare, and Government Work Programs.* New Brunswick: Rutgers University Press.

Ross, Peter H. and Katherine C. Lyall. 1976. *Reforming Public Welfare: A Critique of the Negative Income Tax Experiment.* New York: Russel Sage.

Said, Edward. 1994. *Representations of the Intellectual: The Reith Lectures.* New York: Pantheon.

Sanjek, Roger. 2009. *Gray Panthers.* Philadelphia: University of Pennsylvania Press.

Schulman, Bruce. 2001. *The Seventies: The Great Shift in American Culture, Society and Politics.* Cambridge: Da Capo Press.

Scott, Daryl Michael. 1997. *Contempt and Pity: Social Policy and the Image of the Damaged Black Psyche, 1880–1996.* University of North Carolina Press: Chapel Hill.

Self, Robert. 2003. *American Babylon: Class, Race, and Power in Oakland and the East Bay, 1945–1978*. Princeton: Princeton University Press.

SenGupta, Gunja. 2009. *From Slavery to Poverty: The Racial Origins of Welfare in New York, 1840–1918*. New York: New York University Press.

Shapiro, Thomas. 1985. *Population Control Politics: Women, Sterilization and Reproductive Choice*. Philadelphia: Temple University Press.

Sheared, Vanessa. 1998. *Race, Gender, and Welfare Reform: The Elusive Quest for Self-Determination*. New York: Garland Publishing.

Sitkoff, Harvard. 1981. *Struggle for Black Equality, 1954–1980*. New York: Hill and Wang.

Skocpol, Theda. 1992. *Protecting Soldiers and Mothers: The Origins of Social Policy in the United States*. Cambridge: Harvard University Press.

Solinger, Rickie. 1994. *Wake up Little Susie: Single Pregnancy and Race Before Roe v. Wade*. New York: Routledge.

Solinger, Rickie. 2001. *Beggars and Choosers: How the Politics of Choice Shapes Adoption, Abortion, and Welfare in the United States*. New York: Hill & Wang.

Steiner, Gilbert. 1966. *Social Insecurity: The Politics of Welfare*. Chicago: Rand McNally & Co.

Steiner, Gilbert. 1971. *The State of Welfare*. Washington, D.C.: Brookings Institution.

Street, David, George T. Martin, Jr., and Laura Kramer Gordon. 1979. *The Welfare Industry: Functionaries and Recipients of Public Aid*. Beverly Hills: SAGE.

Sugrue, Thomas. 1996. *The Origins of the Urban Crisis: Race and Inequality in Postwar Detroit*. Princeton: Princeton University Press.

Sugrue, Thomas, 2008. *Sweet Land of Liberty: The Forgotten Struggle for Civil Rights in the North*. New York: Random House.

Terkel, Studs. 1992. *Race: How Black and Whites Think and Feel About the American Obsession*. New York: New Press.

Theobald, Robert. 1965. *Free Men and Free Markets*. Garden City: Doubleday & Co.

Theobald, Robert. 1966. *The Guaranteed Income: The Next Step in Economic Evolution?* New York: Doubleday.

Theoharis, Jeanne and Komozi Woodard, eds. 2003. *Freedom North: Black Freedom Struggles Outside the South, 1940–1980*. New York: Palgrave.

Tyson, Timothy. 1999. *Radio Free Dixie: Robert F. Williams and the Roots of Black Power*. Chapel Hill: University of North Carolina Press.

Van Deburg, William. 1992. *New Day in Babylon: The Black Power Movement and American Culture, 1965–1975*. Chicago: University of Chicago Press.

Weisbrot, Robert. 1990. *Freedom Bound: A History of the Civil Rights Movement*. New York: W.W. Norton.

West, Guida. 1981. *The National Welfare Rights Organization: The Social Protest of Poor Women*. New York: Praeger.

White, Deborah Gray. 1999. *Too Heavy a Load: Black Women in Defense of Themselves, 1894–1994*. New York: W.W. Norton.

Williams, Juan. 1987. *Eyes on the Prize: America's Civil Rights Years, 1954–1965*. New York: Penguin.

Williams, Patricia. 1987. *The Truly Disadvantaged: The Inner City, The Underclass, and Public Policy*. Chicago: University of Chicago Press.

Williams, Patricia. 1991. *The Alchemy of Race and Rights*. Cambridge: Harvard University Press.

Williams, Rhonda. 2005. *The Politics of Public Housing: Black Women's Struggles Against Urban Inequality*. Cambridge: Oxford University Press.

Woodward, Komozi. 1999. *A Nation Within a Nation: Amiri Baraka (LeRoi Jones) and Black Power Politics*. Chapel Hill: University of North Carolina Press.

Wray, Matt and Annalee Newitz, eds. 1996. *White Trash: Race and Class in America*. New York: Routledge.

Zucchino, David. 1997. *Myth of the Welfare Queen*. New York: Simon & Schuster.

Articles

Appelbaum, Diana Karter. 1977. The Level of the Poverty Line: A Historical Survey. *Social Service Review*. 51: 514–523.

Berliner, Milton. 1966. Welfare Voice: We are Living Like Dogs. *Daily News*, April 27, Whitaker Papers, box 3, folder 14.

Boris, Eileen. 1993. The Power of Motherhood: Black and White Activist Women Redefine the Political. In *Mothers of a New World: Maternalist Politics and the Origins of the Welfare States*, eds. Seth Koven and Sonya Michel, 213–245. New York: Routledge.

Brody, David. 1993. Workplace Contractualism in Comparative Perspective. In *Industrial Democracy in America: The Ambiguous Promise*, eds. Nelson Lichtenstein and Howell Harris, 176–205. Boston: Cambridge University Press.

Brown, Scot. 2003. The Politics of Culture: The US Organization and the Quest for Black "Unity." In *Freedom North: Black Freedom Struggles Outside the South, 1940–1980*, eds. Jeanne Theoharis and Komozi Woodard, 223–253. New York: Palgrave.

Cade, Toni. 1970. The Pill: Genocide or Liberation. In *The Black Woman: An Anthology*, ed. Toni Cade Bambara, 162–169. New York: New American Library.

Chappell, Marisa. 2002. Rethinking Women's Politics in the 1970s: The League of Women's Voters and the National Organization for Women Confront Poverty. *Journal of Women's History* 13: 155–179.

Cloward, Richard. 1965. The War on Poverty: Are the Poor Left Out? *The Nation*, August 2: 55–60.

Cloward, Richard and Frances Fox Piven. 1966. A Strategy to End Poverty. *The Nation*, May 2: 510–517.

Couto, Richard. 1978 Mud Creed, Kentucky: Sick for Clinics. *Southern Exposure* 6: 76–79.

Crosby, Emilye J. 2002. "This nonviolent stuff ain't no Good. It'll get ya killed": Teaching About Self-Defense in the African American Freedom Struggle. In *Teaching the American Civil Rights Movement: Freedom's Bittersweet Song*, eds. Julie B. Armstrong, Susan H. Edwards, Houstan B. Roberson, and Rhonda Y. Williams, 159–169. New York: Routledge.

Davis, Martha. 1996. Welfare Rights and Women's Rights in the 1960s. *Journal of Policy History* 8: 144–165.

Duncan, Ruby. 1997. "'I Got to Dreamin': An Interview with Ruby Duncan", conducted and edited by Annelise Orleck. In *The Politics of Motherhood: Activist Voices From Left to Right*, eds. Alexis Jetter, Annelise Orleck, and Diana Taylor, 119–126. Hanover, NH: University Press of New England.

Edmonds-Cady, Cynthia. 2009. *Mobilizing Motherhood: Race, Class, and the Uses of Maternalism in the Welfare Rights Movement*. *Women's Studies Quarterly* 37, 3 & 4(Fall/Winter): 206–222.

Fraser, Nancy and Linda Gordon. 1994. A Genealogy of Dependency: Tracing a Keyword of the U.S. Welfare State. *Signs* 19: 303–336.

Gelb, Joyce and Alice Sardell. 1975. Organizing the Poor: A Brief Analysis of the Politics of the Welfare Rights Movement. *Policy Studies Journal* 3: 346–354.

Gil, David G. 1968. Mothers' Wages or Social Security for Mothers: An Alternative Approach to Attack Poverty. Paper presented at Brandeis University, July 23, ACLU Archives, boxes 1134–1136.

Goodwin, Joanne L. 1995. "Employable Mothers" and "Suitable Work": A Re-Evaluation of Welfare and Wage Earning for Women in the Twentieth-Century United States. *Journal of Social History* 29: 253–274.

Hall, Simon. 2007. The NAACP, Black Power, and the African American Freedom Struggle, 1966–69. *The Historian* 69: 49–82.

Higginbotham, Evelyn Brooks. 1992. African-American Women's History and the Metalanguage of Race. *Signs* 17: 251–274.

Horner, Grier. 1967. PAPAW: How It Started, What It's Hoping To Do. *Berkshire Eagle*, June 30: 15.

King, Deborah. 1988. Multiple Jeopardy, Multiple Consciousness: The Context of a Black Feminist Ideology. *Signs* 14: 42–72.

Kunzel, Regina. 1994. White Neurosis, Black Pathology: Constructing Out-of-Wedlock Pregnancy in the Wartime and Postwar United States. In *Not June Cleaver: Women and Gender in Postwar America, 1945–1960*, ed. Joanne Meyeerowitz, 304–331. Philadelphia: Temple University Press.

Lack, Lawrence H. 1967. People on Welfare Form Union. *Los Angeles Free Press*, April 28, Whitaker Papers, box 1, folder 19.

Larabee, Mary S. Unmarried Parenthood Under the Social Security Act. *Proceedings of the National Conference of Social Work, 1939*. New York: Columbia University Press, 1939.

Levenstein, Lisa. 2000. From Innocent Children to Unwanted Migrants and Unwed Moms: Two Chapters in the Public Discourse on Welfare in the United States, 1960–1961. *Journal of Women's History* 11: 10–33.

Marchevsky, Alejandra and Jeanne Theoharris. 2000. Welfare Reform, Globalization, and the Racialization of Entitlement. *American Studies* 41: 235–265.

Morrissey, Megan H. 1990. The Downtown Welfare Advocate Center: A Case Study of a Welfare Rights Organization. *Social Service Review* 64: 189–207.

Nadasen, Premilla. 2008. "Welfare's a Green Problem": Cross-Race Coalitions in Welfare Rights Organizing. In *Feminist Coalition: Historical Perspectives on Second-Wave Feminism in the United States*, ed. Stephanie Gilmore, 178–195. Urbana: University of Illinois Press.

Nadasen, Premilla. 2009. "We Do Whatever Becomes Necessary": Johnnie Tillmon, Welfare Rights, and Black Power. In *Want to Start a Revolution? Radical Women in the Black Freedom Struggle*, eds. Dayo F. Gore, Jeanne Theoharis, and Komozi Woodard, 317–338. New York: New York University Press.

Naples, Nancy A. 1992. Activist Mothering: Cross-Generational Continuity in the Community Work of Women from Low-Income Urban Neighborhoods. *Gender and Society* 6: 441–463.

Nelson, Barbara. 1990. The Origins of the Two-Channel Welfare State: Workmen's Compensation and Mothers' Aid. In *Women, The State, and Welfare*, ed. Linda Gordon, 123–151. Madison: University of Wisconsin Press.

Orleck, Annalise. 1997. "If it Wasn't For You I'd Have Shoes for My Children": The Political Education of Las Vegas Welfare Mothers. In *The Politics of Motherhood: Activist*

Voices from Left to Right, eds. Alexis Jetter, Annelise Orleck and Diana Taylor, 102–118. Hanover: University Press of New England.

Polatnick, M. Rivka. 1996. Diversity in Women's Liberation Ideology: How a Black and a White Group of the 1960s Viewed Motherhood. *Signs* 21: 679–706.

Quadagno, Jill. 1990. Race, Class, and Gender in the U.S. Welfare State: Nixon's Failed Family Assistance Plan. *American Sociological Review* 55: 11–28.

Reich, Charles. 1964. New Property. *Yale Law Journal* 73: 733–787.

Reich, Charles. 1965. Individual Rights and Social Welfare: The Emerging Legal Issues. *Yale Law Journal* 74: 1245–1257.

Rosenblatt, Rand E. 1982. Social Duties and the Problem of Rights in the American Welfare State. In *The Politics of Law: A Progressive Critique*, ed. David Kairys, 90–114. New York: Pantheon Books.

Spivak, Gayatri. 1988. Can the Subaltern Speak? In *Marxism and the Interpretation of Culture*, eds. Cary Nelson and Lawrence Grossberg, 271–313. Chicago: University of Illinois Press.

Taylor, Ula. 2003. Elijah Muhammad's Nation of Islam: Separatism, Regendering, and a Secular Approach to Black Power after Malcolm X (1965–1975). In *Freedom North: Black Freedom Struggles Outside the South, 1940–1980*, eds. Jeanne Theoharis and Komozi Woodard, 177–198. New York: Palgrave.

Vincent, Bill. 1973. Operation Life Has Brought Hope. *The Nevadan*, January 28, Wiley Papers, box 25, folder 6.

Valk, Anne. 2000. Mother Power: The Movement for Welfare Rights in Washington, D.C., 1966–1972. *Journal of Women's History* 11: 34–58.

Wallace, Mary. 1968. $60 ADC Grants to be Ready Monday. *Ann Arbor News*, September 7, Wiley Papers.

Wallace, Mary. 1968. Welfare Mothers Seek Clothing Funds. *Ann Arbor News*, September 4, Wiley Papers.

Welsh, James. 1973. Welfare Reform: Born Aug. 8, 1969; Died, Oct. 4, 1972: A Sad Case Study of the American Political Process. *New York Times Magazine*, January 7: 14–22.

Williams, Rhonda. 2001. "We're tired of being treated like dogs": Poor Women and Power Politics in Black Baltimore. *Black Scholar* 31(3–4): 31–41.

Williams, Rhonda. 2005. Nonviolence and Long Hot Summers: Black Women and Welfare Rights Struggles in the 1960s. *Borderlands E Journal*, 4(3): 2–4.

Williamson, John. 1973. Beliefs about the Welfare Poor. *Sociology and Social Research* 58: 163–175.

Witmer, Lawrence and Gibson Winter. 1968. The Problem of Power in Community Organization. Paper presented at Conference on Community Organization, University of Chicago, April 12, MFY Papers, box 27.

Wright, Gerald C. 1976. Racism and Welfare Policy in America. *Social Science Quarterly* 57: 718–730.

Unpublished Works

Chappell, Marisa. 2002. From Welfare Rights to Welfare Reform: The Politics of AFDC, 1964–1984. Ph.D. diss., Northwestern University.

Frost, Jennifer Ann. 1996. Participatory Politics: Community Organizing, Gender, and the New Left in the 1960s. Ph.D. diss., University of Wisconsin.

Kornbluh, Felicia. 2000. A Right to Welfare? Poor Women, Professionals, and Poverty Programs, 1935–1975. Ph.D. diss., Princeton University.

Lim, Hilary. 1991. Mapping Welfare Rights. Ph.D. diss., University of Calgary.

Martin, George. 1972. Emergence and Development of a Social Movement Organization among the Underclass: A Case Study of the National Welfare Rights Organization. Ph.D. diss., University of Chicago.

O'Connor, Alice. 1991. From Lower Class to Underclass: The Poor in American Social Science, 1930–1970. Ph.D. diss., Johns Hopkins University.

Rose, Kenneth Wayne. 1988. The Politics of Social Reform in Cleveland, 1945–1967: Civil Rights, Welfare Rights, and the Response of Civic Leaders. Ph.D. diss., Case Western Reserve University.

Sachs, Andrea Jule. 2001. The Politics of Poverty: Race, Class, Motherhood, and the National Welfare Rights Organization, 1965–75. Ph.D. diss., University of Minnesota.

Shreshinsky, Naomi Gottlieb. 1970. Welfare Rights Organizations and the Public Welfare System: An Interaction Study. Ph.D. diss., University of California.

Spitzer, Scott J. 2000. The Liberal Dilemma: Welfare and Race, 1960–1975. Ph.D. diss., Columbia University.

Van Til, Jon. 1970. Becoming Participants: Dynamics of Access among the Welfare Poor. Ph.D. diss., University of California, Berkeley.

Williams, Rhonda Y. 1998. Living Just Enough in the City: Change and Activism in Baltimore's Public Housing, 1940–1980. Ph.D. diss., University of Pennsylvania.

Zylan, Yvonne. 1994. The Divided Female State: Gender, Citizenship and US Social Policy Development, 1945–1990. Ph.D. diss., New York University.

INDEX